theatre journal
1960–1974

theatre journal
reviews from *The Village Voice*
1960–1974

by Michael Townsend Smith

FAST BOOKS

In Memoriam

John Albano	Neil Flanagan	Joseph Papp
Seth Allen	Allen Ginsberg	Harold Pinter
Richard Barr	Jerzy Grotowski	José Quintero
Edward Barton	George Harris II	Hanon Reznikov
Julian Beck	George Harris III	Jerome Robbins
Samuel Beckett	Peter Hartman	Gregory Rozakis
George Birimisa	Fred Herko	Arthur Sainer
Julie Bovasso	Eugene Ionesco	Alan Schneider
Scott Burton	H. M. Koutoukas	Charles Stanley
Al Carmines	Victor LiPari	Ellen Stewart
Joseph Chaikin	Charles Ludlam	Burt Supree
Remy Charlip	Norman Mailer	Jerry Tallmer
Joe Cino	Judith Malina	Harvey Tavel
Frederick Combs	Alan Marlowe	Ronald Tavel
Ralph Cook	John H. McDowell	Luke Theodore
Peter Craig	Taylor Mead	Andy Warhol
Jackie Curtis	Leonard Melfi	James Waring
Denis Deegan	Arthur Miller	Tennessee Williams
John P. Dodd	Frank O'Hara	Lanford Wilson
Tom Eyen	Tom O'Horgan	Daniel Wolf

Cover photographs by Fred W. McDarrah

Fast Books are edited and published by Michael Smith
P. O. Box 1268, Silverton, OR 97381

ISBN 978-0-9887162-7-8

Copyright © 2015 by Michael Townsend Smith

Table of Contents

Introduction	1
Off-Broadway (1960–63)	
The Fantasticks	5
One-Way Pendulum	7
Desire Under the Elms	8
The Blacks	11
Beckett, Albee (1960–65)	
Waiting for Godot	14
Who's Afraid of Virginia Woolf?	15
The American Dream, The Zoo Story	19
Play	21
Tiny Alice	24
Happy Days	28
Unique and Memorable (1961–64)	
Four Dancers	31
The Laundry	32
Meat Joy	34
Caffè Cino I (1962–65)	
The Rue Garden	38
So Who's Afraid of Edward Albee?	39
The Madness of Lady Bright	39
Incidents	41
The Haunted Host	42
Cino fire: interview with Joe Cino	42

Judson Poets' Theatre (1963–67)
    What Happened   49
    Home Movies   50
    Sing Ho for a Bear!   51
    A Beautiful Day, Play I Play II Play III   53
    Song of Songs   58

La Mama (1962–68)
    The Room   61
    The People vs. Ranchman (Firehouse)   62
    Sarah B. Divine!   65
    The Moon Dreamers   66

Pinter, Ionesco (1962–64)
    The Dumbwaiter, The Collection   71
    The Bald Soprano, The Lesson   73
    The New Tenant, Victims of Duty   76
    The Room, A Slight Ache   79

Albee-Barr-Wilder (1962–64)
    Endgame, Bertha   82
    Gallows Humor, The Sandbox   84
    Deathwatch, Picnic on the Battlefield   85
    Funnyhouse of a Negro   87

Broadway (1963–64)
    The Beauty Part   89
    The Milk Train Doesn't Stop Here Anymore   90
    Oh Dad, Poor Dad…   93
    Oh, What a Lovely War!   95

The Living Theatre (1962–73)
    The Brig   98

The Maids	101
Frankenstein	103
Seven Meditations on Political Sado-Masochism	108

Grand Tour (1963–66)
Berliner Ensemble	111
Polish Lab Theatre	113
Rome, Paris	118
Peter Brook's US	122

Off-Broadway (1964)
In the Summer House	129
The Slave, The Toilet	133

Poets in the Theatre (1963–67)
Diane di Prima, George Dennison	139
LeRoi Jones	140
Frank O'Hara, LeRoi Jones	141
Peter Hartman, Wallace Stevens	144
Michael McClure	145

Repertory Company of Lincoln Center (1964–65)
After the Fall	149
Marco Millions	155
Tartuffe	158

Shakespeare (1964–68)
Burton's Hamlet	162
Othello in Central Park	165
A Midsummer Night's Dream	168
Papp's Hamlet	172

Theatre Genesis (1964–72)
    Cowboys, The Rock Garden   176
    Chicago   178
    The Hawk   179
    Willie the Germ   182

Notable Playwrights (1964–68)
    Terrence McNally   184
    Lanford Wilson   186
    Ronald Ribman   188
    George Birimisa   190
    Rochelle Owens   193

H. M. Koutoukas (1965–67)
    Only a Countess May Dance When She's Crazy 197
    Medea   198
    All Day for a Dollar   199
    When Clowns Play Hamlet   200

Caffè Cino II (1965–67)
    Directing Icarus's Mother   203
    Moon   204
    News report: Death of Joe Cino   205
    The Clown   207
    This Is the Rill Speaking   208
    The Brown Clown   209
    News report: Caffè Cino Closed   210

Broadway (1966–67)
    Marat/Sade   216
    The Homecoming   219
    Rosencrantz and Guildenstern Are Dead   220

The Ridiculous I (1966–67)
    The Life of Lady Godiva   222
    The Life of Juanita Castro, Kitchenette   224
    Gorilla Queen   226
    Conquest of the Universe   229

Tom O'Horgan (1963–71)
    Love and Variations   233
    Futz   233
    Tom Paine   235
    Hair   240
    Jesus Christ Superstar, Lenny, Inner City   241

Off-Broadway (1967–68)
    The Deer Park   246
    The Boys in the Band   250
    Red Cross, Muzeeka   252

Memorable Outliers (1967–73)
    San Francisco Mime Troupe   254
    And They Put Handcuffs on the Flowers   256
    In Search of the Cobra Jewels   257
    Hot Peaches: The Magic Hype   259

New Forms (1967–73)
    Environmental Theatre   262
    Scott Burton   265
    Richard Foreman   267
    The People Show   269
    Peter Schumann   271
    Meredith Monk   272
    Robert Wilson   273

Personalities (1972–74)
    Allen Ginsberg   278
    Charles Stanley   281
    Gertrude Stein   282
    Joseph Chaikin   284
    Jackie Curtis   287

The Ridiculous II (1972–73)
    The Trojan Women   289
    Eunuchs of the Forbidden City   291
    Sissy   293
    Corn   296
    The Magic Show of Dr. Ma-gico   298

Notable Playwrights (1972–73)
    Murray Mednick   301
    Robert Patrick   304
    Rosalyn Drexler   305
    Arthur Sainer   306
    Jeff Weiss   309

Theater for the New City (1972–73)
    Petit Cabaret Solenelle   312
    Angels of Light: Gossamer Wings   314
    Ten Best Martyrs of the Year   316

Last Columns (1974)
    State of the Theatre   318
    McDowell, Fierstein, Trocks   320
    On Richard Foreman (with Arthur Sainer)   324
    Ave atque vale   329

Index   332

Introduction

I wanted to be a writer so Serena Stewart's friend Betty Rollin took me to meet Dan Wolf and Ed Fancher, the editor and publisher of a weekly newspaper in Greenwich Village called *The Village Voice*. The two-year-old paper had cachet, thanks to Norman Mailer's early participation, but in these early years it was barely surviving from week to week, and writers were not paid. I said I'd write anything they needed. They gave me a bi-weekly column about sports cars.

I liked producing usable copy and being published, and it was sometimes fun: I covered the unveiling of the Edsel at the Waldorf. But cars were an enthusiasm I had outgrown. I had come to New York to become a director; my principal interest was theatre.

In October 1957, barely twenty-two, I o'erleapt the bounds of my automotive beat and turned in a soul-searching essay on two new works everybody was talking about, John Osborne's play "Look Back in Anger" and Jack Kerouac's novel "On the Road." Jerry Tallmer, the paper's theatre critic and associate editor, had the moxie to accept this and began sending me out to write short reviews of plays he was too busy to cover himself. I gladly yielded the car column to Dan List, the *Voice's* distributor and an enthusiastic rallyist. And I gradually became a theatre critic.

Jerry Tallmer was responsible for editing the paper's arts coverage, and because of his devotion to theatre, he gave it a generous proportion of the available space. A superior model as a critic and editor, Jerry taught me whatever I know about writing reviews and pointed me toward a taste for the unusual. In the paper's first year, 1955, he had founded the Obies—the *Village Voice* Awards for Off-Broadway Theatre—and gave a top award to Julie Bovasso for producing Genet's "The Maids" in her homemade theatre on St. Mark's Place. He admired the revolutionary, experimental Living Theatre, taking them as seriously as the better-funded show business professionals uptown. I followed his example, looking for theatre in out-of-the-way places as well as the mainstream, coming to prefer it up close and personal.

Theatre was at the heart of American culture in those days, and we wanted to be part of the conversation, which still pivoted on Broadway. It turned out that more interesting work was being done around the edges.

I considered the theatre not just a diversion, but an essential ingredient of a civilized life. Going to the theatre was a communal ritual I could embrace, connecting people in real time by way of guided collective exercise of imagination. It was an enormous pleasure when it worked. I loved it and wanted other people to enjoy it as much as I did.

Initially assuming that a critic's job was to criticize, that is, point out flaws and weaknesses, I scrutinized, analyzed, made a case for my opinion. Jerry took all the best plays for himself so for the first few years that I was writing for *The Voice* I got the leftovers. My early reviews were often extremely short—I might get three inches. Too often I spent my precious words delineating supposed "faults" in writing, production, and performance. What did I know? Nothing. I learned by seeing and doing and thinking about it, and gradually came around to a different approach, essentially reporting on my own experience, on what I actually saw and felt.

In addition to writing reviews, I took on paid work at *The Voice*, proofreading and assisting Jerry Tallmer with the copy-editing. When Jerry left in 1962 to write for the *New York Post*, then a strong liberal paper with many first-class writers, I got his job. A few months later the Newspaper Guild went out on strike, the city's seven (!) daily newspapers suspended publication for sixteen weeks, and *The Village Voice* went city-wide, gaining readers and beginning the phenomenal growth of the next decade. Till then we were averaging sixteen pages, twenty in a good week; by the time I left, in 1974, the paper was running 120 pages or more.

In later years, post-*Voice*, I became a reviewer of classical music. A key difference between music and theatre is that concerts are almost always good. Musicians don't get out on the stage unless they can play their instruments with some competence, and the music they perform is usually time-tested and great. Theatre on the other hand is often terrible. People go onstage who can't act; there are no real standards for good acting, though you know it when you see it. Actors often have trouble learning lines and may say only an approximation of what the author wrote. Directors may grossly distort the playwright's intention. Shows go wrong and nobody knows why. Vast sums and skills are regularly invested in Broadway plays and musicals that turn out to be complete duds and close as soon as they open.

I saw and reviewed hundreds of plays for *The Voice*—809 by my count. I was open to anything and responded to a wide variety of theatre. I saw great musicals and most of the great British and American actors of my time. Broadway was often extraordinary. Increasingly, I found myself more interested in writing about what you might call "art" theatre than commercial plays and musicals, just as I prefer classical music to pop. Simultaneously, I embraced a bohemian lifestyle and became alienated from the bourgeois audiences that supported the uptown theatre. In sync with my time—living in Greenwich Village and writing for "the newspaper of the trendmakers"—I was looking for authenticity, immediacy, intimacy, and the breaking of all boundaries.

Many of my friends were active in the theatre. I myself wrote, directed, produced, and designed the lighting for quite a number of plays while I was a critic. My own productions never broke through to a wide public, but they were what I wanted to do. I greatly valued the tiny do-it-yourself theatres like Caffè Cino, Theatre Genesis, La Mama, and eventually many more that made such work possible, free of pressure to sell thousands of tickets and play the celebrity game.

This book represents only a fraction of the reviews I wrote for *The Village Voice* in those magical years of my youth. Even so, I think you will be amazed, as I was, to be reminded of how much happened in a short time. Like any reporter, what I was given to write about was serendipitous; the coverage is unavoidably hit-or-miss. But I went to the theatre steadily for months and years at a time, and I wound up seeing and writing about most of what was most interesting in the period when I was reviewing. I especially liked pointing readers to unusual work they might not otherwise hear about, hoping they would go see it and discover its virtues for themselves.

Silverton, Oregon
June 2015

Off-Broadway
1960–63

The Fantasticks

A musical by Tom Jones and Harvey Schmidt, directed by Word Baker, presented by Lore Noto at the Sullivan Street Playhouse.

I am sadly out of practice at writing raves. It is easier to describe a production's flaws than its virtues, and I am hard-pressed to account for "The Fantasticks" being so irresistibly good. With this in mind, I did something for the first time. Having seen the show for free last Tuesday, its opening night, I bought tickets and went again on Thursday. My mother was in town, and I knew she'd like it.

There are a boy and a girl. They are in love. Their love is especially romantic because their fathers are feuding and they can only meet by climbing trees on either side of a wall. The fathers, secretly pals, hire a "professional" to stage a "rape." The boy comes to the girl's rescue, defeats the rapist in a duel, becomes a hero. Rapture.

This is the first act, and it is a measure of the show's daring that at intermission the story seems to have been concluded. It isn't, of course, and I enjoyed the second act as much as the first.

The play's notion that "without a hurt the heart is hollow" is alarmingly romantic these days, and the most elaborate and sophisticated art is employed to catch the audience in its simplicity. Tom Jones's book and lyrics achieve a breathtaking balance between worldly wit and commitment to naïveté; he obviously knows better than to rhyme "tender" with "September," but traps us with his willingness to take a sentimental chance. Harvey Schmidt's songs sound like the best Walt Disney tunes given vocal arrangements and accompaniments (on piano and harp) of high originality and effectiveness. Director Word Baker has rehearsed his cast to highly styled relaxation; their timing and interplay are impeccable, and no effort shows.

And the cast. For one thing, everybody can sing. For another, everybody plays in a perfect style for romantic fantasy, a style that makes the most ridiculous attitude believable and enthralling. Kenneth Nelson and Rita Gardner, as the boy and girl, have conviction and range. William Larsen and Hugh Thomas, as their fathers, are pitiable and hilarious. Jerry Orbach, playing the narrator and the professional rapist, is perfect because he is a little clumsy, a little less (and more) than the ideal romantic figure. There is something of the hick in his performance; every time the evening starts to be fey, he pulls it back to reality. Author Jones, calling himself "Thomas Bruce," plays an aging Shakespearean actor with a deft sense of fun. George Curley is his sidekick, whose acting talents are limited to dying. Richard Stauffer, a mime portraying the wall and silently hovering, observing the human comedy, exemplifies the immaculate care applied to the whole production.

The theatre is tiny, the actors close to you. What are usually limitations off Broadway become advantages. I might go see it yet again. 5/11/60

One Way Pendulum

A play by N. F. Simpson, directed by Douglas Seale, presented by Caroline Swann at the Phoenix 74th Street Theatre.

British weighing machines talk. There you stand, and the machine rasps: "Fourteen stone, ten pounds" (assuming you weigh 206). As "One Way Pendulum" opens, Kirby Groomkirby is in the attic teaching a battery of these machines to sing the Hallelujah Chorus. His dream is to lure millions of music-lovers to the North Pole and have them jump up and down, thereby tilting the earth and improving England's climate. Preferring black clothes, and being highly logical, Kirby has to commit constant murders in order to be in constant mourning.

Downstairs in the living room his father constructs a full-scale, roof-splitting replica of the Old Bailey. His aunt querulously rhapsodizes about transport. His sister combs and spray-nets a hairpiece. His mother tries against all odds to keep a neat house. The maid comes in three times a week to consume the gross excesses of the food industry. And so on.

The playwright, N. F. Simpson, who invented, built, and ignited this ingenious missile and aimed it at a strategic cluster of targets, unfortunately forgot to install a guidance system. By mid-second act the play has soared off into the author's hopelessly private outer space, and even the hardiest sky-watcher dozes at his post. Douglas Seale's deadpan, dragging direction doesn't help matters, but sly Gerald Hiken as the father, housewifely Betty Leighton as the mother, and matter-of-fact Anna Russell as the maid are much to the point, if only there were one. 9/28/61

Desire Under the Elms

The play by Eugene O'Neill, directed by José Quintero, presented by Theodore Mann and José Quintero at the Circle in the Square.

The Circle in the Square demonstrates what good theatre is. You begin with a great play. Your hire superb actors for the leading roles. Your director works with the single aim of illuminating what the playwright has put into the script. And the result is theatre as it should be, with stature and meaning and distinction.

There are other ways. There is the director's theatre, in which the play is staged—or choreographed—with such imagination and vitality that one marvels at the director's work. There is the star's theatre, where a single performance dominates the entire event and may leave the audience gasping out bravos for the sheer virtuosity of the display. There is the designer's theatre, which can be a feast of visual pleasures.

But for a demonstration of what theatre itself is, stripped bare and working straight through to the emotional core of experience, go to the Circle in the Square and see "Desire Under the Elms."

Eugene O'Neill's play is the nearest thing there is to an American classic, and José Quintero's production shows us why. The play moves with economy and inevitability. It does not progress so much as it uncoils, turn on turn, gradually revealing what O'Neill has packed away. The end is there from the moment the play begins; we sit hypnotized but wholly alert until the final loop is strung out before us.

The play is concerned with how men live. Ephraim Cabot is a hard man. He has spent his life clearing rocks from his fields and piling them into rock walls. Now he is old. Two wives have borne him sons and then died, too soft to survive or to understand him. At seventy-six, he marries again, to Abbie Putnam, a woman of thirty-five who seems at first to be as hard as he is, clenched like a man in her cold determination to take possession of the farm. Sharing the farmhouse, sharing the work, and disputing the ownership of the land is twenty-five-year-old Eben, Ephraim's son. Eben is haunted by the memory of his mother, destroyed by Ephraim's hardness. The farm, she had claimed, was hers; Eben is resolved that it shall be his. And so the scene is set. To be sure of the farm, Abbie must have a son—always a son; for herself she must have a man. Eben wants her as he wants everything that is his father's, and the son that Abbie bears is Eben's, not Ephraim's. Knowing this or not, Ephraim tells Eben that the farm will go to Abbie on his death, and the love in Eben turns to dry, despairing hate. Abbie by now has cut herself off entirely from Ephraim, and clings to the only thing she has left, her love for Eben. In desperation, for she can think of no way to make things right, she proves the purity of her love by murdering the child. Unbelievably, it works, Eben sees through the hateful act to the love—what kind of love does O'Neill see? Abbie and Eben, in love, are taken away to justice, and Ephraim is left on his beautiful farm, surrounded by his rock walls, alone with his hard God.

This is theatre, not a novel: the eloquence and penetration of it comes in performance. George C. Scott as Ephraim commits his whole being as an actor to animating this elemental character. He succeeds superbly. It is Ephraim who speaks to us here, who stands against these assaults, who stands and survives like the trees and rocks.

Colleen Dewhurst, playing Abbie, is an actress of enormous presence, with the power to convey whole chapters in an extended look or a stance or the way she sits in a chair.

As she taunts Eben and manipulates Ephraim, womanly and knowing in her strength, she is magnificent. Perhaps she misses the weakness in Abbie—what it is that makes her, after she has mothered Eben and seduced him, want to be mothered herself, want desperately to be taken care of; what it is that she must overcome in herself, the weakness she fears and denies. But what she gives us in Abbie is almost everything, and it is unforgettable.

Rip Torn, as Eben, is an actor of extraordinary subtlety. The first moment of the play as written is painfully bare. Eben comes out on the porch at sunset, rings the dinner bell, looks at the sky, and says: "God. Purty." Mr. Torn's eloquence, in this scene, the richness he instills in it, is enough to set up the whole play. I can't believe that O'Neill expected as much. Throughout Mr. Torn demonstrates—in his face, in the way his body reacts—an extreme and constantly useful sensitivity as an actor. His limitation is vocal, a tendency to fall into mannerism in his speech, and this slightly lessens the impact of his performance in the final scenes.

José Quintero's staging is richly imaginative in its use of the Circle's long, narrow, three-sided play area, but his work is almost always unobtrusive, held subservient to the events of the play. Locus of action is indicated almost casually as the lights change (credit David Hays) and the characters move from bedroom to kitchen to yard. There is none of the usual miming of doorways and unseen walls; we are only told as much as we need to know.

Quintero's skill is most evident in the scenes he must animate. The third act opening, with a party in progress and attention shifting awkwardly from the guests to isolated dialogues between the principals, is transformed into a canon by Quintero's staging. When the script does not need his manipulating hand, he has the discretion and humility

to leave his actors alone, free from the compulsion to "keep things moving." He knows that if a great speech is being spoken there is no need to "liven it up" with superimposed movement or side action.
This is the real thing. 1/17/63

The Blacks

The play by Jean Genet, directed by Gene Frankel, at the St. Mark's Playhouse.

More than two years have passed since "The Blacks" came to America. Busy years. The play is an undoubted work of genius, and it has become more relevant in the time that has passed, not for Genet's meaning but for his means and manner. Layer and layer of role and image peels away; and like an onion, the play consists not in the meat or meaning found at the core but in the sting. An onion is what makes you cry when you cut into it. "The Blacks" is not merely a play within a play but a confrontation between black actors playing blacks and whites within a confrontation of these actors with a white audience within a society in which blacks and whites confront each other ever more directly and dangerously.

The occasion for these words is the return of much of the original cast to the production of "The Blacks" at St. Mark's Playhouse. They play it now with even more conviction, more directness, more extravagance, literalness, and personal concern, more balls than they did before. The performance of performances is that of James Earl Jones as Village, caught between his instinct to love and his obligation—the obligation of all Genet's blacks—to hate and kill. Jones is torn apart as character, as actor playing actor, hypnotized by the conflict, then released into action with undiluted commitment. He wields an extraordinary and magical talent. Roscoe Lee Brown is brilliantly his opposite, ice cold and calculating and coldly committed to duty and necessity, as Wellington to the master of grisly ceremonies. Brunetta Barnett as Felicity, Louise Stubbs as Snow, Godfrey M. Cambridge as Diouf, Roxie Roker as the "white" queen, Cynthia Belgrave as Bobo, Morris Erby as Newport News are deadly right.

Nobody in that theatre forgets that the skin colors opposed between players and audience are those that met in Birmingham, and the actors never fear to remember. Think of Birmingham, read *Muhammad Speaks*, reread Marlene Nadle's article on the March on Washington in last week's *Voice*, remember Algeria, see "The Blacks." It does not have much to do with what Genet was actually writing about— this is in reality a chapter in his metaphysic of perversity, his glorification of criminality and homosexuality and the underside of everything, in which the ultimate act of love is murder, in which blacks are beautiful and adored because they are despised. The play that works here has little to do with that, because we are too caught up in our history, in a present physical reality of threat and change, to have access now to its metaphysics. But it is our limitation only, for Genet's "play" is only aided. The black actors look at the white audience and see that they are white, and the pale audience knows what the blacks see.

If the production at the St. Mark's Playhouse does not strike much terror into the audience, which it should, it is nonetheless electrifying for fully half the time it lasts. The stage is too small for the grandeur of ceremony the play requires, and there is something too smooth inside all the excellences of Gene Frankel's direction. The ritual savagery of the blacks and the civilized ritual of the white court do not contrast hard enough, Genet's fabulous assault of language is held too rigorously to literal sense, the contrasts and fissures of reality and "illusion" are hidden in skilled modulations. And the final scene in which the blacks onstage murder the whites onstage who die and live and mask and unmask their black faces is playful when it should be grotesque, shocking, horrible. It is good theatre, but the first act is great theatre. I urge you to see it. 9/12/63

Samuel Beckett, Edward Albee 1960–65

Waiting for Godot

The play by Samuel Beckett, directed by Burt Brinckerhoff, at the Actors Repertory Theatre Workshop.

Friday night, supperless and rather tired, I climbed creaky stairs to an unprepossessing loft at 498 Third Avenue and witnessed an excellent revival of Samuel Beckett's "Waiting for Godot." By any standards the acting and direction were admirable; under the circumstances they were astounding. Tony Lo Bianco made Didi professorial, slightly dandified, immensely gentle. Becklan Algan's Gogo was an overgrown, overage child, sweet, eager to please and be pleased, irrepressible against all odds. Together the two men were tender, respectful, showing such warmth and love toward one another that the play became something new. Paul Lally's Pozzo was somewhat less successful, the actor not old enough or practiced enough to play the absurd dignity of the first act. As Lucky, John Horn displayed the necessary virtuosity with apparent ease. I wished that director Burt Brinckerhoff hadn't let the play end quite so slowly, but his overall approach was right—simple, sensitive, intelligent.

What was new for me was the revelation that what Norman Mailer called "the total lack of hope" is not the point of "Waiting for Godot" but rather the basic condition from which the play proceeds. The play describes the futility of expecting the absolute and, in the most unsentimental terms, the necessity of remaining human anyway. 3/2/60

Who's Afraid of Virginia Woolf?

Do not be fooled by appearances. Edward Albee has written a play about truth and illusion, and the evening's number one illusion is that this is a conventional play—extraordinary in its emotional persistence, its vital language and coruscating wit, and its all-round technical superiority, but conventional and ordinary in its form and devices. This is, I repeat, an illusion. "Who's Afraid of Virginia Woolf?" (*at the Billy Rose*) is, subtly but critically, a new kind of play.

Edward Albee, whose reputation previously had—by his own admission—outstripped his achievement, has now stepped clear of the derivativeness, self-consciousness and technical angularity of his first works and come up with what is first of all a real play. The characters are specific and identifiable and entirely credible. The play's events happen in a real place and a real time span. No event occurs on the stage that could not actually happen in this living room of this college assistant professor. There are, in short, no tricks; the audience is not held by theatrical gimmicks. What happens on the stage is exactly what we think of as drama: people talking to one another, interacting, revealing themselves to each other and to us, revealing more than they want each other to know, rising to emotional challenges and crumbling beneath them. And this is executed so excellently—by the playwright and his director and actors—that the audience is held for three and a half hours, longer than any Broadway play has held it since "Long Day's Journey into Night."

But this superior drama is all a disguise; it is what holds us, but it is not what hooks into our minds, what finally engages us. Since the play is not in its innards a conventional drama, it has a number of faults when it is seen as one, and these give the clue to what it really is. It is too long for the material of its plot, what there is of plot: why? It is written and played at a high but almost uniform emotional pitch: why? Its characters do not captivate us the way we expect to be captivated, we do not like them, we cannot identify with them, we cannot empathize with them, we do not really care what happens to them: why? And the conclusion of the play, the final revelation, is distinctly out of key with the kind of resolution that lets us leave the theatre feeling, for want of a better word, satisfied: why?

The first clue is the play's length. It goes on and on and on and on and on, with no real justification except completeness—the play occupies the same time-span as its events. The structure is something like variations on a theme, the theme being people destroying one another and the variations being four of the hilarious, vicious games they play. The basic material is stated at the outset, and for the next three hours we go deeper into the familiar mire. The play settles, immediately after the bitchy hilarity of the opening, at an intense level of mutual hatred and stays there, with slight and brief modulations up and down, clear through to about five minutes before the end. The tones of voice and the actions, the anguishes and the buffooneries, are strung out in perfectly even undulations, like what I imagine to be a banshee wail. After the first forty-five minutes we are virtually incapable of being surprised by anything, although things happen that in other circumstances would be jolting. We are practically numb, with no reliable sense of time or of emotional balance. At the ends of the second and third acts, this hypnotic rhythm is augmented by, respectively, a series of offstage sounds—voices and laughter—that seem to be coming from underwater and an interminable chant in Latin. Leaving the theatre at the end, or thinking back on the experience an hour later, we realize that although we know these characters intimately, we do not exactly know them as individuals. They are utterly specific, but we do not feel for them in any way, they have immediately ceased to exist, there is something general and almost mechanistic about them: we remember them in detail but through an emotional fog, as if we had met them when we were drugged or drunk—although it is they who have been drunk, throughout the play. We have believed—or accepted—them in every minute thing they have said and done, but we do not think for a minute that they actually exist, that the play reproduces reality, that we might meet them someday on some street. In a sense we might become them, but it would take an act of dark magic to transform us. They are, in short, inevitable more than real.

These three characteristics, which one at first puts down as faults, exist for a purpose. Albee's jumping-off place for this play was experimental drama, drama that attempts to enlarge the theatre by breaking down its habitual forms. Despite the trappings of naturalism, "Who's Afraid of Virginia Woolf?" is a continuation of this effort, infinitely more daring, valuable, and successful than any he has given us before. Albee has thrown out the fundamentally sentimental means—basically, inducing the spectator to identify with the hero or heroine—by which the ordinary naturalist play "moves" its audience, and for them he has substituted a kind of ritual. He has written many riotously funny moments, but the laughter is always bitter, always at someone's expense. It is genuine laughter, but it is never free of cruel mockery, and its purpose is only to lull us into going along.

We are not moved or entertained by this play, we are transfixed. We are drawn smoothly into a world that we manage only to skirt in our ordinary lives, and then the gates are locked behind us, and the leafy hedges separating us from the people next door become impenetrable walls, and the clocks are stopped, and we are denied any reference to the selected reality we try, and ordinarily manage, to see around us.

The final moment and final "fault" of the play is as devious as the rest. We are given a sham resolution, a reconnection with reality which we can, if we absolutely need to, see as a potential up-turning in these ruined lives before us and in us; but this ending is equivocal in the extreme, not really a resolution or finality at all, and we leaving the theatre knowing for sure—though not knowing why—we have not got away unscarred.

Alan Schneider, directing, has confronted the challenge of the script directly and unblinkingly, and his work is a complete success. The actors—Arthur Hill, Uta Hagen, George Grizzard, Melinda Dillon—give performances that could not be better: they have with courage and determination given us the play itself. William Ritman has created a perfect setting. Richard Barr and Clinton Wilder (Theatre 1963) are the producers.

The experience is irreplaceable. Edward Albee has found fire in the soggy ashes of naturalism and forged a technique of inestimable potential. This is a crucial event in the birth of a contemporary American theatre.   10/18/62

The American Dream
The Zoo Story

Two plays by Edward Albee, presented by Theatre 1964 (Richard Barr and Clinton Wilder) at the Cherry Lane Theatre.

Edward Albee's two short plays are becoming an institution, something like the Oberammergau Passion Play: they are back at the Cherry Lane now in their fourth and fifth New York incarnations since January 1960. In the interim they have become easier to categorize—as the flawed, awkward, somewhat tentative early manifestations of an extraordinarily talented playwright. They retain their uniqueness as personal and vivid theatrical statements.

The difficulty with "The Zoo Story," which chronicles the encounter of an Establishment Man with an Outsider one sunny Sunday afternoon in Central Park, is still the question of whether the latter, Jerry, is insane. The possibility of psychosis lurks everywhere beneath the lines, constantly threatening to undermine and invalidate the universality of the play's content. Albee has since learned to keep Freud in his place. The climax still seems forced, arbitrary, not quite credible. Nonetheless, the play has a starkness of energy, an unrelenting directness and precision of image, that cuts through its awkwardness and scratches at the audience's skin.

"The American Dream" is a nasty, hilarious, extravagant satire for its first two-thirds—with an unmistakable debt to Ionesco—then careens sharply and unsuccessfully into horribleness: the young man of the title enters and reveals how he has been rendered "incomplete," and Grandma choruses "Oh, my child" in sympathy. The tone is sentimental, and for all its felicity of expression the material simply refuses to mesh with what preceded it. Yet the first section is brilliant, and the final moments nearly fuse farce and grotesque realism. Albee learned a clear lesson from the play, for in "Who's Afraid of Virginia Woolf?" he makes comedy and tragedy, to their mutual advantage, operate at the same time.

Sudie Bond recreates her exquisite portrayal of Grandma, and Jane Hoffman and Alice Drummond are excellent as Mommy and Mrs. Barker. As Daddy, David Hooks injects a note of irony and masked strength. Jered Barclay, insecure in his initial narcissism as the Young Man, brings a fine earnest intelligence to its development.

Mr. Barclay and Mr. Hooks play Jerry and Peter in "The Zoo Story." Peter emerges clearly and accurately—despite an unfortunate tendency to engage the audience as allies at the outset. Mr. Barclay's Jerry is garbled, boring, and disagreeable, and the play sags. His performance is too well worked out, with every line, practically every individual word given a special reading, a special calculated attitude, a special weight. The lines are burdened with more significance than they have, and the character's intensity seems false. In concentrating on the word-by-word emotional content of the lines, Mr. Barclay has lost sight of their sense. This is confusing to the audience and apparently confusing to the actor as well, for on opening night a good-sized chunk of the central "Story of Jerry and the Dog" was missing.

Perhaps this a price of institutionalization. In this revival the producers chose not to hire a director, and "The Zoo Story" needs one badly. The program also does not credit a designer, and the production has a decidedly slapdash look.

6/6/63

Play

A play by Samuel Beckett, directed by Alan Schneider, presented by Theatre 1964 (Richard Barr, Clinton Wilder, Edward Albee) at the Cherry Lane Theatre.

Samuel Beckett is the master. With each utterance he further refines a craft that has been irreproachable for years, and at the same time bears down harder and harder to embody his vision with purity, intensity, inevitability. Already he has given us at least two masterpieces—"Waiting for Godot" and "Happy Days"— "Endgame" may be another. His new work, "Play," an eighteen-minute one-act which has just opened at the Cherry Lane (on a double bill with Pinter's funny-peculiar "The Lover"), is a summary and step beyond.

Beckett has been moving his characters steadily away from everyday reality toward immobility. Vladimir and Estragon in "Godot" wait on a bleak country road; Hamm and Clov in "Endgame" are in a "bare interior" in a ruined or abandoned world, with Hamm confined to a chair and his parents in ash cans; Winnie in "Happy Days" is sinking into a mound that is up to her chin by the second act.

The three nameless characters of "Play" are dead, which Beckett images as confinement up to their necks in separate but adjacent urns. Unable to see or hear one another, they are bathed in a "hellish half-light," and they are being played with. A brighter shaft of light moves from one to the other of them, seemingly at random, and as they are revealed to the eye they reveal themselves to the ear. As the light strikes, each speaks his mind.

The play is in two sections, the first concerned with memory. As the finger of light prods them they bring up fragments of the dreary, banal relationship that constituted their meaning and led to their deaths. Woman 1 was the wife of Man, whose mistress was Woman 2. The three of them met in various combinations from time to time and variously deceived and misunderstood one another as they struggled with the geometry of what they saw as love. The recollections, for all their stark detachment and austerity of emotion, sparkle with humor, and although the fragmenting and dislocation of sequence makes the details of the story difficult to follow, its factual spirit is communicated with great efficiency. The sequence lasts no more than ten minutes, and we know these people as well as they can be known.

The memories end at the characters' deaths. Woman 2 and Man disappear; Woman 1, having gone to seek them, dies in an auto crash on her way home. Man seems to have committed suicide, for Woman 2 remembers burning his clothes. After seeing the play twice I am not certain how Woman 2 died.

The second section of the play is concerned with their present, the experience of death. Previously the finger of light has been only a neutral instrument revealing thoughts-in-progress. Now it is experienced as an inscrutable accuser: when the light strikes them it demands some response, but no particular response is specified or, apparently, accepted. Their circular memories of inconclusive life are exhausted; now they must face circular, inconclusive death.

Woman 1 begs from the start, with mounting insistence, "Get off me!" and wonders whether she should do something with her face other than "utter" or weep. "How the mind works still," she muses, "how the mind works still, to be sure." Woman 2 concedes that "there are endurable moments"— she means the dark silences when the light is off her—but then reflects that "things may disimprove; she wonders if she has become "a little unhinged," then judges coldly, "I doubt it"; within seven or eight minutes she is driven to hysteria. Man, between hiccoughing and begging "Pardon," wonders whether it is some truth that is being asked for, and he and the others offer all the truth they can find. Finding nothing that affects the senseless movement of the light, unable to admit that the movement is senseless, he has the courage to ask the question which must not be answered as it can only be answered, the question: "Am I as much as being seen?" The light goes out, the hellish half-light persists, the light comes on, he says, "We were not long together," the light goes out, the hellish half-light persists...

In these rarefied strata Beckett retains his earthy Irish wit. His choice of a corny romantic triangle to carry his meaning is rooted in the sense that the best of us are predictable, dull, and wracked with trivial self-deceptions, goading ourselves into action by pretense, hot in pursuit of anything that comforts. The color of life is drab, not motley; and Beckett's commitment to reality requires him to forego the "realism" of conventional theatre.

All this by now is presupposition to Beckett, whose surfaces exist only to reflect the depths, but it is extraordinary that he can this bluntly and uncoyly make of death a metaphor for life. For Beckett, unlike Sartre, hell is not other people but one's own consciousness guilt-ridden in its own eternity. Given all this, the surprising thing is that "Play" seems to me another statement of hope. Again and again Beckett reaffirms the possibility of waiting for Godot and asking questions. The barest suspicion that one is "as much as being seen" is an assertion of hope.

When this nearest approach to despair can rouse itself to work of such excellence, no matter how dark the vision, it is enormously vitalizing. The particular method of Beckett's excellence is to work directly in stage imagery. His play is neither wholly aural nor visual but functions as a unit. Sight is essential to understanding the sound, the finger of light is as vocal as the actors. Like a jewel the play would disintegrate if it were flawed and should be wrongly struck.

Alan Schneider has communicated Beckett's eternity perfectly. His perfect actors are Marian Reardon, Michael Lipton, and Frances Sternhagen, and the movements of the light are expressively controlled by Robert D. Currie. William Ritman designed the perfect urns and created the hellish half-light. All together they make perfect chamber music, absolute theatre. 1/9/64

Tiny Alice

Edward Albee is more interested in failure than other writers are in success. With "Tiny Alice" (*at the Billy Rose*), Albee overreaches himself, and while the play is more ambitious in scope than was "Who's Afraid of Virginia Woolf?", it is less successful in execution. Still, the new play is Albee's most provocative. Audiences continue to react to it well after the evening has ended. Albee has such talent and skill at his disposal that he is provocative almost by reflex; but "Tiny Alice" lacks evidence of the further transformation that might have turned its provocations into dramatic statement. The play is a brilliant first draft.

Formally, the play exists on two levels, the naturalistic and the mythic. Each is fascinating as far as it goes, but the intended interaction barely occurs.

The "real" story concerns the corruption of an innocent. Brother Julian, a lay brother acting as secretary to a cardinal, becomes the Church's intermediary to a vastly rich woman, Miss Alice, who is giving them a stupendous sum of money.

Miss Alice turns out to be one member of a trio with her butler and her lawyer, her past and present lovers, the three of them mysteriously co-involved in altering Julian's life. Julian moves into Alice's house, becomes involved with wines, with horses, finally with Miss Alice herself. At last he marries her, renouncing his vows and abjuring his formal identity. Julian has been rendered apostate; it is for this privilege that the money is given. The money has bought Julian's soul, on the most obvious level; once the transaction is completed, its agents have no more interest in him.

The naturalistic level wears increasingly thin as the evening advances. Some elements of the mythic level are immediately apparent. The lawyer is repeatedly identified as Satan. Butler is a servitor angel, or possibly the demiurgos—here my knowledge of Christian myth is inadequate. Julian is Christ at least (as well as a Faust figure). Alice is both Marys and also the godhead—also an ally or aspect of Satan.

The play resists interpretation as allegory—its correspondences are too willfully disarrayed—but is a mythical statement in its own right. The density is extraordinary. Still, it is not evidence of genuine obscurity that one is unable to resolve the elements into a coherent mythology. What is needed is not smarter detective work but more clues; on both the play's levels—the murder mystery as well—Albee has left frustrating gaps. He continually hints at some central revelation that would make everything fit together. "I live here...with a secret," says Miss Alice portentously in the first act. But this is just teasing: the secret is never revealed, and one doubts if it exists. The play is incomplete. Albee may have fully conceived his mythology, but he has not put it fully into this play.

Superficially it is concerned with faith of the theological kind. Julian describes a crisis of faith some years earlier that was the critical event of his life. He says: "My faith and my sanity...they are one and the same." The play also tackles the interpenetration of reality and illusion—or the isolation of reality within experience. Julian asks: "Is the memory of something having happened the same as it having happened?" Well, no, but Albee has set up several inventive demonstrations of the instability of "reality." The play is also preoccupied with betrayal. (The viewpoint is bleak: twice Julian is in a sexual relationship with a woman, both times she is symbolically his mother, and both encounters result in deaths.) Beneath it all is the pedal point of myth that would give everything substance if only it could be felt.

The play is eloquent on the sanity aspects of Julian's crisis, less convincing on its religious side. Julian says, rather airily, that the crisis was brought on by "the chasm between the nature of God and the use to which men put...God." Albee is determined not to be psychological, and yet in this instance he offers no alternative: Julian's God seems to be nothing but a fragile device for deceiving internal chaos. It is unfortunate that Albee has used Christian myth as a basis for his play, since the reality-illusion conundrums cannot be brought into it without undermining Julian's character. This is the script's worst misstep—that the characters' reality is continually diluted, often quite casually, by the other levels of the play, until we can neither make sense of them nor feel anything for them. Julian's anguish is meaningless if it makes no difference whether he believes in God or in Alice—he is betraying only the words.

Albee pokes malicious fun at the personnel and functional structure of the church, as if contrasting these to the purity of direct faith in God. In reality his thinking is alien not only to the church but to the absolutist assumptions behind it, to the very idea of God. His concept of faith has to do with existence, not with divinity. If the play's final confrontation is anything, it is a demand that Julian transfer his faith away from God into the existential void—that he make a leap into faith in confounded existence itself. Yet this is not what is dramatized. All the preparation for this scene goes to waste, since what is actually going on is a shift in terms of reference, a redefinition of the play's vocabulary.

Conceived on an ambitious scale, the play remains fragmented, its pieces uneven in quality, structurally out of control. It needs a further step, the application of mind to the raw creation. The writing is best in the most incidental moments—as in the opening scene, which is reminiscent of Albee's past work, wonderfully effective, and irrelevant to the present play. (A scene between lawyer and butler in Act II could be excised without loss.) The author is infectiously delighted at many of his inventions, but he has not always judged whether they advance or merely confuse his explorations. The big moments in the play are weak because general. Miss Alice's Act II monologue is hollow and disappointing—her pain and terror lack reference. The "ceremony" that should resolve the play's tensions is formless and vague, and Julian's final speech occurs in an emotional vacuum. The ending, in which lighting and sound effects are employed for the first time, is a gross violation of style.

The production emphasizes the play's faults. Using superior actors, director Alan Schneider has concentrated almost entirely on the play's naturalistic level. (William Ritman's sets would have permitted other solutions.) But the play is insufficient on this level. Schneider fits it all together as smoothly as if it made perfect sense; as a result the actors often appear victimized by the play's style rather than attuned to it. John Gielgud plays Julian with superb concentration and eloquent moment-to-moment intensity—he is a great actor—and Irene Worth is an apt and potent Miss Alice. Both do what they do superbly—but they are doing the wrong thing. The play cannot be played realistically because it won't hold together. Granted that no production can perfect a flawed play, it is disappointing that Schneider did not attempt a bolder answer to the problems the author handed him. William Hutt fares better as the lawyer, a crisper role that he plays with assurance and dispatch. John Heffernan and Eric Berry are satisfactory as Butler and Cardinal.

The play's principal virtue is its resonance. The language is continually alive, continually aware of itself on many levels—so much so that self-consciousness sometimes breaks into the open. Albee is brilliantly attuned to experience but unsure of his identity at this point in his career. It is heartening that he is not satisfied to repeat what he can do well. The sensibility behind the play is contemporary, original, and authentic. 1/14/65

Happy Days

A play by Samuel Beckett, directed by Alan Schneider, presented by Theatre 1966 (Richard Barr, Clinton Wilder, Edward Albee) at the Cherry Lane Theatre.

Hooray for "Happy Days," one of my all-time favorite plays and theatre delights, which is here again with Ruth White playing Winnie again. There is a widespread impression that the title of "Happy Days" is ironic, that the actual play is bleak and depressing. Not so! The play is invigorating, an anthem to the resourcefulness and buoyancy of the human spirit. One witnesses a human being sunk (literally) to appalling depths, deprived of mobility, distractions, even hope, and still managing to have happy days; the human condition is stated with unsurpassed grimness, yet the human spirit survives, prevails, transcends.

Of course I am a minority. I see many of Samuel Beckett's works from this angle and find it enormously rewarding. The secret is to pay attention to the whole play, not just its outline. In "Happy Days" the principal character, Winnie, appears during the first act buried to just below her breasts in the earth; in the second act only her head protrudes/ In the first act she has the consolation of a parasol and a large bag full of equipment with which to occupy herself—toothbrush and toothpaste, a mirror, a hairbrush, a revolver; in the second act she is reduced to words. Her husband, Willie, a sluggish, mole-like creature, in the first act occasionally shows himself and acknowledges that he can hear her; in the second, he has disappeared, perhaps died. For all she knows, Winnie is talking into a void, although she declines to believe it.

All this, however, is only the background, the situation. This much is Beckett's very striking metaphor for the human condition—but it is far from all he has to say, not in fact the content of the play. This much is the way things are, Beckett says: but see what happens then. See whom it's happening to. The situation is dismaying to an unparalleled degree, but Winnie is largely undismayed. Like anyone else she has good moments and bad ones, moments of exhilaration and moments of exhaustion; she has happy days and presumably unhappy ones. But it never seriously occurs to her to despair. The revolver is always there—"ever uppermost," in fact—but there is never a chance that she will use it. Winnie is completely a realist, well aware of the state of things, without the tendency or evident desire to flee into comforting fantasy. She is not at all heroic, there is nothing exceptional about her, and so Beckett seems to suggest that her nobility is available in every woman or man. The locus of meaning, it seems to me, lies not in the kind of world we find ourself facing but in our response to it, and Winnie is magnificent.

Magnificent is also the word for Ruth White's performance. She is more than faultless; to an exactly faithful performance of the script she adds endless warmth, variety, animation, humanness. Winnie's commitment is to nothing less than life, and the fullness of life in Ruth White's performance is exalting. Alan Schneider, the director, as her collaborator earns a similar measure of praise, and John C. Becher is perfect as Willie. I urge you to see "Happy Days" not just because it is a supreme work of dramatic literature superbly performed but for the bounty of pleasure it offers to its audience. 10/7/65

Unique and Memorable
1961–64

Four Dancers

It was an easy hour-and-a-half (or less) of dance Monday night at the Living Theatre. To be sure, it got off to a less than scrutable start with James Waring's "Little Kooch Piece No. 2." My program scribbles read: "disintegration-separation seen as humor, in terms of specifically comic movements—except not laughable because of the bleakness, barrenness..." This is the humor of despair. Mr. Waring's eccentricities all but destroy communication, and perhaps that is the point.

Yvonne Rainer's two solos, "Three Satie Spoons" and "The Bells," are studies in form. Movements, sounds, spoken words are repeated in various juxtapositions, and this concern with structure is effective in holding attention. I wonder what it has to do, though, with an audience. "The Bells" is funny, maybe for the wrong reasons; the "Satie Spoons" is bleak, introspective, fascinating, private.

Aileen Passloff's "Rosefish" is, to a verbal mind, about a hopeless desire to escape. From what, you tell me. The feeling is of a fish wishing it had other extremities than fins and lived in some other element than water. It was danced with fine authority.

In this bleak landscape it is good to learn from Fred Herko's "Possibilities for a Pleasant Outing" that something as simple as "pleasant" is still possible. Mr. Herko seems, more than the others, to derive direct delight from moving, which I'd think would be the basis of all dance. This work refers to the child's pre-rational pleasure in expending energy, to his conflict with the inhibiting adult world, to the possibility of expressing yourself anyway.   8/3/61

The Laundry

A play adapted from the French of David Guerdon by Howard Richardson, directed by Nicolas Bataille, at the Gate Theatre.

Tipped off in advance that "The Laundry" has to do with Theseus, Ariadne, Pasiphaë, the Cretan labyrinth, and the monster inside, I spent the first act trying to piece things together. From my sketchy memory of the myth I picked out Mama Yvonne as Pasiphaë, her late husband Papa George as Minos, Laurent as Theseus. I am still confused whether Lena or Estelle is Ariadne—Lena is Laurent's wife, but it is Estelle whom he tries to seduce into giving him the key to the "secret room." Señor Armando, who must be a version of Daedalus, the architect of the labyrinth, doesn't appear until the second act. Daniel, the mysterious son locked away in that room, was clearly to be the Minotaur.

Such thoughts of the ancients distracted me from the first act of "The Laundry." Papa George had just died. His widow Yvonne, proprietress of a laundry in a provincial French town, was in an elaborate form of mourning. Her daughter Lena, married to Laurent, is chafing at the drudgery, eager to get away. Estelle, the girl-of-all-work, prowled about with something heavy on her mind. And the unseen Daniel, key to it all, was locked up in a secret room, waiting for Laurent to find his way in.

In the second act the play began to overpower the myth. These became ordinary people in an ordinary town faced with an extraordinary problem. Locked in that room was a monster-child now nearly twenty years old, a son whose very visage provoked fear and shame—and at the same time love—in his mother. Lazy, coarse, grasping Laurent saw the monster-child as a way out of a dreary life. By the end of the act the whole family was negotiating with the impresario and artiste Señor Armando to sell Daniel to his circus. Now the play was working marvelously; the familiar and the bizarre invaded each other and were transformed by each other; at one moment we were watching a conventional family quarrel, then we were buying and selling human flesh, then we were deep in the uncoilings of myth; then back again, until all we saw wore a glowing haze of theatricality.

In the third act messages started creeping forth. Daniel was revealed. It was no shock that he wore the head of a bull, for the story was studded with sly references to its mythic origins, but his mask (made by Ralph Lee) was startlingly beautiful. At Señor Armando's bidding a great crowd gathered before the laundry-palace. Yvonne, all the while insisting, "I am a laundress," became the queen-mother. Estelle was transformed into Mary Magdalene. The minotaur Daniel became Christ returned.

By now the play had rather fallen apart. Too much significance was heaped onto this shy bull-man, including confessions by Laurent, who had killed his childhood friend (Daniel became that friend), and Yvonne, who confessed the monster's conception, until the drama had again withdrawn behind its meanings. When everything is universal, nothing remains particular. In the end, when all was lost when all might so easily have been won, the tragedy was antic and charming but no longer tragic.

Playing up the fanciful Frenchness of the play, the production is highly entertaining, if at times a bit less off-hand than it might be. It was directed by Nicolas Bataille, whose historic production of Ionesco's "The Bald Soprano" is still running in Paris, and achieves a polished air of amateurism that complements the whimsical significating of the script. Fran Malis romps through the role of Yvonne like a great tragedienne in her cups. Elisa Loti as the pregnant Lena is bouncy and adorable. Négro Verdié's Laurent is vain, surly, and neurotic, just as he should be. Linda Marsh is all seductress as Estelle, Robert Smith all bombast as Armando, and Carl Jablonski makes a most delicate monster. Merrill Sindler designed the set, which is attractive, faintly threatening, and extremely useful.   2/21/63

Meat Joy

A happening by Carolee Schneemann, presented by Judson Dance Theatre at Judson Memorial Church.

Images: a brilliantly lit, vast cascade of paper pouring, pouring down from the balcony to the floor of the church; two pairs of embracing bodies clad in bikinis and paper and rolling, rolling about the floor, through the piles of paper, while another couple stalks slowly, formally, in a great circuit slowly undressing one another; girls buried in paper, only their legs waving in the open air; darkness, red and green lights whirled wildly like bolas, strange membranous creatures emerging squirming from the floor, girls in plastic wrapping silhouetted in the dim, creeping, pouncing light; a woman painting a man, brushing on bright colors, then a man painting a woman, then the man and woman rubbing their painted bodies together, spreading and smearing the colors; men arranging girls' bodies, improvising patterns, four and four; and then the meat, principally fish and fowl, dead fish and plucked chickens and sausages from a serving tray thrown onto a pile of bikini-clad male and female bodies in the center of the big open space in bright theatre lights, and games with the raw food, hitting and rubbing and throwing and waving games, writhing, playing; finally more painting, the men painting the women, painting themselves, all of them jumbled together with the fish and chickens and sausages on the huge plastic sheets covering the floor of the church with an audience of hundreds watching from a ring of pews.

"Meat Joy" proposes images that are not only non-dramatic but non-theatrical. Carolee Schneemann is a painter. The images are static rather than dynamic. They succeed one another in a more or less regular pattern but do not develop, do not have a structure of meaning but only a rising curve of complexity and intensity. The basic pattern of "Meat Joy" is simple: it gets messier and messier. There is no increase of tension, no suspense. The "meaningful" elements function as direct images: "meat" is a single idea which, once introduced, does not change, is not developed, commented upon, but simply stated.

It would be a mistake, however, to suggest that "Meat Joy" is painterly because it is primarily visual; the distinction of the kind of work from theatre, as in all the happenings by painters that I have seen (as opposed, for example, to the work of Ken Dewey), lies in the basic nature of the images—that they are single, simple, static in concept (not in execution).

The result, unexpected in "Meat Joy" but fairly typical of happenings (and, for me, of painting exhibits), is that the spectator is left coolly detached from the work. The experience is different from theatre in kind, not in value. One is not drawn in as by a play, in which to some degree one identifies with the characters, lives through their experiences (however abstract); here one simply looks, observes, registers, one is permitted to explore but not required to experience. This is, incidentally, nothing like the Brechtian principle of "alienation." Brecht was practical; Schneemann is poetic. Brecht concretized the effective principle, generalized, caricatured practicality in action; Schneemann abstracts, removes all social context, alters and distorts reality instead of moving toward its essence: her images are nearly unrecognizable. By further contrast to the theatre, to a play, "Meat Joy" is timeless—as LaMonte Young's music is timeless by contrast to a classical symphony. It is not a line but a series of discontinuous points.

Knowing the ingredients of "Meat Joy" in advance, I had expected (and wanted) it to be a violent, frightening, threatening, transgressive, possibly embarrassing experience. Instead it was pleasant. Several of the images—particularly the earliest ones—I found stunning, breathtakingly sustained. I wanted it to continue for a much longer time. Yet somehow as it continued it became less and less exciting; I kept wishing it would go further, become wilder, accelerate kinetically to an orgiastic level of energy. When it ended I felt disappointed, that its promise has not been fulfilled. It was what it was, not what I wanted it to be.

I suspect my disappointment was the product of certain stylistic confusions in the work. One was an early scene in which a woman lay in bed while a man undressed to get into bed with her; the impulse was naturalistic, despite its stylized rendition; it not only distracted from but diluted the strong abstract images surrounding it. Another, more crucial issue was the musical score: a succession of popular rock-and-roll songs that imposed an artificial time-sense on everything that happened, a rhythm from outside. I was continually aware of one song ending and another beginning, of the recorded minutes passing, of the untransformed beat.

As a painting exists outside time (unlike a play or a piece of music), so should "Meat Joy" have cancelled out the audience's customary sense of duration and created a new time zone of its own. This would have been an impressive achievement, and it was possible. But the music imposed ordinariness on one's sense of time.

I sense a "literary" meaning in the "meat." These dead creatures, this violated food, are as decorative as paint, have as much objectness as the human body, possess more sensory possibilities than those encountered in cooking and eating them. Here the impulse begins to be theatrical—just as painting has moved toward the literary in the present period: away from the pure image toward the comment, from detachment toward involvement, toward a fusion (a refusion) of the two streams that has been largely missing since the decline of religious painting. Miss Schneemann hasn't quite decided, she doesn't know whether she wants to "do something" with her images or simply state them; the work is performed with a cool lack of personality that further decreases its urgency and further removes the actual experience from the implicit content. 11/26/64

Caffè Cino I
1962–65

The Rue Garden

A play by Claris Nelson, directed by Marshall W. Mason, at the Caffè Cino.

Agatha Apfeather and her aunt live in isolation behind walls. Agatha's fiancé, Henery Chiggins, left seven years ago, stifled by the sadness; Agatha has planted a sprig of rue every day since his departure. When there is need of a chambermaid, Jennifer materializes at the gate. Although she is happy selling roses, one a year, Jennifer is bullied into taking the job.
At this point Henery returns. "Come away with me," he says to Agatha, "the world is beautiful."
"Can you promise me there will be no pain?" she demands.
"No," he must reply, "I cannot promise." And Henery leaves with Jennifer.
Linda Eskenas was glorious as Agatha, a performance to be marveled at. Her timing and sense of detail were exquisite; she was by turns hilarious and heart-breaking: a triumph of style. The other performances were less effective, Claris Nelson, author of "The Rue Garden," a bit too wistful as Jennifer, Lin Kennedy too abandoned as Prudence. The play itself, fathered by Lewis Carroll and obviously nourished on nothing but rose petals and tears, is almost pure magic, and Marshall W. Mason did an admirable job of staging it.

8/16/62

So Who's Afraid of Edward Albee?

A play by David Starkweather, directed by Robert Dagny, at the Caffè Cino.

Two weeks running the Caffè Cino has given premiere productions of plays by David Starkweather. The current one, playing through Saturday, is a striking romp called "So Who's Afraid of Edward Albee?" Obviously Mr. Starkweather is not, and need not be. His one-act play gambols through the field of Albeean symbolism like a ram in spring. Scattering absurd techniques right and left and blithely ignoring all rules of structure, he nonetheless manages to evoke hilarity, sympathy, and bizarre terror by turns. It adds up to an action-packed forty-five minutes. The production is frantic and excellent, with Neil Flanagan and Brandy Carson turning in pointed, resourceful performances under Robert Dagny's direction and Jonathan Torrey's lighting.

Starkweather's effort the previous week, "You Can Go Home Again," was a pretentious, tiresome amalgam of Thornton Wilder and the heavier sort of expressionism, and actor-director Richard Smithies did very badly by it.

2/28/63

The Madness of Lady Bright

A play by Lanford Wilson, directed by Denis Deegan, at the Caffè Cino.

Lanford Wilson's unmistakable talent for swift, biting characterization and adroit dialogue is once more on display at the Caffè Cino. This time the subject under examination is an aging homosexual, Leslie Bright, camping away a hot afternoon in his cramped apartment and gradually losing his mind. The lines the author has written for his desperate hero are poignant and funny. "There's no question about it anymore," he tells his reflection flatly, "you're a faggot. You're funny, but you are a faggot." Examining his lost looks item by item, he reflects, "Beauty isn't everything. But then, what is?" Communing with his memories, all of whom have autographed the wall over the bed, he assures himself, "Old hustlers never die, they just start buying it back."

Wilson in this play has also made an interesting technical maneuver. In the apartment with Leslie Bright are a boy and a girl, the makings of a triangle that never quite comes alive, and these two figures are smoothly generalized as the play develops. The boy becomes Adam, the one true love of Leslie's life, giving his name to the wall but nothing more. They also become the voices of ridicule, of torment, pushing toward madness. The writing here is uneven; Wilson writes best when he is being most specific, and the play sometimes slides toward sentiment and moralizing. But the essential strength of writing is above the ordinary, and the play certainly has more than routine interest.

Under Denis Deegan's direction, the performance is marked by spirit, telling detail, and an assured control of the space. Neil Flanagan's portrayal of Leslie Bright is expert and delightful, with a clear sense of modulations between joy and manic desperation. Flanagan makes every shading of the character his own; his work is beautifully precise. The other performances, by Carolina Lobravico and Eddie Kenmore, are less effective but unobtrusive. The play is Lady Bright's, and Flanagan makes the most of it. 5/21/64

Incidents

A performance by Yvonne Rainer and Larry Loonin, at the Caffè Cino.

By this time I can recognize an avant-garde idea when I see one, and so my interest at a semi-chance program like this one is quickly focused on the question of how the instructions have been formulated. There is a certain structure, which consists in this case of preset periods of time, words, relationships, props, locations—the instructions—and within this structure the performers react to whatever happens, according to their ability. The incidents at the performance I witnessed were four: an audience-moving sequence; a rehearsal of a brief play; a double event in which Larry Loonin attempted to memorize a short passage about the duties of a special tax agent and Yvonne Rainer became involved with books, a telephone, and a few words; and a closing reversion and surprise. The suspense lies in not letting the audience know what is predetermined and what is new, and much of the fascination has to do with the performers' composure. Rainer's concentration is legendary. Loonin is somewhat less compelling as a performer, but the two of them are personable and adroit in their manipulation of these techniques. My reservation about the result as a public entertainment is that it remains at the level of technique, like most improvisational theatre, and not terribly interesting once the novelty has worn off. Its content is accidental and trivial except in those moments when Rainer's personal style of movement becomes dominant, a hesitant, seemingly painful, highly developed style that seems to express a vision of life. These incidents have value as a concise demonstration of one stream of experimental thinking.   6/11/64

The Haunted Host

A play by Robert Patrick, directed by Marshall W. Mason, at the Caffè Cino.

"That's what the theatre needs, depraved queers and simple country boys!" The speaker is Jay, the host, who has been acting very much like a depraved queer all evening. His listener is a simple country boy. The line is spoken in heavy irony, as are about three-quarters of the lines in "The Haunted Host," and yet the play is oddly convincing. Robert Patrick's central character is so elaborately twisty and continually witty at the expense of his own self-image that the play has intensity and application far beyond the narrow, obsessive situation it describes. The plot is less clear than it might be, and occasionally the technical devices are self-conscious; but the play is obviously the work of a sophisticated and talented writer.

In the title role, the author gives perfect line readings but lacks a sure sense of pacing, with the result that the play proceeds in leaps and spurts and seems more shapeless than it is. William M. Hoffman is convincing in the thankless role of his foil. Director Marshall W. Mason and lighting designer Dennis Parichy move the play through its various moods and moments effectively. 12/10/64

News report and interview
Joe Cino's World Goes Up In Flames

The Caffè Cino was destroyed by fire on Ash Wednesday morning. The modest Italian coffee house at 31 Cornelia Street opened in December, 1958, and became important as New York's most tenacious and active café theatre. For several years the Cino has been presenting plays, changing the program every week, and an emphasis on original scripts has led to the discovery of several talented new playwrights as well as actors, directors, and designers.

The fire, thought to have been caused by a gas leak, completely destroyed the interior of the café; the structure of the building was not affected. The café occupies the ground floor of a tenement building. Credit for containing the fire goes to the fireproof ceiling of the café, recently installed as part of a new lighting system. Ironically, the final payment for the ceiling had been made two days prior to the fire.

Immediately after the fire plans were undertaken for the rebuilding of the Caffè Cino. Joseph Cino, founder and proprietor of the café and impresario of its plays, has been given a temporary home-in-exile at the Café La Mama, where Ellen Stewart has created a café theatre partly modeled on the Cino; on Sunday and Monday nights for the next few weeks Café La Mama will be run by Joe Cino and his staff, and plays scheduled for the Caffè Cino will be performed there.

Meanwhile a group of actors, directors, and playwrights who have worked at the Caffè Cino have banded together to raise money for reconstruction, and benefits are planned.

One night after the fire Joe Cino reminisced about the café and about his life, which have become almost inseparable. He recalled his arrival in New York by bus during a blizzard on February 7, 1948. He was sixteen. "I didn't have a dime," he said, "and I don't have one now." Raised in upstate New York, Cino's theatre background consisted of an appearance on Uncle Ben's Liberty Shoe Hour, singing "I'm Beginning to See the Light," at the age of twelve. In New York he took a succession of jobs—at the Penn Station YMCA, at Howard

Johnson's, at the Hotel Statler. "When I got the job at the Statler, I enrolled in the Henry Street Playhouse and took courses in everything—acting, dancing, speech, makeup, things like that. I was there for two years." Concentrating on dance, he was given a scholarship to Jacob's Pillow during the summer of 1953. Later he danced with Mary Anthony, and in March 1957 went on tour with Maxine Munt and Alfred Brooks. In 1958 he opened the Caffè Cino.

Joe Cino describes how it all began:

"I started thinking about the café in 1954. It would just come and go. It would usually go when there were too many people trying to have a part in it. I would talk about it with close friends and it would just dissolve away into nothing.

"My idea was always to start with a beautiful, intimate, warm, non-commercial, friendly atmosphere where people could come and not feel pressured or harassed and anything could happen. I knew a lot of painters, so my thought immediately was, I'll hang all their work. I was thinking of a café with poetry readings, with lectures, maybe with dance concerts. The one thing I never thought of was fully staged productions of plays. I thought of doing readings, but I never thought any of the technical things would be important."

Cino opened the café in partnership with Ed Franzen, a painter. "Ed was working at NYU, in the printing department. He was looking for a studio to paint in and exhibit his work, and he knew that I was looking for a place of some kind. He called me one day in November 1958 and said, 'I just walked down Cornelia Street, and hanging on this piece of manila rope is a sign saying, For Rent.' And I said, 'What does it look like?' And he said, 'It looks like a big storefront studio.'

"When I got there Ed was in conversation with Josie, the landlady, who was hanging out the upstairs window with blonde sausage curls. He said, 'This is Mrs. Lemma.' I said,

'Oh, you're Italian.' She says, 'Yes, what are you?' I said, "Sicilian.' So she said, 'I don't even have to come down, I'll throw the keys.' She threw the keys and we went in and viewed the ruins. The first thing you saw when you looked down the room was the toilet at the back. I thought, 'There's a toilet, and there's a sink, and there's a fireplace. This will be a counter, a coffee machine here, a little private area.' I turned around and looked and said. 'This is the room. I have no idea what to do with it.'

"We opened on a Friday night in early December 1958. There were thirty people in there, and they were friends. We had one of those old coffee machines, like a Vittorio Arduino, with the eagles on it. It turned out the machine had no gaskets in it, and at pressure the coffee gushed out all over the place. So I borrowed coffee pots all over the neighborhood and set them up under the counter and pretended I was getting the coffee out of the machine. I had never thought of having a waiter, so one of the friends took care of the other friends.

"We started doing poetry readings, and we had the Risa Corsin Chamber Theatre Group. It turned out to be a bunch of poets. What a farce! They were given every second Sunday, a matinee and an evening. This went on maybe for five months.

"What came right after that was Sunday night readings at a long pine table. The first reading we had was Jean-Paul Sartre's 'No Exit.' They did it with three chairs and three scripts. The room was packed, but I didn't even think of doing it again. I thought there were people who didn't want to see this, and I didn't want to disturb the rhythm of the room. That was a Sunday reading, and soon after that we added Monday. It was one performance a night, and before long we added Tuesday, and so on. The hardest thing was to avoid having performances on the weekend. It took almost two years to get from those Sunday readings to a full week. It was always something different every week. They went into staging right away.

"The biggest thing was two performances a night. It seemed very challenging to have an 11 o'clock performance. There were many nights when we went on with no people there, just performing for the room. I feel the room is grateful, something happens to the walls. We started doing two a night by January 1961, and the play was one of the most beautiful things we had at the Cino, an adaptation of Lewis Carroll's 'Alice in Wonderland.' It was thirty-two minutes long. Johnny Dodd did the lighting, and it was very tight just for the actors in the performing areas. The rest of the room was dark. I think it was the first time we had that kind of magic."

During the first years of the café, until 1960, Cino continued in a daytime job at the American Laundry Machinery Company that enabled him to support the café. The initial capital, $400, he had saved by working at the Playhouse Café on weekends. "I learned about espresso, and learned what not to do. I saved every penny I made there. I knew the next thing would be my own room. I saved all the money in a drawer, and I emptied the drawer out into a paper bag and took it to the bank, and it was $400."

At first the performances at the café were put on by a close circle of Cino's friends, but the personnel has widened over the years. Cino himself does not perform. He thinks of himself as a café proprietor rather than a theatrical producer, and his role is to provide opportunities for people to work. The Caffè Cino developed its identity not according to any plan of its creator but was permitted to create itself.

"Once we had started doing the play readings, that was it, it never stopped from then on."

The Caffè Cino's importance to the theatre has been as an arena for new work, primarily for new plays, The Cino's development coincided with the change of Off-Broadway from an inexpensive, relatively informal place for experimental work not requiring mass audiences to a formalized professional institution as much controlled by unions and real estate considerations as Broadway and economically almost as prohibitive to the rise of new work. The Cino represented an alternative, where plays of uncertain finish could be given at small expense for a week's run and continued work, with none of the outside pressures of the commercial theatre.

"We would have long stretches of scenes from 'Separate Tables' and one-act plays by William Inge and Tennessee Williams. We've always done new playwrights in and out. Jim Howard was the first, and then Doric Wilson's plays were beautiful. Jane Lowry was in his plays. She made her return on the last night of the café, in 'War' by Jean-Claude van Itallie, and the same magic came back again. We did Beckett and Pinter, too, the first productions in this country of 'Embers' and 'A Slight Ache.'"

Two of the Cino's playwrights, Lanford Wilson and Paul Foster, have plays on the current new playwrights series at the Cherry Lane Theatre. Cino remembers many more of the playwrights whose work he has sponsored: "David Starkweather's 'So Who's Afraid of Edward Albee?' was one of the high points. We did five plays by Jerry Caruana. A Korean playwright, Pagoon, had two plays at the Cino. There were five by Lance Wilson. We did plays by Paul Foster, Michael Locascio, Harry Koutoukas, Ruth Yorck, Ronald Colby, Donald Kvares, Barbara Guest, Claris Nelson. For a long time we did plays seven nights a week, fifty-two different plays a year."

Cino talks about the café as a going concern. He emphasizes that it is a café, not a theatre. "We're not off-off-Broadway." he says, "we're in-café.

"I firmly believe that there is a definite place for café theatre and really to the letter of café, where hot coffee or hot anything may be spilled on an actor if he doesn't pay attention to the audience. It's very exciting to be working so close to people.

"The way we are doing things, there is no end to the possibilities of improvement. This is without becoming a theatre. There is more than enough to do forever as a café theatre. My only thoughts about expanding are not commercial but only to make it more difficult. Good always comes from what is supposedly bad. What we need now is the room to be open again as soon as possible. I'm very anxious to get open again and continue what we're doing. It is all worth it, forever." 3/11/65

Judson Poets' Theatre
1963–67

What Happened

"What Happened," a play by Gertrude Stein, music by Al Carmines, directed by Lawrence Kornfeld, presented by Judson Poets' Theatre at Judson Memorial Church.

Lawrence Kornfeld's production of Gertrude Stein's first play, "What Happened," is pure lyric theatre, a direct lyrical experience that has no counterpart in logical words or concepts or ideas. There is not much I can say about it except that I expect to go a couple more times during its run at Judson Church, and I hope to see you there.

I will briefly tell you that Kornfeld has taken Miss Stein's open-minded words and made them into a visual anthem, if that makes any sense. He uses five girl dancers who move, act, and speak. The correspondences between the words and the actions are on some other level then sense or reason can determine, but unquestionably they connect. Everything that happens has the casual inevitability of great art. In addition to the young women, Kornfeld has used four men as singers. One of them is Al Carmines, who has composed a delightful score that contains more tunes than "My Fair Lady." He plays it on the piano and sings and moves around all at the same time.

There is a strong form to the play we see, presumably suggested or inspired by the Stein words. (Kornfeld responds to Stein the way Balanchine responds to Stravinsky in, say, "Agon.") Each of the young women distinguishes herself at various times during the performance, and I will let you discover their wonders for yourself. All five are extraordinary. Larry Siegel made a backdrop that is perfect for the play. It is a theatrical fountain of youth. Go, drink.

10/3/63

Home Movies

"Home Movies," a play by Rosalyn Drexler, with music by Al Carmines, directed by Lawrence Kornfeld, presented by Judson Poets' Theatre at Judson Memorial Church.

The main thing I remember about "Home Movies" is that I loved it. I remember somebody slapping a nun in the head. I remember a song about peanuts; a frank and hilarious loving-and-wrestling match on a big satin bed; a whole series of improbable exits and entrances; the vivid confrontation of Freddie Herko with the audience, which has nothing to do with literature; and Sudie Bond's daisies, which you should see for yourself. I remember the infectious rhythm of the play. I can't remember how it all fit together, except that it did, delightfully.

We know the genre: a collaboration between director Lawrence Kornfeld and composer-pianist Al Carmines working with material that permits itself to be molded. Their former triumph in this vein was Gertrude Stein's "What Happened." Rosalyn Drexler's "Home Movies"—a series of improbable tableaux vivants of domestic life—is not nearly so abstract but permits the same freedom of interpretation. Carmines's music is freshly heart-warming and energetic, and Kornfeld has once again contrived an experience that functions in direct theatrical terms: the emotional content is conveyed by the shape of the event rather than in its "meaning." Memory finds nothing verbal to attach itself to, but the sense lingers of an hour joyfully spent.

Kornfeld's method as a director is to release and use the personalities of his performers; the play is not "acted" in a normal sense. When he finds performers with the energy and presence of Herko, George Bartenieff, Barbara Ann Teer, Sudie Bond, Carmines himself, and Gretel Cummings, the results are marvelous and make ordinary theatre look contrived and unconvincing. Hooray for "Home Movies"!

3/26/64

Sing Ho for a Bear!

A musical adapted by Robert Sargent and Lawrence Kornfeld from stories by A. A. Milne, music by Al Carmines, directed by Mr. Kornfeld, presented by Judson Poets' Theatre at Judson Memorial Church.

Al Carmines as Winnie the Pooh! It's an outlandish idea, almost a frightening idea. Winnie the Pooh is a sacred character, after all: we've been carrying him around in our minds since childhood, which means devastating competition for anybody who tries to change our Pooh by externalizing and becoming him. Al Carmines is not even an actor, he is a minister, a song-writer of ability ("What Happened," "Home Movies"), the catalyst of Judson Poets' Theatre and Judson Dance Theatre. The idea of his playing Pooh Bear...

The experience is authentic. Al Carmines *is* Winnie the Pooh while the play is on. He does not supplant the Pooh of the mind but refers to it, complements it, pays homage to it, and it is a pleasure to yield to him. Clad in a furry tunic, adorned with two furry ears, he is irresistibly beguiling and at times incredibly, delicately apt in voicing the spirit of the familiar lines. Resistance to him or any part of the production would be profitless.

By emphasizing Al Carmines's success as an actor, I do not mean to slight his infectiously charming and disarming music. The production is a full two-act musical, and its twenty-six musical numbers give Carmines opportunity for various styles that serve their occasions exactly. Much of the music is built on simple harmonic patterns, which yields an ingenuous, childlike feeling perfect for this work; the composer also shows himself capable of great density of writing.

By emphasizing Al Carmines's music, I certainly do not mean to slight the rest of the cast and production. In these adventures Pooh encounters Rabbit (George Bartenieff), Piglet (Joyce Aaron), Eeyore (Eric Nord), Owl (Florence Tarlow), Kanga (Gretel Cummings), Roo (Susan Kaufman), and Tigger (Christopher Jones). Christopher Robin leads them all on an expedition to the North Pole; Jane Harris at age nine looks much like the famous E. H. Shepard drawings of Christopher Robin, with pageboy bob and mary-janes. This near approximation of "reality" illustrates what an advantage the other actors have. All adult humans, they produce delight and even illusion not by identity with their roles but by contrast. Florence Tarlow is obviously not an owl, for example, and so her owlishness can be stylized and controlled to wonderful effect. We are never jarred by her lapses into humanness, instead constantly surprised at how whimsically owlish she becomes. The very impossibility of playing an owl enables her to relish the fantasy, releasing the audience from preoccupation with its own nature.

Such speculations are irrelevant to the experience. Better to think of Miss Aaron's Piglet in pink padding, flat on her back in a blue spotlight singing "All Alone in the Moon." Or

Miss Kaufman's bouncing Baby Roo. Or Miss Cummings singing an incredible full-blown aria in full voice and full kangaroo guise. Or Mr. Nord's grey gloom as Eeyore on his birthday, or the energetic matter-of-fact sneaky Rabbityness of Mr. Bartenieff. Many of the good things in the evening are ensemble work, when the performing (not exactly acting) is perfectly coordinated by Lawrence Kornfeld's direction—brisk, easy entrances and exits, a constantly expressive sense of the performing space, emphasis on what his performers can do with no regret for their lacks. (In this context wit and enthusiasm easily replace professional polish.) Much credit is also due to the delightfully witty, inventive, lyrical "additional choreography" of Remy Charlip with Marilyn Wood. The production is a complete treat.   12/24/64

A Beautiful Day
Play I Play II Play III

"A Beautiful Day," by Ruth Krauss, music by Al Carmines, choreographed and directed by Remy Charlip, and "Play I Play II Play III," by Gertrude Stein, directed by Lawrence Kornfeld, presented by Judson Poets' Theatre at Judson Memorial Church.

Watching the Saturday night performance of "A Beautiful Day" I found myself thinking, several times, "Remy Charlip is a genius." The word is dangerous in a critic's vocabulary, but I kept thinking it. Remy Charlip choreographed and directed "A Beautiful Day." Ruth Krauss wrote the dozen-plus poem-plays it consists of, and Al Carmines wrote the music, and perhaps they are geniuses too. Certainly their encounter has had miraculous results.

What kind of geniuses? Light, elusive, personal and

particular, instantaneous. They are operating in delicate areas of sensibility, not among the grand passions. Their subject emotions are tenderness, surprise, amusement, comfort, nostalgia. But delicate emotions are not necessarily weak, and the production proves as well that sweetness and charm are not necessarily cloying and precious, that sentimentality is not necessarily soft or false. All these dangers are almost perfectly avoided. "A Beautiful Day" is insistently human, grounded in the reality of human feeling and experience; despite its lightness it never floats into the looser, more detached regions of fairy tale and fantasy. Its distinct and incisive bite produces the nourishment of astonishment and delight.

Ruth Krauss's writing is the basis. The show is a group of her poem-plays, which extend in form from tiny blackout skits to elaborate narratives. Their content is simple, charming, often sentimental, but they are saved from sentimentality's traps by two characteristics in the writing. One is its range and specificity of reference, which by bringing together disparate fragments from the most widely separated fields places events in the context of the real wide world. Second is its pure verbal felicity, which occurs mainly in the variations of rhythm and sound patterns and by graceful irregularity keeps the ear and mind alert. An example of both is a line from "This Breast," a long poem-song that opens the show: "This breast, suggesting by turns the mother, the mistress, the father, the church, Ireland, England, Greenland, Tierra del Fuego, and the boot of Italy."

Al Carmines's music is more varied, responsive, and complex than ever before, without any loss of charm. His inventiveness seems unlimited. He bounces from mood to mood with unflagging ease, writing brief lyrical or comical snatches as readily as extended vocal ensembles. The music contains stylistic references in wide variety but almost never seems merely derivative or pastiche. The sheer quantity of it is amazing; he leaves dozens of good ideas casually suggested. The music is pleasantly unassuming, devoted to theatrical service rather than its own development. Carmines is without question one of the most prodigious and effective composers writing for theatre.

Remy Charlip's work is distinct from anyone else's because of its perfect clarity. Even when he is abstract his intention is clear, the emotional content readily accessible. Charlip's background is dance and children's theatre, and he has written and illustrated a number of children's books. His work on "A Beautiful Day" reflects this. Often he illustrates the text directly, inventing gestures and actions that specifically demonstrate, elucidate, intensify, or comment upon the meaning. At other times he creates abstract movement for the same purpose or in counterpoint; in three pieces he uses dance as dance. His third strength is pure style. His use of space, visual wit, and sense of timing are impeccable. Several pieces are spectacular for the originality and simplicity of his imagination and the exactitude with which he has carried it out. The entire production radiates his concern and feeling for the material, an unmistakable devotion to showing it and the performers to best advantage.

The theatrical occasion comes into being when Ruth Krauss, Al Carmines, and Remy Charlip encounter particular performers. Florence Tarlow in "This Breast" and "A Beautiful Day," Aileen Passloff in "Onward" and "A Show a Play: It's a Girl," and Sheindi Tokayer in "As I Passed the Andy Auto Body" and "A Show a Play" are the outstanding examples. Miss Tarlow's performance of "This Breast" is an astonishing tour de force, and Miss Passloff's dancing of "Onward" is exquisite and breathtaking. (If you have never seen Miss Passloff dance, you have a special pleasure ahead.) Both are perfect encounters between creator and interpreters, and the results in each instance are lovely. Several group works are also marvelously effective, with excellent performances given at various times by David Vaughan, Charles Adams, John Herbert McDowell, Gretel Cummings, Jamil Zakkai, and Burton Supree.

Contributing to the success of "A Beautiful Day" are the lighting by John P. Dodd, the set pieces by Malcolm Spooner, and the costumes by Maria Irene Fornés and Sue Smith. I participated in the production by running the lights for some performances. As a result I have witnessed the superior service given by the stage manager, Lee Guilliatt. Good stage managers are rare and rarely given credit for their work, which is exacting and essential.

"A Beautiful Day" is perhaps somewhat less effective as a whole than in its parts, although it has been assembled with care and skill. Its form is that of a revue, i.e., fragmented and discontinuous, which prevents "A Beautiful Day" from quite cohering as a major theatrical event. Nonetheless, it is a superbly entertaining collaboration, and contains some of the best and most delightful theatre work I have seen in a long dry time.

Preceding "A Beautiful Day" on Judson's double bill is "Play I Play II Play III," by Gertrude Stein, as directed by Lawrence Kornfeld. Kornfeld, an exceptionally creative director, has fashioned a piece of pure theatre music. Gertrude Stein's words, four actors, a narrator, and some flute music by Telemann have been ordered into a unified stage event. Its organization is based on the formal tools of classical music: themes (in word and in action) are stated, varied, recapitulated; dynamics are structured to produce tension, climax, and release; variations of rhythm and tempo proceed in precise patterns; the play seems even to break down into movements.

Kornfeld knows exactly what he is doing, and he is very very good at it. The piece is fascinating to watch and occasionally brilliant. It is almost without human content, however; as a result, the few moments when Kornfeld's invention flags are completely blank. The technique is intricate and extremely clever, but once it has been grasped there is little else to hold one's attention. Stein's words are stated and repeated and repeated and varied and re-arranged until they are reduced to abstract patterns of sound and their associative impact is exhausted. Toward the end, the piece is engaging only in flashes. Kornfeld has not provided an equivalent intensity on the level of abstract movement (as he did in "What Happened," using dancers), and the piece is visually dull. He is most fortunate in his quartet of actors— George Bartenieff, Crystal Field, Robert Frink, and Marcia Jean Kurtz—who perform with terrific zest and humanize the piece considerably.

The work seems to be entirely Kornfeld's—a one-man show. He is functioning as a choreographer, not a director. This is his right, of course, and in so far as he succeeds, I give him credit. But it seems an unwholesome approach for a director of plays, who should to a great extent be an interpretive artist rather than a creator, or at least a collaborative creator. Every element of the production—including the script and the actors—is here turned to the director's purpose as if it had no purpose of its own. The approach is too anti-literary for me. Kornfeld can do it to Gertrude Stein, whose writing can survive anything. Here his method suggests a distrust of the writer, or a preference for himself. Despite the insistence in the performance that this is "one play," Kornfeld evidently feels that Stein did not write the play but only provided the

raw materials for him to make the play from.
One further impression I have is of a certain coldness. What content the produced play has concerns human relationships and culminates in a double wedding climaxed by the kiss, when the newlywed husbands switch wives and continue coolly kissing. This is a cold point (it has Stein's style but not her personality). The particular chill I am concerned about is on another level. The aim of the production seems to be perfection. It is as detached as a solo high-wire walk; and while I believe the theatre needs this element of virtuosity, I doubt that it should sacrifice its collaborative warmth in order to get it. 12/16/65

Song of Songs

An adaptation with music and direction by Al Carmines, presented by Judson Poets' Theatre at Judson Memorial Church.

"Song of Songs" is a musical setting by Al Carmines of the Biblical book about "profane" love—in full, "The Song of Songs Which Is Solomon's." Carmines calls the work an opera. More accurately, it is an oratorio with dances and sparse action. In Carmines's own staging at Judson Church, the action vaguely resembles four phases of wedding festivities—the preparation, the night before, the betrothal, the celebration. The setting suggests a palace banquet hall in remote times. The six singers seem at times to have characters, the four dancers to be entertainers at the nuptial feast. But the dramatic impulses are fugitive. Really it's just songs and dances of love. Carmines sits at a grand piano on the stage playing, speaking, singing.

The score is more ambitious than any Carmines has previously attempted. It is eclectic and (in the formal sense) primitive, echoing composers as disparate as Honegger, Orff, and Gordon Jenkins. What gives this music its uncommon weight is its emotional honesty: it is explicitly expressive of important, beautiful, specific feelings. Unlike previous Carmines scores, it never takes evasive action in irony, parody, or self-mockery. This time he means it. The text is from the Bible, and Carmines is a Christian minister. Nor is the content anything but straight: the subject is love, not the popular romance of frustration indulged, not the ever-so-hackneyed word, but the consuming desire of one human being for another. At its best, "Song of Songs" rises gloriously to its occasion.

The high points are simple and memorable. Carmines sings "I am the rose of Sharon" while Aileen Pasloff dances, and together these two extraordinary performers achieve a definitive statement of what it is to be sick with love. Lee Guilliatt sings the rousing "Prince's Daughter," as extravagant and detailed a tribute as any lover could dream. When Christopher Holt wanders through playing a flute solo it is a tender theatrical masterstroke. The climax of the evening is the text "I am my beloved's," thrillingly sung by Andrew Roman and danced by Remy Charlip and Miss Passloff, a rhapsodic, breathtaking expression of yielding to love. This and "The Rose of Sharon" are gorgeous songs by any standard. (Curiously, but only a little distractingly, sex is often reversed from text to performance.) "Song of Songs" is a rich experience for these moments alone. In others and as a whole, it is less clear, less convincingly simple, less than totally effective, but never less than a pleasure.

Nancy Christofferson's costumes can only be described as brilliantly eccentric. The performers are all dressed in different styles, evoking an apparently random range of images and periods. I suspect the choices refer to the individual performers rather than to their barely defined roles or the presumptive setting; but each is imaginative and meticulous. The show gains needed coherence of rhythm and style from John P. Dodd's lighting, saturated in color, pulsing and throbbing like love itself, sustaining in its surge the passion to which the event pays homage. Tim Oksman made a revolving orange tent that provides an original means for entrances and exits without interruption of the flow.

"Song of Songs" is an authentic ceremony of reverence for the beauty and personal force of human love, and as such has my glad assent. 5/4/67

La Mama
1962–68

The Room

A play by Harold Pinter, directed by John Chace, presented by Ellen Stewart at Café La Mama, 321½ East Ninth Street.

Café La Mama is a tiny, dark, cozy, thoroughly pleasant coffee house in a cellar on East Ninth Street. Plays are done there more or less regularly, and the whole operation just about justifies the Lower East Side's being called the East Village.

The current attraction is Harold Pinter's one-act play "The Room." This is the first play Pinter wrote, and while it is not well produced, the opportunity to see it is valuable. For all its immaturities—the nearly sophomoric whims of misleading, the deliberate "absurdity," and the heavy air of symbolism—the play is taut with hints of the power Pinter was soon to discover. One can see him in the act of learning that irrationality doesn't have to be forced to be terrifying, especially when the circumstances seem immutably ordinary.

It is this ordinariness that the cast, under John Chace's direction, fails to convey. Naomi Riseman in the leading role tends to load her lines with unwarranted significance, and with the exceptions of George Kearns, Bruce Sparks, and Donald Julian, the other actors are as yet ill at ease in the public eye. But the production and the place for it are welcome. 11/15/62

The People vs Ranchman

A play by Megan Terry, directed by Sydney Schubert Walter, presented by the Firehouse Theatre of Minneapolis at La Mama.

Under the direction of Sydney Schubert Walter, an Open Theatre alumnus and Off-Off-Broadway veteran, the Firehouse Theatre in Minneapolis has taken a courageous stand for theatrical innovation and political morality. A small, independent, shoestring group, the Firehouse is closer in kind to old-fashioned community theatre than to the glossy temples of regional repertory that get the foundation funds. Devoted to theatre, rather than to culture, it has been running experimental acting workshops and begun to build a company devoted to genuine contemporaneity, and it already has an impressive record of producing difficult, even dangerous plays by new playwrights.

Megan Terry's "The People vs Ranchman," which they brought to La Mama last week, was an impressive example of its lonely enterprise. The play is radical on several levels. In content it explores the subject of violence and repression in America, which the director identifies in a program note as the root cause of the Vietnam war; then moves on to the alternative vision, roughly that of Norman O. Brown in *Love's Body*. In form the play uses many of the devices, generally described as "transformation," staked out in Terry's earlier plays and in the work of the Open Theatre. The production exemplifies a free use of space, reconstruction of the actor-audience relationship, and abstract, expressive use of sound-and-movement dynamics.

The play's hero, Ranchman, is tried, convicted, and executed for sex crimes. He is polymorphously perverse—therefore, an enemy of society, and simultaneously its hero and hope, threatening prophet of the new life. In the trial he is confronted by his supposed victims, accused and condemned by their protectors, executed by the social order from which he has snatched them loose. After his death he meets them again: and now it is clear that they are not damaged but dazzled by exposure to the taboo reality of life in the body. If they are unfit or unable or unsatisfied to live in society, the fault is not Ranchman's but society's. The play concludes with Ranchman's paean and plea to his destroyers, to the audience: "Someone sits next to you," he says. "Someone sits next to you. Enjoy him while you can."

Walter's supercharged production scattered the action throughout La Mama. He used the cast as a chorus, moving together and apart, straining to make contact, fearful, hysterical; rushing in a body from one area to another; chanting, sometimes singing, tapping and beating on noise-making metal props. Alternately they were a mob of bloodthirsty avengers, suppliants desperate for a hero and savior, the people coldly looking on, the jury passing public judgment. By moving into the audience and by direct address, they implicated the spectator in each of these attitudes. From this group emerged the specific characters—the judge, the prosecutor, the victims and their guardians—while Ranchman alone remained intransigently himself.

Despite moments of stridency and pretension, the effect of all this was extraordinary. The spectator was continually forced to take an attitude toward what was happening, to define his own relationship to the attitudes represented in the play. Faced with Ranchman the victim, one's first response was liberal clichés—capital punishment should be abolished, he is to be pitied not condemned, cured not punished. Then Ranchman became the hero and plunged us from this shallow comfortable piety into the depths of

Freud's dark vision of society. Then, step three, Ranchman asserted himself not as a symptom but as a human being like each of us, demanding that we recognize and embrace him not for himself but in and for each our own selves. In this final leap the play transcended itself and became a beautiful, moving experience.

In "The People vs Ranchman" Terry has carried her inventive techniques beyond exercise and experiment and used them to project an authentic personal and universal vision; it seems to me much the best play she has yet written. Its moments of tenderness are particularly good. Its faults are a tendency toward the obvious and melodramatic and a certain sketchiness in the writing—she seems at times to deal in signals, not realities, perhaps leaving too much for the audience to fill in. But these limitations do not seriously reduce her achievement.

Walter's production was impressive in imagination and finish, although it's a style I don't really like. The elaborately choreographed movements, the intricately synchronized sounds were undeniably expressive, but they continually called attention to themselves as much as to the emotional realities they serve. The cast was superbly disciplined, their ensemble work impeccable, if too generally at the cost of individual spirit and personality. The performance that stands out is, not surprisingly, that of Paul Boesing as Ranchman. Boesing is a superb actor, forceful without tension, casual without slackness, impulsive without loss of control.

This is one of several out-of-town and international productions that Ellen Stewart plans to bring to La Mama. This import project promises to be as fruitful as La Mama's export of new American plays to Europe. 5/18/67

Sarah B. Divine! (Part 1)

A musical play in progress by Tom Eyen, with music by John Kramer, directed by the author, at La Mama.

Tom Eyen's "Sarah B. Divine!" uses simplistic farce to reach genuine tenderness. The play is a brisk biography of Sarah Bernhardt ("Sarah, be divine!") jam-packed with theatrical trickery. Eyen has a cast of thirteen, often using those not involved in a scene for background decoration or comment. The role of Bernhardt is divided among three actresses, who portray her from childhood to death and in a variety of roles: Phèdre, Marguerite, Medea, Jeanne d'Arc. The narrative is fragmented in time and space into brief scenes linked and woven together by varieties of choral speaking and crisply patterned movement. Sometimes Eyen is whizzing through classical devices of staging, sometimes toying with figure-ground ambiguity. The play goes in and out of focus as it skips along, one minute a flurry of inevitable Sarah Bernhardt jokes, the next a vividly caricatured confrontation scene, the next a modulation via sound and movement from one mode into another. The flow is maintained almost perfectly from beginning to end—it is a tour de force of both writing and staging.

"Sarah B. Divine!" is a musical; the composer, John Kramer, appears on stage with guitar as Maurice Bernhardt, the Divine's neglected son. The music is in a delicate, very pretty folk style. Kramer plays the guitar gently and sings in a high, sweet voice. The contrast between this music and the slapstick vulgarity of much of the action makes the leaps of mood happen.

The play is outrageously silly, an irreverent cartoon version of Bernhardt's character and career. Eyen stoops

to anything for an effect or a laugh. His sense of humor is appallingly, irresistibly eclectic, and much of the play is hilarious. Its special feature is the flip-side mood, a smooth, sweetly ironic, tender regard for Bernhardt and theatre tradition that comes through surprisingly direct and touching. (This is supposedly the first of several parts, in several styles, of an eventual large-scale "Sarah B. Divine!")
Eyen's direction is impressive for its intricacy, swiftness, suavity, and sustained invention. The cast is disciplined and cohesive but far from faceless: Eyen capitalizes on personality as well as acting ability. Outstanding are the three Sarahs: Helen Hanft as Bernhardt, her Medea, and her mother; Karole Kaye Stevenson, big, beautiful, and knowing, as most of Bernhardt, including Phèdre and Marguerite; and Elsa Tresko as old Bernhardt playing young Jeanne. Also specially good are Bobo Legendre as Eleanore Duse, Kathleen Dabney as a would-be Ophelia, Dan Mason as Dumas, Tarina Lewis as Sarah's "Little Mother," Carole Silon as a wise-cracker, William Duffy as Oscar Wilde, and John Kramer. The production is handsomely set, lit, and costumed, to the designs variously of Saito, Rene Gonzales, Michael Warren Powell, and Mary Nichols. 6/8/67

The Moon Dreamers

A play by Julie Bovasso, directed by the author, at La Mama Experimental Theatre Club.

Julie Bovasso is author, director, and leading actress of "The Moon Dreamers," a mammoth production continuing through this week at La Mama. The play has a cast of thirty and runs nearly three hours. It is in two parts, a musical prologue and the play itself. The whole thing is so big, complicated, and chock full that the sum effect is mind-numbing. It's difficult to think about it coherently, much less describe or account for it. The forty-five-minute prologue is patriotic in theme and heavily satirical in tone. Miss Bovasso makes her initial appearance as a stunningly cool, long-stemmed emcee named Mimi, whose off-hand introductions make the show's elaborately tacky, overcrowded manner seem a deviously subtle formal irony. It starts off in a deliberately deadly rhythm presenting peculiarly half-baked tableaux for the audience's contemplation while ridiculous old-time records are played loudly. First there is a quartet of Citizens: a pair of fake Indians and a bride and groom. Then a trio of grotesquely maimed soldiers from various American wars, a vapid beauty queen, a chorus of nurses doing a hospital ballet, a trio of dancing Negro stockbrokers, an anguished solo dance to "Strange Fruit," finally a trio of whistling schoolboy angels. The whole spectacle is presented with enough razzmatazz bravado to turn La Mama into, say, the Apollo were it not for the blatantly sardonic point of view. Everything that such pageants normally celebrate is here shown to be fake, rotten, cruel, loathsome, and pathological; the content contradicts the style to demonstrate the self-betrayal of the American dream.

The stockbrokers' dance, performed by Barry Montcrease, Clay Taliaferro and Bert Rose, is particularly exquisite and dazzling, and the constant presence of the three crippled soldiers—beautifully played by Norman Hall, Alex White, and Buddy Teljelo—is chilling. The selection of recorded music, including several songs barked by dogs, is amazing; its excessiveness in both quantity and volume adds to its expressive success. The ideas of the prologue, its blunt dead-pan presentation, and the staging—in which Miss

Bovasso was assisted by choreographer Buzz Miller—are inspired. The whole effect is devastating.

The prologue leads immdiately, if not directly, into the play itself, and here the mind really begins to boggle. "The Moon Dreamers" plays on the basic triangle—Sandra has just caught her husband, René Utray, with his mistress, Mimi. One of them has to go, and as they seek a solution, the play interminably balloons into elephantine low farce. Sandra's mother comes over followed by a lawyer, a doctor, an oriental Indian chief and his squaw, two Irish cops, a midget French police chief, a poet, a belly dancer, the bride and groom, and various others, all ridiculous individually as well as generically. It is so grossly excessive, so plainly much too much, all of it in every way, that it would be tautology to criticize it for excess—like saying a three-ring circus lacks focus. To a considerable extent, though, the play is unmistakably self-sabotaging: the manic comic invention piles up until the mind can take no more, no matter how hilarious it is. Much of the audience is turned off and many people leave at intermission, if not before. I'm not at all sure this is a fault or failure in the play so much as its nature. Miss Bovasso has gone to such an extreme that one can hardly imagine she intended the fine tuning and meticulous pace of conventional farce. It's my impression that her bloating of these techniques, to the point of grotesque malformation, is as basic to her theme as the crippled soldiers in the prologue. If the play's subject is contemporary America, its pernicious excess and ill-proportioned overabundance are relevant; and their embodiment in its form is a mark of deep sophistication.

Where the play seems to go wrong is in the central character of Mimi, played by Miss Bovasso herself, who spends most of the play in a deep sleep often mistaken for death. At one point she falls or jumps out a window and lies for a time face down in the mud. In her semi-waking moments she speaks from a dream or trance, in a poetic monotone, almost chanting, slowly, ceremoniously, and incomprehensibly. She is presumably the central moon dreamer, but her dream is impenetrable, at least in this farce context, making her sections of the play dull. I got the impression toward the end that she was aiming at parody, not the pretentious poesy I'd first thought; it's so hard to pay attention to her speeches that my final impression is of stylistic vagueness and blank confusion.

The play's title becomes explicit near the end of the play with the arrival of Ira, somebody's son the astronaut, just back from the moon with a message. Life on the moon, he says, is wonderful; "The earth is populated entirely with moon rejects." Earthly discontents are those, in short, of exiles, suffering because they're out of place, dreaming of an unsuspected world where they truly belong. When this deus ex machina, by some miracle it's too late to understand, offers to take them with him, home to the moon, their squabbles are forgotten and they go. Only Mimi stays behind—and then a man comes for her, just a man. The moon is Eden in the Heavens, a paradise of cheese or paper, it matters not, because the image rings clear, resonating specifically with the world we live in, filling the play with compassion. Mimi may be the only realist: Miss Bovasso does not suggest that the moon dream is true, only that it may bring some comfort to the pitiful farceurs crowded on the earthly stage.

I can't say the play is a success, only that it is an enterprise of great originality and of greater coherence and density than is apparent from its peculiar appearances. The fact that it fails to get through to much of the audience, which at La Mama is earnest and interested, counts against it, though one wishes the audience would realize its anticipations are being manipulated, not thwarted—or would at least be more patient. Three hours isn't such a long time, and no one could say the play lacks interest. By classical standards—"less is more," for example—the play is monstrously inefficient, but this is essential to its theme. The sensation it imposes on the spectator feels something like boredom but is closer to the kind of stupor that comes from overeating or the semiconscious, quasi-hypnotized state induced by overexposure to, say, pre-Christmas crowds at Macy's. You can resist it, put it down, turn it off, or leave; if you stick it out and let it have its way with you, it sucks you into a world that is crazy but complete and weirdly familiar, compelling not so much to the mind as to the spirit. The play's honesty, passion, and relevance are beyond doubt, despite its resemblance to a giant put-on. What is dubious is whether audiences will or can subject themselves to such an experience. I found it difficult, more rewarding in retrospect than at the time.

2/18/68

Harold Pinter, Eugene Ionesco
1962–64

The Dumbwaiter
The Collection

Two plays by Harold Pinter, directed by Alan Schneider, presented by Caroline Swann at the Cherry Lane Theatre.

"The Dumbwaiter," the first of the two one-act plays by Harold Pinter currently playing at the Cherry Lane, is a flip transposition of "Waiting for Godot." Two men are waiting in a cellar for a summons that will send them out on a mysterious, unsavory "job." They chat and bicker. Messages begin to arrive from above via a dumbwaiter and a speaking tube, nonsensical messages ordering food. The two men scramble to comply with these sourceless orders. They send up everything they have, although they clearly do not have what is wanted. Their substitutions are not punished or even noticed; orders keep coming. The play ends with a sharp wrench which I will not disclose.

The meaning of this brief anecdote—at least up until the end, which seems to me arbitrary—is obvious to the point of tedium, although Pinter writes with such skill and wit that one is always kept alert. It is excellently played by Dana Elcar and John C. Becher.

"The Collection," the evening's longer work, is more original and exceptionally diverting. It concerns two couples—one marital, the other male-male—and their intricate interinvolvement in an event that may or may not have occurred. The play—originally written for television—shows Pinter in unerring control of his technique. The play leaps between the two couples' homes via a telephone booth and a bit of sidewalk, with a mastery of timing that sharpens the effects rather than distracting from them. The confrontations assume the patterns of an elegant but mad dance, and the lines of communication tangle hopelessly. The way individual scenes combine realism with unreason is electrifying.

Despite my admiration for the skill with which Pinter wields his chosen technique, both plays left me with the feeling that it is severely limited. It seems to me an afterthought to explain Pinter's refusal to resolve and clarify his situations as an expression of the unclarity and irresolution of life. This way lies a theatre of cerebral games—and I want more than bright entertainment from the theatre. The content of these plays is virtually nil; their fascination is technical. But there is something innately youthful about the fooling Pinter indulges in here, and his talent is enormous, and perhaps he will transcend his exuberance and write something of more weight.

Alan Schneider, who directed these plays, has become the best director now working in New York, and he has made the absolute most of the material at hand. There is a moment in "The Dumbwaiter" when the two men sit back to back on a bed reciting the litany of their furtive plan; Mr. Schneider modulates the tone of the entire play, through this moment, with faultless control. There is a moment in "The Collection" when the husband and the kept boy confront one another in a perfect orgy of restraint, where Mr. Schneider's discretion and taste as a director are unforgettable. The actors in "The Collection"—James Patterson, James Ray, Patricia Roe, Henderson Forsythe—reward him and us with their performances. In particular, Mr. Patterson's subtlety and intelligence are extraordinary, especially considering that the nature of Pinter's technique provides everyone with incompletely written characters. William Ritman is responsible for the sets, which broaden one's idea of what a small stage can encompass. Lloyd Burlingame did the meticulous lighting. 11/29/62

The Bald Soprano
The Lesson

Two plays by Eugene Ionesco, translated by Donald M. Allen, directed by James Nisbet Clark, at the Gate Theatre.

I saw Ionesco's two well-known one-act plays last summer in Paris, where they are still running strong after eight years. "The Lesson" in particular, which I had begun to grow tired of after productions at the Phoenix and elsewhere, had the demonic energy of a Bartok quartet and amazed me by the violent directness of its style. "The Bald Soprano" I knew only from reading and, with limited French, could less well appreciate; the acting had a crisp disdain of personality that wholly suited the anti-play at hand. The Théâtre de la Huchette, on a narrow street off Place St. Michel, is preposterously tiny and cramped for audience and actors alike. The stage is crowded when there are four people on it. The sets must have been bought as junk from a fourth-rate touring company of "Hedda Gabler." In Nicolas Bataille's production, it all fuses, it all coheres, the plays are conveyed entirely.

The present revival at the Gate Theatre more or less attempts to reproduce the style of the Paris production, and succeeds rather less than more. The trick with "The Bald Soprano" is to find a balance between real and artificial. The play's energy is in the conflict between the reality of actors on stage and the unreality of the characters they play, who are only the surfaces they present, whose behavior is arbitrary. They are defined by their actions, costumes, patterns of communication—the content of what they say and do and are is not important and must be kept at arms' length. The dialectic of the play might be: if nothing seems true or real, then we can believe everything.

In the production at the Gate, the actors try to make sense, and the characters sound stupid. It is not the characters who free-associate but the author; the actors are not obliged to "act" the characters, merely to present their behavior. These American actors are steeped in the naturalistic tradition and can't help trying to be real; they seem to feel that they must be interesting, must interest us in themselves, and what they do becomes a barrier between us and the play. A corollary of the attempt to make sense is that they are afraid to play at full speed.

I should add that the performances they give are good performances, and they are skilled actors. Fran Malis is comic and unhappy as Mrs. Smith, Gerald E. McGonagill amusingly obtuse as her husband. But why must they characterize at all? George Reinholt as Mr. Martin comes closest to the impersonality Ionesco wants. William V. Metzo, Thea Ruth, and Jane Cronin are competent in the other roles, all of them, however, too much slaves to the idea of personality.

"The Lesson," following the script fanatically, is solidly conceived in most of its details. It is funnier and livelier in effect than "The Bald Soprano." I must praise Ronald Weyand for the concentration and controlled hysteria he brings to the Professor. Yet this rendition of the play almost completely lacks form.

This play raises a very different production problem. There is much more naturalism here. It is almost a direct horror melodrama. The line of action is almost clear, the plot structure simple. The "absurdity" lies in the wacky absence of content and in the grotesque relationship between the substance and the style of the antagonism that develops. Mr. Weyand and Thea Ruth, as the Pupil, do very well in establishing their characters, and the events move along quite efficiently. Just beneath the surface, though, it is apparent that they are playing from moment to moment. They are not listening for the inner dynamics of the play, and they have a shade too much tendency to dramatize, to make each moment "dramatic" in a more conventional sense than is needed. These hints of misconception and misdirection are fatal to the music at the heart of the play: the abstract, obsessive counterpoint in which Ionesco screws tight on our nerve ends and produces his climax. Against the increasingly meaningless and contentless chant of fake-language names from the Professor, Ionesco plays the frantic crescendo of cries of "I've got a toothache" from the Pupil until he succeeds in driving us mad just as they drive each other mad.

It doesn't quite happen at the Gate, for all the worthy effort. I suspect there is, in fact, too much effort and sense of worth. Neither of the plays is allowed to become really madcap, as when in Paris the maid Marie is matter-of-factly played by a mustachioed man. Why? you may ask. If you are confounded by my replying Why not?, never mind.

9/26/63

The New Tenant
Victims of Duty

Two plays by Eugene Ionesco, translated by Donald Watson, directed by Michael Kahn, at Writers' Stage.

Eugene Ionesco is a completely modern playwright, and if the current production slightly misses the ideal performance style, it still makes a pointed and delightful evening. The essence of Ionesco lies, modernly, in the experience itself rather than in ideas or meanings that can be deduced from the experience. The critic thus faces the depressing alternative of either mouthing platitudes—noncommunication, alienation, existential angst, etc.—or saying nothing and abdicating his own role and identity. Criticism has to do with reasoned discussion, but reason has less than the last word to say about Ionesco's plays.

"The New Tenant" is Ionesco in his Pinter mode—writing better Pinter than Pinter writes—while "Victims of Duty" is Ionesco at his most Ionescoesque. In "The New Tenant": a man moves into an apartment, he is lengthily besieged with conversation by the landlady, movers arrive, so much furniture is moved in that the new tenant is squeezed into a tiny space in the middle of a jam of things—a preserve of things, perhaps a jelly. What is Pinteresque about the play is its "comedy of menace" mood and the antic simplicity with which its facts are distorted to produce an air of mystery. The landlady is, for example, both childless and polymaternal. Pinter does this kind of thing often, disconcerting his audience, using mystification to produce the suspense that naturalist playwrights achieved through plot and character.

Ionesco, however, is more subtle and less purposive.

Ionesco does not alter facts so much as he permits them to change. The play lives in its dialogue and events, instead of existing as an intention that dialogue and events are invented to disclose. Objects—human, artifactual, or fantastic—have their own energy on Ionesco's stage and tend to take possession of it, rendering impossible the idea of drama that produced drama of ideas. Once the wife in "Victims of Duty" starts bringing in cups of coffee, she brings in so many that the stage is filled.

If witnessing the proliferation of objects is not enough for you, if you must have an explanation of what it all means, you will miss Ionesco. (You will also miss living, my Ionesco moral for the moment.) Ionesco is creating theatre, not literature—although his theatre is certainly literary in its wit and sophistication. Furniture and coffee cups in extravagant numbers are not on Ionesco's stage to illustrate an idea but to be looked at. Ionesco gives us direct stage images that illuminate the way we experience existence; he is in combat with idea theatre, which screens us from being itself.

It is as difficult to perform Ionesco's plays as it is easy to write gibberish about them. Ionesco himself has made many statements about how they should be acted, frequently contradicting himself, opening up avenues that invite exploration but may not lead to an accessible performance style. Michael Kahn, director of the present production, has evidently not quite made up his mind how the plays ought to be projected, and the members of his cast have therefore gone several ways. They are exceptionally talented, and many of the results are very good, but "Victims of Duty" is seriously fragmented by this variety of styles.

Charlotte Rae is expertly comic in both plays. Her portrayal of the landlady in "The New Tenant" cannot be faulted. In "Victims of Duty," however, her personality proves a mite solid, the required transformations indicated mainly by cliché gestures. Michael Howard as Choubert seems earthbound in a different way. The role requires him to tunnel through the earth and climb higher than Mont Blanc, all within a living room set; his means of performing these feats seemed centered on his own sensations rather than a demonstration for the audience.

Anthony Holland and Joseph Chaikin offer more promising approaches. As the new tenant, Holland cultivates an extreme mannered detachment that removes him to a separate plane: he takes on the appearance of a tintype or a waxwork, with a personality so cool as to deny its own flesh. His intense passivity is so convincing that the plethora of furniture seems hardly unusual. As Nicholas Tou, the poet in "Victims of Duty," who is proud to admit that he is not a writer, Holland manifests Ionesco's self-satire by broadly kidding his own characterization, practically winking at the audience, having fun at his own expense and thus beguiling us into perceiving the character on its proper level. With a red beard he achieves a dashing, zany presence that melodramatizes his gestures happily.

Chaikin, dissimilarly, plays the detective with violent alterations of personality and mood, lurching from the smiling charm of his entrance, for example, into harsh bullying without visible transition. Within each of its sharply differentiated zones, his acting has a heightened clarity and intensity that leads us to accept it absolutely, though never naturalistically. The character is thus defined by its inconsistencies rather than by familiar patterns. The method pays off brilliantly in the despairing soliloquy, in which the detective enacts Choubert's father. It is Chaikin's performance that gives "Victims of Duty" its rhythm and shape.

The physical production is satisfactory except for problems at the end of each play. The final installment of furniture in "The New Tenant" arrives through a trapdoor in the ceiling, here anticlimactically represented by a decorated bamboo screen. The excess of bread-eating in the end of "Victims of Duty" is played out so literally that I was distracted with worry about how Michael Howard was going to swallow it all. 6/4/64

The Room
A Slight Ache

Two plays by Harold Pinter, directed by Word Baker, presented by Caroline Swann and Martin Lee at the Writers Stage Theatre.

A story has reached me about "The Room," Harold Pinter's first play, which I pass on not because it seems true or false but because of the interesting questions it raises. According to the story, Pinter, an actor, wrote "The Room" (in 1957) as a joke, a parodistic burlesque on the then novel styles of Samuel Beckett and Eugene Ionesco. The play was done at a drama festival, and Harold Hobson, the drama critic of the London *Sunday Times*, hailed it as the first manifestation of a major new playwriting talent.

The play itself, which outlives the intention behind it, is charmingly written in the light, flexible, allusive, suggestive style that distinguishes all of Pinter's plays, telling a parable-like story heavy with provocation and mystery. Those who attempt to unravel the parable will be frustrated; its "meaning" lies in the telling, not in any symbolic correspondences with outside reality.

Today we face some disturbing doubts as to what

"seriousness" is. The revolutions early in this century, by which free association and chance became valid subjects and tools of art, suggested that the most "playful" attitudes and techniques might produce the most "serious" work and, further, made the discipline of academic training seem irrelevant. More recently, "serious" art has become a field separate from "popular" (or "semi-classical") art; the serious artist is denied the ambition of simply pleasing his audience. (Real art is a serious matter; some art is a tax-loss opportunity, some is just entertainment; some art carries status, some gives pleasure.) Part of the problem is the age's, a by-product of the "cultural explosion" that levels distinctions of all kinds, in which the artist is the dupe of popularized misunderstanding of his function. Another aspect is the artist's ever-increasing self-awareness—he sees himself at what seems like the end of history but is denied the reassurance of a live tradition.

As a result, today's artist can trust nothing but the process of his art. His rational mind has been discredited, the traditional techniques seem exhausted. Pinter finds a way to let the play "write itself" in much the same way than an action painter's work is one of the gestures of his life or chance music is made to happen "spontaneously." It becomes difficult and almost meaningless to speak of content as distinguished from form and manner, or to break the processes of writing up into serious or trivial.

Pinter's distinction, which enables him to sidestep the more enervating elements of this situation, is that he is a highly entertaining playwright, and he should be greatly valued for that. The nature of his initial impulse is irrelevant, except that it shows a new way talent can discover itself. His works are fascinating if not profound, whether written in his (possibly) joking beginning manner or later, when he became serious. He draws character with wit and precision in the tradition of English polite comedy; events and language continually hint at mysteries that might hold profound significance but are never elucidated. The energy that moves his works reflects a familiar contemporary anxiety about the safety of ordinary assumptions. His meanings seem to me not so much deep as broad, not bottomless like Beckett's or topless like Ionesco's, but sideless, lacking the definition of corner and edge.

"The Room" and "A Slight Ache" are well produced under Word Baker's direction. Frances Sternhagen is excellent in both plays, drab in the former, bright in the latter, exquisitely in tune with the shifting dynamics of language. The evening is hers, and she carries it. The plays are thoroughly diverting, which sets them above most of their more unquestionably serious competition. 12/17/64

Albee-Barr-Wilder
1962–64

Endgame
Bertha

"Endgame," by Samuel Beckett, directed by Alan Schneider, and "Bertha," by Kenneth Koch, directed by Nicola Cernovich, presented by Theatre 1962 (Richard Barr and Clinton Wilder) at the Cherry Lane Theatre.

Kenneth Koch's "Bertha" is one of the silliest plays I have ever seen. It chronicles the life of Bertha, Queen of Norway, in ten blackout scenes and about ten minutes, and is very funny about eight times, chopping away with a sharp if tiny ax at the foibles of power-wielders, women, and women power-wielders. Sudie Bond does Bertha slyly and near-perfectly. The witty sets and costumes by Remy Charlip are half professional, half high-school, which fits.

Samuel Beckett's "Endgame," which precedes "Bertha" on the first program in the "Theatre of the Absurd" series at the Cherry Lane, is not silly. Beckett is the master among contemporary playwrights. His language is inexhaustibly resourceful; he operates on multiple levels—in multiple modes of thought—simultaneously and consistently; his emotional scope is narrow but implacable; his vision is insufferable and inescapable. One is reduced to negatives.

I have always seen—tried to see—Beckett as not so negative, because he fills his plays with a humanness that is to me inherently optimistic. After all, I tell myself, his characters do survive, so their hopelessness (or despair) is beside the point. They speak of death, but they do not die. Nell, Hamm's mother in "Endgame," probably does die, as a matter of fact, but our evidence is only: "Looks like it." Hamm's father, legless in his ashcan, is seen crying. "Then he's living," says Hamm.

My hope is vain. Hamm asks his servant, Clov: "Did you ever have an instant of happiness?" Clov replies: "Not to my knowledge." Clov in violent bitterness defines "yesterday" as "that bloody awful day, long ago, before this bloody awful day. I use the words you taught me. If they don't mean anything anymore, teach me others. Or let me be silent." Twice in the play Hamm admonishes himself: "Use your head, can't you, use your head, you're on earth, there's no cure for that!"

I am at length convinced that Beckett means all his meanings. The text of "Endgame" is marked throughout with extravagant care for detail, with taut balancings of structure. In the theatre the play is irreplaceable, like nothing else, boring, engrossing, appalling, wildly funny, savagely whimsical, grindingly, grotesquely sad.

The Cherry Lane production under Alan Schneider's direction is faithful and expert. Vincent Gardenia as Hamm surpasses himself; his performance is flawless. Sudie Bond and John C. Becher are perfect as the parents. But Ben Piazza as Clov is too young, too healthy, and too American; for all his skill and effort, I cannot always believe him.

"Endgame" must be seen. 2/15/62

The Sandbox
Gallows Humor

"The Sandbox," by Edward Albee, directed by the author, and "Gallows Humor," by Jack Richardson, directed by George L. Sherman, presented by Theatre 1962 (Richard Barr and Clinton Wilder) at the Cherry Lane Theatre.

Edward Albee's "The Sandbox" is a beautiful play, his most emotionally accessible work and his best to date. It is a tender and delicate twelve-minute tribute to his grandmother and to courage in the face of mistreatment and death. Funny, precise, and perfectly economical, it is greatly to be admired. Under the author's direction, the Cherry Lane revival is impeccable. The cast: Jane Hoffman, John C. Becher, Herman Price, Vincent Romeo, and Sudie Bond as Grandma.

Jack Richardson's "Gallows Humor" impresses me less than it did a year ago at the Gramercy Arts, although it is undeniably intelligent, inventive, and perceptive. I see two main problems. One is that it doesn't hold together as a single play. The subject is death—more specifically, the present-day overlapping of the quick and the dead. The play opens with an ironic prologue delivered by Death, a character out of a morality play. There follows a long deathhouse scene in which a prostitute tries to revitalize a man about to be hanged. And finally comes a scene in the hangman's house, when he tries to break out of his dead life patterns and fails because his wife won't let him think it's possible.

By the end of the play, in short, Richardson strays far from his stated theme. And this brings us to the second problem. The final segment of the play—and finally the play itself—is too specifically psychological. As analysis of

deadly marriage it is chilling, but as drama it is narrow. The hero confronts and succumbs to personal tragedy, but his anguish is not related to anything beyond his own weakness and his own wife's strength. Death-in-marriage is not a sufficient metaphor for death-in-life.
The production is all right. Vincent Gardenia and Alice Drummond are sharp and comic and credible, but Arthur Anderson as the almost dead hero is often dull. George L. Sherman's direction, despite bright flashes of theatricality, fails to give shape to a flawed but valuable play.   2/22/62

Deathwatch
Picnic on the Battlefield

"Deathwatch," by Jean Genet, directed by Donald Davis, and "Picnic on the Battlefield," by Fernando Arrabal, directed by Gene Feist, presented by Theatre 1962 (Richard Barr and Clinton Wilder) at the Cherry Lane Theatre.

To like "Deathwatch" you have to be intrigued with Jean Genet's very special turn of mind. "Deathwatch" belongs in the Genet canon with *Our Lady of the Flowers* and *The Thief's Journal*. It is fantasy autobiography. Genet's mind is here characterized by adoration of the sick and the self-destructive. He romanticizes crime and homosexuality, attaches some kind of mystic aura to both, and merges them. The ultimate criminal — the murderer — is the ultimately desirable lover.

Three men are in a prison cell. One of them, Green Eyes, is a murderer condemned to death. The larger of the others, Lefranc, envies his "eminence." The smaller, Maurice, directly desires Green Eyes. There is much talk about Green

Eyes's "woman"—who may in fact be a man: another Genet concealment. Green Eyes is willing to give her away to anyone at all. The action circles this situation several times. Then Lefranc sees what he must do to become as great as Green Eyes: murder Maurice. And he does. And Green Eyes scorns him.

Green Eyes distinguishes his own murder from Lefranc's: "I didn't want anything. I didn't want what happened to me. It was all a gift. I didn't know I was strangling the girl... You don't know the first thing about misfortune if you think you can choose it." We are carried straight back to Lafcadio and right up to the present, to the beats, to the glorification of the cool.

Still I find the play tedious. I do not find pathology enchanting, and Genet's fantasies are too emotionally loaded for him to have given the play a satisfactory structure. In the current revival, director Donald Davis pursued Sartre's speculation that the play is a dream. This led him to stylize the action, ask his actors to freeze in place at moments, use lighting semi-symbolically. Perhaps too it led to the monotone in which Ben Piazza speaks most of his role as Green Eyes. If so, it is a good example of the harm an intellectual concept can do in the theatre: the monotone adds greatly to the tedium. The other principals, Mylo Quam and Vincent Romeo, are intense and exciting to watch.

"Picnic on the Battlefield," which follows, is a pleasant, whimsical piece of anti-war propaganda by Fernando Arrabal, adroitly directed by Gene Feist. Three of the four main actors—John C. Becher, Jane Hoffman, and Vincent Romeo—are excellent. 3/1/62

Funnyhouse of a Negro

A play by Adrienne Kennedy, directed by Michael Kahn, presented by Theatre 1964 (Richard Barr, Clinton Wilder, Edward Albee) at the East End Theatre.

"Hide me!" cries out the Negro girl to the funnyhouse man. "Hide me from the jungle!" Sarah cries most directly, most piercingly in the guise of the Duchess of Hapsburg, one of her selves. As Queen Victoria Regina, monarch of England, she recalls: "My mother looked like a white woman." As Patrice Lumumba, her black father, she is dead by her own hand, hanged in a Harlem hotel. Her fourth self of Jesus is an almost wordless martyred figure of anguish. These selves circle her in the top-floor room she rents in a brownstone in the west nineties. The terror they hold for her is real if they are not. Her face says, "Say it's not so!"

She wants to be white. Her idol Victoria is there with her, an over-scale white plaster statue seated in state. In addition to the selves, she has men in her mind: Raymond ("He's a poet and he's Jewish and he's very interested in Negroes"), God, Maximillian, Albert Saxe-Coburg. Her mother moves through the room, bald. Her mother looked like a white woman and when the black man her husband touched her she began to lose her hair and her mind. The girl Sarah finds a wad of kinky black hair fallen out on her own pillow on the day the play occurs; with her we live through these and her other obsessions and that ultimate dreadful double fact—she is a Negro, she wants to be white—within the span of the day and of the play she is hanging before us.

I do not know how to evaluate this play as art or craft, but as an obsessive, cruelly honest statement of self it is extraordinary and devastating. Although I am leery of ad hominem criticism, it seemingly must be taken as a personal testament. The character's obsessions are presented in a frantic, lacerating jumble that bears little evidence of transformation and objectification and yet is the inescapable form for the inescapable content. Honesty is, for the character, extended to the point of self-destruction; one cannot avoid the thought that writing it must have been nearly as painful for the author. There are no heroics and essentially no pretenses. The play has its existence on a level to which criticism is nearly irrelevant.

The obsessions are animated with clarity and impact in Michael Kahn's production. The best performance is that of Ellen Holly as the Duchess of Hapsburg, whose one brief scene pushes the play into universality. Leonard Frey, Cynthia Belgrave, and Gus Williams are also excellent. Billie Allen does all the right things in the central role of Sarah—at times she is brilliant—but perhaps lacks the special quality that would focus the play on her presence and make its elements cohere. William Ritman's set is imaginative, moody, functional, if a shade too literal in its Germanic distortions; Willa Kim's costumes are excellent.

The play runs just under forty-five minutes, which for most people is less than the time it takes to get there and back. It seems unfortunate that the producers chose not to pair it with another one-act play to make a longer evening.

1/23/64

Broadway
1963–64

Anything for a Laugh

S. J. Perelman's "The Beauty Part" (*at the Music Box*) is a cross between "Auntie Mame" and "The Bald Soprano," or so I happily thought for the whole first scene. There was Alice Ghostley, done up in the phoniest grandeur, draped along a ghastly settee in a rich, hideous, flimsy-looking library, casually discussing her husband's didoes with private eye David Doyle. There came her husband Bert Lahr, the king of the garbage industry, and son Larry Hagman, much too fresh from New Haven's so–called groves of academe. The whole quartet spoke perfectly awful, giddily high-flown dialogue in the most serious of put-on manners. The sound of pretensions being punctured was inaudible only because of the laughter.

Now, it is a lovely idea to piece together styles of humor in this motley way. Auntie Mame is an American icon, and "The Bald Soprano" has been running for years in Paris. But it is not such a good idea to apply this bizarre technique to such tired topics as Greenwich Village girls, sell-out artists, and Method actors, or to graft in a mocking theme of the search for identity unless you really think it's mockable—or to demand that Bert Lahr play this highly verbal style of comedy.

That first scene is the evening's peak of originality and leads one to expect something quite different from what follows. Out of the library we go, and everyone but Hagman changes guise as we whirl through a chichi beatnik pad, a fashion magazine HQ, a painter's studio, an employment agency in Santa Barbara, California, the kitchen of a couple of Civil War novelists, a right-wing millionaire's conservatory, a Hollywood scene shop, a TV-dominated courtroom, and back. Perelman seems to stay behind in the library, making up names for the characters and waiting to show his antic hand once more in the final scene. Here and there along the way Lahr cuts loose with comedy of definitive proportions. As the paranoid millionaire, he is irrepressible and completely irresistible.

If I laughed almost all the time, I felt that the play is somehow doubly a pity. Perelman is a verbal ironist, Lahr a farceur. Whatever Perelman had in mind got lost somewhere along the way; Lahr kept being held off-stage while Perelman spoke his mind. One hit, in short, might make two smash hits.

Director Noel Willman keeps things moving at an exhausting pace. His eye for comic invention is superb, and I suppose it doesn't matter that he seems to have no standards: anything for a laugh. Charlotte Rae is wonderful in a variety of characterizations, and the rest of the cast is enriched by the flexible talents of Arnold Soboloff, Mr. Doyle, and a host of others. 1/3/63

The Milk Train Doesn't Stop Here Anymore

Tennessee William's new play shares the rueful tone of his novel *The Roman Spring of Mrs. Stone*. That book's title was ironic; the season was really Indian summer, and Mrs. Stone was growing old. The play's title is not an irony. Milk equals youth, or that which gives life, or both; but Williams's newest heroine, Flora Goforth, is old and dying and knows it every minute of these final episodes of her life. She can't even fool herself, Williams tells us. Does it make much difference that her death is a little more imminent than Mrs. Stone's? At its best, "The Milk Train Doesn't Stop Here Anymore" (*at the Morosco*) is a profoundly cynical, corrupt, disgusted play. Williams spells it out in a program note: Flora Goforth "is not a human being but a universal condition of human beings." Her life has been an irredeemable succession of trivia, some of them frivolous and gay, some of them grotesque and mock-tragic. Even the struggle against death has no value in it. Flora indulges herself, debases herself, desperately reveals herself—and everything she does is useless, as useless in life as it is useless against death.

Williams balances against Flora the poet and artist Christopher Flanders, the latest incarnation of his ever-aging young man, who seems to have sold his body and his youth but has actually given them away, who is profoundly tired, who tries to help and protect and save but is always misunderstood and mistrusted. Chris comes to Flora in her complex of villas on the Divina Costiera. Penniless, he has walked up a steep goat-path to reach her, carrying in his knapsack a book of poems, a verse translation of a book of Hindu philosophy, and the mobile he has made. Flora is living in emphatic isolation, dictating her memoirs frantically to a secretary, Frances Black, who is obsessed with the memory of the physicist husband who died recently in terrible pain. Flora, in pain, calls the agony of dying after an empty life "neuralgia" or "allergies." Chris tries to save them both and to save himself through them. But his words are rejected, his mobile is scorned, he himself is feared. Flora grotesquely tries to seduce him; but he is drained by now, purified too much, and can no longer give himself. Instead he hangs the huge mobile from her chandelier and leaves it turning there before her.

Chris is Christ, thus far we can go in the parable, but having made this step we find ourselves stranded, because Williams does not carry us farther. Christ comes to the overblown, dying Flora and can give her nothing but an empty, antic symbol. Still, the material of the play, even if it is not worked through, is extraordinary, taking on nothing less than life and death, and confronting them directly. The vision it reveals, if not clear, is chilling. Williams shows us what he sees without holding back; the disappointment is that he does not see further, beyond obsession, that having gone this far he stops (he seems to want to tell us what is in Chris's Hindu book). He cannot quite bring the vision to life, for his writing has gone curiously dead.

These characters do not breathe. Where we expect revelations of character, Williams gives us only the glittering surfaces of empty people in an empty world. To make them interesting he surrounds them with the trappings of chic. Flora is a cliché, speaks in clichés, is described in clichés and revealed only in clichés, which is to say she is not revealed at all. Chris has been purified in the writing to the point where his part is only outlined, where the "meaning" displaces life. Frances is nothing but a mourner, condemned to sounding one note throughout the drama. If the technique is true to the vision, it is unaffecting in the theatre.

Williams is badly served by the production. Director Herbert Machiz has allowed Hermione Baddeley every kind of excess as Flora; she needs help, and clearly no one has given it to her. Her suffering seems grotesque theatrically as well as in terms of the character. Paul Roebling plays Chris with extreme elegance and simplicity, but Chris is written as a symbol, and no amount of dedication and skill can bring him to life. Ann Williams plays Frances's one note well; inevitably it grows tiresome. Only Mildred Dunnock comes off well as an actor in the comic role of Vera Ridgeway Condotti, the "witch of Capri," which suits her formidable talents. The production seems to obscure what Williams is getting at, and as a theatre experience the play is extremely unsatisfactory. Jo Mielziner designed an elaborate, beautiful, awkward setting that hangs between decadent luxury and the burned-out isolation of Williams's double conception. Director Machiz seems to have mistaken the surface—the gimmicks, the distractions, the talk of Hispano-Suizas and costume balls, Chris's apparent corruption—for the essence. The emphases fall in all the wrong places; the play plays dreadfully badly. But the intensity and insistence of Tennessee Williams's vision is everywhere behind it, still developing, unmistakable. 1/24/63

Oh Dad, Poor Dad...

It seems to have become fashionable to trivialize Arthur L. Kopit's first, fabulously successful play, "Oh Dad, Poor Dad, Mamma's Hung You in the Closet and I'm Feelin' So Sad," which after a long off-Broadway run at the Phoenix and a national tour has now been revived for a limited Broadway engagement (*at the Morosco*). The play offers easy targets for sophisticated archers: the familiar momism of its subject, the self-consciousness of its title, the frequent cuteness of its humor, the over-publicizing of its author, the play's briefness and narrow scope, and the contrastingly big-time aid of producer Roger Stevens, director Jerome Robbins, and original star Jo Van Fleet, whose triple presence off-Broadway could presumably turn anything into a hit. Such powers seldom invade off-Broadway in avant-garde trappings, and when they do we are right to be wary. The fact is, "Oh Dad" has moments of extraordinary high comedy and of equally extraordinary poignancy, and while it is a very rickety piece of work, it is much superior to many of the plays that come to the stage in more serious, earnest, openly hard-working guise.

The play is improved in its Broadway rejuvenation. Hermione Gingold has replaced Miss Van Fleet as the voracious man-hanger of the title, and she is a great improvement. The tone of the play is lightened, one is less aware of the work going into the performance, one can laugh with the character as well as at her—she is a good-humored monster—her performance allows a certain faint shade of sympathy in spite of everything—she is lethal, but she has style. Miss Gingold seems to appreciate the humor of it all much more than Miss Van Fleet did, and since Mr. Kopit approaches his quasi-tragedy through comedy, that's the main thing. Miss Gingold does not indulge her comedienne self most of the time but engages the meat of the script as an actress, with considerable success, although she does not always make the words understood.

Also new to the cast is Sam Waterston as son Jonathan (or Edward or Albert or Robinson), and he is super good. His stammer is fabulous, his stream of single-mindednesses exact and heartbreaking, and his final moment of attempted contact with the passing airplane is beautiful. Absent is the faintly repulsive quality Austin Pendleton brought to the role at the Phoenix. I'm not sure it's missed.

The new Rosalie is Alix Elias, who exactly reproduces the vocal inspirations of Barbara Harris and never quite makes the part her own. The Balthusian attitudes of the bedroom scene are still magnificent—they are director Robbins's doing—but now the scene winds down instead of up. Sandor Szabo is still doomed to play Commodore Roseabove, that hideously unplayable foil for the mother.

Despite all the good things, there are dreary stretches of bad writing and inexact imagining that disfigure the play. Some of it works in print but fails on the stage. Madame Rosepettle's monologue is the outstanding flop: I fell sound asleep the first time I heard it and couldn't keep my mind from wandering the second. Mr. Kopit's baroque diction makes it impossible to follow his train of thought, which, when finally traced through, turns out to be clumsily conceived and pointless. And yet the speech goes on for nearly fifteen minutes. The scene preceding it is a hodgepodge of tones and directions, which neutralize one another and leave a vacuum. It is not only Jonathan who can never come to the point with Rosalie, it is Kopit, who hadn't yet the craft to build a climax cleanly.

Robbins's main achievement was to make this most awkwardly constructed of plays function as a unit. He has made inspired use of music, of filmed entr'actes, and of lighting to achieve this. His actual staging is not always so sure: the opening procession of bellboys, for example, is flat, and when the script lets the actors down, so generally does he. But he and Kopit can and do modulate moods from star-spangled to mauve like nobody's business. 9/5/63

Oh, What a Lovely War!

I am shocked at the reviews that Walter Kerr and Harold Clurman wrote of Joan Littlewood's "Oh, What a Lovely War!" (*at the Broadhurst*). To my mind it is the single indispensable production now playing in a New York theatre (and probably also the most joyous). It is not on the question of quality that I am shocked. Mr. Kerr took the attitude that we know all about pacifism and, consequently, are properly uninterested in the subject after the first or second mention. Mr. Clurman took the line that this is the sort of thing the American theatre is much better at (giving not one single example) and concluded as follows: "There is something depressingly sentimental about protesting the ravages of war when so little is ever done to fortify ourselves in the day-to-day conflict of living before war breaks out." There is something depressing about such a sentence coming from Harold Clurman.

"Oh, What a Lovely War!" is a demonstration of the murder of innocence. It is a reenactment of the First World War slanted to reveal its arbitrariness, stupidity, ugliness, to illuminate the irrelevance of virtue on a level of intensity that has moral echoes far deeper than mere "pacifism." "Oh, What a Lovely War!" is not opposed to war but to inhumanity, of which war is a special case. It proves a point that Mr. Clurman, in his preoccupation with sentimentality, apparently missed: that the amenities of "the day-to-day conflict of living," of individual people learning to know and love one another, are useless in a world that pridefully would destroy its citizens in units of hundred-thousands.

"Oh, What a Lovely War!" does not preach or cite text and principle. Its device is presentation—this is what the war was like, the songs they sang, the letters they wrote, here are photographs and scenes, can you not see the grotesque pointlessness of it? To me it is devastating, devastating, to see men destroyed by other men who have forgotten what a man is, who can order thousands to their deaths on a theory, out of pride, out of ambition. I am already convinced, I am moved by the terrible sadness of something I already know to renounce. What happens to those in the audience who believe in war? What do those feel who support the business in Vietnam, who wish we would invade Cuba, who are ready to risk nuclear war in defense of "freedom"? I don't think it changes their minds. I wish it did, but I imagine that they, like Kerr and Clurman, laugh at its jokes, cavil over its techniques, and dismiss its content.

Unlike other morality exercises (lest all this scare you away), "Oh, What a Lovely War!" is not self-righteous and aggressive toward its audience but beguiling. Ordinarily in the theatre the audience identifies with the characters; here an identification is deliberately set up between the audience and the actors themselves: one feels not preached to but coinvolved. The play is as anti-Puritan in impulse as it is anti-war; it joins the two hand in hand. Implicit in its form and spirit is a vision of life as joyous and expansive: it is this that makes the issue worth arguing. Thus the play takes the form of a musical entertainment that is largely light-hearted, sentimental, charming, often uproariously funny. The difference between standard World War I chauvinistic esprit and Miss Littlewood's is subtle but complete. That carnage was inspired, supposedly, by idealism, principles, God; Miss Littlewood's eye is on man.

Enough has been written about the techniques of the production. Miss Littlewood has borrowed from every source with remarkable tact. The actors demonstrate ensemble playing more zestful than any New York has seen since "The Hostage" on Broadway, another Littlewood project. Victor Spinetti, Barbara Windsor, Murray Melvin might be called outstanding—in fact the entire show is outstanding. Believe nothing any critic tells you. See for yourself. 10/15/64

The Living Theatre
1963–73

The Brig

A play by Kenneth H. Brown, directed by Judith Malina, at the Living Theatre.

It is true that "The Brig" isn't a play. Neither are all the events in the Judson dance series dances, nor are Jim Dine's paintings pictures, exactly, nor in normal terms are John Cage's compositions always music. It is meaningless to criticize any of these works in terms they don't use. "The Brig" uses a stage and (in a sense) actors and (in a sense) dialogue—but it does not use story, plot, character, conflict and resolution, or any of the other traditional devices of drama.

"The Brig" is reminiscent of "The Connection" in its emphasis on verisimilitude, although its methods are different. The people on the stage are not required to "act" much; instead they are defined by their activities. "The Brig" goes a step beyond "The Connection"; in the latter the actors were required to pretend, since they presumably weren't actually shooting heroin in performance; in "The Brig," however, with slight exception the actors are made to experience the degradations literally, to perform the appalling tasks, to suffer almost all the pains of their characters. During the performance the actors retain their identities in the same way and to the same extent as do civilians who enlist in the Marines and are thrown into the brig.

Printed in the Living Theatre's program is a series of "Brig Regulations," which for dramaturgical purposes function much the same way as the stringencies a playwright like Beckett imposes on his work: e.g., the mound of muck in which Winnie is buried in "Happy Days." Once the playwright has established this kind of convention, much of his work is dictated by it. Most of the action and dialogue of "The Brig" is dictated by Rule No. 2: "At each exit and entrance within brig boundaries, there is a white line painted on the floor. No prisoner will cross any white line ... without requesting permission to do so, using the form: 'Sir, prisoner number ... requests permission to cross the white line, sir.'" The regulations playwright Brown has imposed upon himself dictate virtually all the dialogue and action, the tone of voice, the costuming, the haircut, the manner of movement, and the props. The playwright has left himself no opportunities.

The event that proceeds from these principles, the event now occurring nightly at the Living Theatre, is a representation of a day in the Marine Corps brig at Camp Fuji, Japan, in March 1957. The ten prisoners are wakened at 4:30 a.m., they dress, make their beds, wash, march off to breakfast; they return, and the day continues. The basic mode of action is brutality: the guards humiliate the prisoners by enforcing preposterously complete discipline. The slightest infraction of any regulation is punished with a punch in the belly. The dialogue consists of bellowed orders, yes-sirs and no-sirs (solo and in chorus), the white-line speech repeated countless times, and very occasional, virtually inaudible exchanges between the guards. The incidents include a rest period in the prison yard during which the smokers, having been separated from the non-smokers, are given their one cigarette of the day with elaborate ritual, during which one prisoner is required to jog around the confine for about fifteen minutes; a "field day," which is a complete scrubbing of the floor of the brig—with brushes, buckets of water, squeegees, and mops—and a complete disassembling of the beds and changing of their linen; several complete dressings and undressings by all the prisoners; the release of one prisoner; the nervous breakdown of another and his removal to the hospital; and the admittance of a new prisoner.

My reaction as audience was to take the first fifteen minutes or so as scene-setting, with the assumption that soon—as soon as we had been given enough of the background—the central characters would emerge from the anonymity of prisoners-and-guards and the dramatic action would begin. This never happens. In a sense the entire play is devoted to scene-setting. Instead of permitting audience-members to identify with characters on an individual basis—essentially a sentimental approach—"The Brig" engages the audience directly with its characters' situation—an approach advocated by Brecht. I am not so much shown a representative of myself suffering in the situation as I am taken personally into the situation and made to suffer through it myself. The norm in the brig is brutality, this norm is stated and illustrated again and again and again, and eventually there is no other norm and no other world. By passively witnessing the real suffering and humiliation of the actors, the audience becomes accomplice to the inflicting of that suffering on the prisoners.

The play achieves its political impact because it is not horrifying. One feels inhuman in watching this play and not being horrified; yet this brig is the direct and inevitable outcome of the Marine Corps system, which is the outcome of ... everything. In order to be horrified by "The Brig," one must be horrified by every act of external discipline, by every arbitrary regulation, by every inflicting of control on the weak by the strong. In order to be horrified by "The

Brig," in short—in order to be human in this context—one must embrace anarchy.

"The Brig" is director Judith Malina's as much as author Kenneth Brown's. The script being animated here is the outline for a theatre piece. (The original script included at least two scenes of Japanese life, outside the brig, which were omitted with the author's consent. The author's statement must have been contained in the contrast between scenes inside and outside the brig.) This "Brig" only has existence as a theatre piece on a stage, and Judith Malina—with set-designer Julian Beck—has brought it into existence with fanatical intensity. The play alternates between total order and total chaos, and the director's control is everywhere subtly in evidence. Her theatrical vision is muscular and obsessed, and it is realized with brilliant devotion. The actors who sacrifice themselves to this vision are Jim Anderson, Henry Howard, Chic Ciccarelli, and Warren Finnerty as the guards; and James Tiroff, Tom Lillard, Rufus Collins, Steve Thompson, Michael Elias, William Shari, Jim Gates, George Bartenieff, Steven Ben Israel, Leonard Kuras, and Henry Proach as the prisoners. If they are denied the satisfactions of conventional acting, they are privileged to be participants in the Living Theatre, which here restates its presence as our most original, profoundly adventurous, and persistently important theatre institution.   5/23/63

The Maids

After the tax-collectors closed the Living Theatre on Fourteenth Street, where its dead shell remains, Julian Beck and Judith Malina took their latest production, Kenneth H. Brown's "The Brig," to London. Out of the cast and crew of "The Brig" evolved the present Living Theatre company, a free-form self-conscious community numbering around thirty people, permanently on the road in Europe. The Living Theatre had played in Europe twice before, performing "The Connection," among other plays, and winning the top prize at the Theatre of Nations festival in Paris. There have been a few long gaps between engagements; living conditions have sometimes been wretched, at best fairly makeshift. But the theatre has survived and continues to make new work and find receptive audiences.

Judith Malina's production of Genet's "The Maids" opened in Berlin in early spring. I saw it in Munich, at the medium-sized, modern Theater in der Leopoldstrasse.

I did not greatly admire the production. Its concept seemed to end at the by-now-familiar trick of having men play the parts, which are all female. (The author wanted boys.) While much of the work was theatrically effective, it relied more on appearances and the players' fierce concentration than on any manifest vision of the play itself. Julian Beck looked extraordinary as Claire and sometimes managed to animate the dense music of Genet's writing; William Shari focused convincingly but too constantly on the breaking edge of Solange's hysteria; Luke Theodore was handsome and stylish as Madame, capitalizing on the contrast between his strong physical presence and the character's fluttery, confused personality. All three performances had gaps in them, and so did the production as a whole—points where the detail was incomplete or vague, where execution fell noticeably short of understanding.

"The Maids" is the most frustrating of plays. Endlessly intriguing as a project, its realization is always a disappointment. I have never known it to come alive dramatically except in fragments and isolated images. The play will not yield itself directly; the audience must always interpret and interpolate. (Sartre's famous introduction to the play is partly at fault for burdening it with the idea of ideas.) The action is confusing, the plot premise weak, the language compressed and energized almost to opacity, and the ritualizing repetition tends to become boring.

Despite its annoying mannerisms and ultimate vacuity, the play is hypnotically engrossing. As I sat among the Germans and watched it and listened to it, I was swallowed up in the intense, obsessional rhythms and emanations. Only afterward did I feel that its pleasures had been peripheral, that the quirks and difficulties were its main interest and had to remain unresolved. Without the sense of incompletion and inevitable frustration, the emotions would seem gratuitous, the themes threadbare. Success with the play, in short, may result from failing to overcome its difficulties.

It is heartening to find, meanwhile, that even if New York will not support an enterprising and devoted professional experimental theatre, the world has not shrunk so small.

8/12/65

Frankenstein

By brilliant luck, I arrived in West Berlin in time for the opening night of the Living Theatre's "Frankenstein" at the Akademie der Künste, where it has just concluded five performances. If I had reviewed it right away, I would have reported a painful disappointment. Having read Saul Gottlieb's descriptions of "Frankenstein" in *The Voice* and in *Tulane Drama Review*, the performance seemed to me nothing more than an enactment of the description. The same events occurred, but actuality had no extra dimension, no magic. The complex, ambitious conception was more engaging as an idea than as experience. Much of the performance, in fact, was boring: the presentation seemed repetitious, needlessly slow, over-emphatic, the acting style clumsy and sometimes amateurish.

This first encounter with "Frankenstein" was painful because my central purpose in coming to Europe was to see the Living Theatre. Its exile had left a hole in New York theatre, which everywhere seems to suffer the lack of any dynamic ideology, any passionate commitment to theatre in the world, to a life in art. Without the Living Theatre, Off-Broadway had lost its focal point, and Off-Off-Broadway too often seemed like play. As much as my life is involved with theatre, I felt this personally. Meanwhile the Living Theatre had not died, it had gone away and gone on, and I came to see it, to see if such a thing as experimental theatre is possible, or if it matters. When I saw "Frankenstein," that first night, I thought in terror that I had found my answer, a flat no. I'd have to look elsewhere or give up the search.

During the next few days, spending time with old and new friends in the Living Theatre company, I was reminded that the Living Theatre is more than just a theatre, it is a community, a way of life, almost a religion. Theatre is the metaphor in which the company lives, but the importance of the Living Theatre is the total gesture in the total context. I needed to rationalize what I saw as the failure of "Frankenstein," and it was surprisingly easy to do so. Broadway has to be concerned with results, with consistency and effectiveness, not the experimental theatre; and the Living Theatre is genuinely, profoundly experimental. Its experiment is not limited to a few onstage tricks and innovations. The entire existence of the company is a provocative, dangerous experiment, and experiment requires the freedom to fail. Experiment is measured not only by its success but also by the boldness, quality, and relevance of its enterprise and the intensity and tenacity of its procedure.

The Living Theatre is experimental on many levels. In its present incarnation—increasingly distinct from its Fourteenth Street life—it is an American theatre itinerant in Europe. It is a theatre in a sense that hardly exists in America: a large, permanent, dynamic company with a repertory of four productions, soon to be five. The company consists at present of twenty-eight adults and five children, who are all dependent on the theatre for their financial and spiritual support as it is dependent on them for its existence. (They are paid a rough equivalent of Off-Broadway minimum.) Judith Malina and Julian Beck are the geniuses of the company, it is unmistakably their theatre, but its operation seems more cooperative now than it ever did in New York. Its communal life is extra intense because the company and the work are the only points of relative stability and permanence: traveling, the theatre must be self-sufficient. The theatre must occupy the center of its members' lives.

The quality of involvement and quantity of energy this situation produces is extraordinary. The theatre work determines the value and meaning of the company's demanding and difficult lives; and in these circumstances there is no comfort for anyone who gives less than his best. The structure of the situation creates for the members of the company a valuable self-esteem as artists and provokes them to excellence, just as the situation in New York suggests that no one should take his art too seriously.

Later I saw another complete performance of "Frankenstein" and watched some parts several times. I discovered that technical mistakes, particularly in the lighting, had seriously marred the opening-night performance in Berlin. I saw an increasing assurance, passion, and coherence among the actors: the play had not been performed for a month, never on this particular awkward stage, and there had been no time for a full rehearsal before opening. The second time I saw the immense quantity of personal detail in the individual performances; what had appeared to be trite, abstract movements were, I discovered, richly particular. Each performance, I realized, is as interesting as the performer giving it, and the Living Theatre company is a group of exceptionally interesting people.

I was learning how to see "Frankenstein," and it isn't easy. The play is unlike any theatre I have seen before. The second time through I could see more of what was happening, on the stage and in the play's mind—which is the collective mind of the Living Theatre, for the play was created by the entire company. I began to see past the tricks, good and bad, to the life of "Frankenstein," which has a grotesque and artificial but authentic life like the creature it describes. It is a single monstrous metaphor, this play, an artifact as well as an image of all the monstrousness in civilization. It is the Living Theatre's personal, eccentric, extravagant indictment of civilization—and it ends in affirmation, in a gesture of acceptance, love, peace.

My initial disappointment with "Frankenstein" had been, then, partly the result of a bad performance, partly a slowness in my own vision. As I began to see "Frankenstein," I also saw that it is not yet fully realized. It is sometimes too hard to follow, needlessly inaccessible. It is sometimes tedious, repetitious, or too slow, and a few parts are too long. A few of the technical devices misfire and throw off the tone and rhythm.

Also, the Living Theatre now lacks good actors more than it did in New York. I mean actors in the conventional sense, and in "Frankenstein" this doesn't too much matter. The roles were created by and for these performers, and in general they do not call for "acting." Instead of acting—that is, pretending to be predefined characters experiencing predefined feelings—"Frankenstein" demands enactment—that is, the performance of actions by the performers themselves. There are only two or three fictional characters in "Frankenstein"; generally, the actors bring themselves onto the stage, without the camouflage of pretense. Occasional "acted" moments in the play are thin and unconvincing, but the redefinition of the actor's task, dictated by need, is exciting and rich in possibilities and leads to high-intensity ensemble work.

"Frankenstein" is constantly changing, still growing. An entire new third act was made this summer. Someday, with continued work and many more performances, it may be finished. It already has the character of a major, revolutionary theatre piece.

I am thus able to rave about "Frankenstein" in spite of not having liked it. And I'm not just saying this: I really have developed a passion about "Frankenstein"—the kind of love-hate-terror one can feel for an especially real person. My impulse comes, I'm sure, from my feeling for the people in the Living Theatre—I like many of them individually, admire and envy their commitment and involvement, and believe in the necessity of the revolution they represent. Their lives demonstrate that Timothy Leary's formula—turn on, tune in, drop out—need not lead to inaction and disaffiliation. Their approach to work proves that theatre is not a dead art. Of all the theatres I have seen, theirs is the most relevant, contemporary, useful, and inspiring.

10/13/66

Seven Meditations on Political Sado-Masochism

Arthur Sainer writes about the company of the Living Theatre as self-sacrificing holy actors, moral vessels, ancient mariners whose teachings can only be echoed, chanted, intoned. Jonas Mekas writes about them as gypsies—"half gods, half humans, unlike any of us." The truth is not so romantic—their concerns are not abstract, not mysterious, but practical. Urgency produces the present style of their work, which is insistently serious, formal, heavy, in your face, meanwhile passionately friendly in its heart. Maybe the work fails, maybe the message doesn't get through. We enshrine them as faithful farthest out opposition and let it go at that, as if they were not using all their art to say something specific.

The Living Theatre urges us to think with them, to apply the analysis of anarchism to our economic, social, personal situation before it's too late. The current work is a cry to us to wake from our dubious dream and thin sleep of well-being, which we protect by talking or not talking of Watergate as if it mattered. Their concern is human suffering, our own and that much greater which we are luckily, momentarily spared, that of the outright victims, from which we hide as best we can. The concern can be practical because much of the suffering is humanly created and so can be overcome by understanding, by change, which they call revolution.

"Seven Meditations on Political Sado-Masochism," which the Living Theatre performed last week at the Washington Square Methodist Church, is a study of this human suffering and an analysis of its causes. It is a series of ritualistic actions illustrating texts on the specific mechanisms that perpetuate the suffering. It ends with a question, "What can we do?" and a series of individual conversations with the spectators. The work has a strong, sure rhythm; the aim is not to drift with it but to come awake. It is frightful, even accusatory—making us face our unconcern and evasion—but it wants us to come forward in the strength of solidarity, not withdraw in guilty helplessness.

Some of the views ring true and brave; others are arguable. The basic sexual image of sado-masochism, of cruelty and suffering seductive in themselves, I doubt but can't replace. In his book *The Life of the Theatre* Julian Beck presents man-woman fucking as inherently sadomasochistic. The first of the seven meditations shows slaves licking water off the floor at their master's feet, welcoming the stroke of his stick, licking honey from his hand, while Judith Malina speaks a text about the State's repression of sexual love. This voluptuous imagery of submissiveness—the master is aloof, unexpressive—has the strange hypnotic power of sexual fantasy.

In the second meditation the people put on chains.

The third is on ownership, and the actors come into the audience and ask the spectators individually, "Am I your slave?" Asked by Judith, I said, "No," thinking I am yours, I am watching your play—no, I am one of you, you are one of us, we are come together to share these meditations. "No," she responded, "I am not your slave." Asked by Julian, my companion answered with feeling, "No!" to which he replied, with shocking, level intensity, "Yes, I am your slave."

The meditation on money with its text by Eric Gutkind gave me a useful insight into my immediate economic slavery and stirred my useless anger against the banks.

The fifth meditation is a literal, horrifying demonstration of a form of electric torture presently used in Brazil and at least twenty-five other countries for political ends, with a chilling text from Cleaver, Alexander Berkman, and Senate Foreign Relations Committee hearings. I have no TV, read little politics, contend that the real news is what happens to me and the people I know, reflect that the one world always holds its balance of suffering and joy, reduce the world to self and expand self to dwarf the planet. But that doesn't help the victims of torture.

The sixth meditation is on the death inherent in all the forms of repression—sexual, economic, racist, intellectual, imperialist. The company does the dance of death, all those repressed energies making jangling puppets of them, till they burn out into a frieze of desperation, an image of the coming judgment. Judith reads the final texts: Malatesta on how the belief in the necessity of masters and governments has become established, Kropotkin on anarchy.

In the rap session afterwards, Judith confronts the old fearful argument that anarchy—which is society without government—equals chaos. It goes like this: while it's true that the authoritarian system represses the natural social order, we're so fucked over that we need authority to keep things together while we get ourselves together. Here and now, Judith argues, we have to see through that fear and break the cycle of conditioning or nothing will ever change. I love the sensuous warmth and strength of the affinity group, and feel my fears rising too, and keep listening and trying to answer.   11/29/73

Grand Tour
1963–66

Berliner Ensemble

Berlin — I came in at the end of the season and only managed to see one production at the Berliner Ensemble, "Die Dreigroschenoper," and I don't know where to begin describing how unexpected it was. It is, first of all, a show that couldn't be duplicated on Broadway for half a million dollars. The Berliner Ensemble, the theatre company established by Brecht and his wife, Helene Weigel, in East Berlin in 1949, demonstrates the advantages of state subsidy. As well as a beautiful playhouse, the company has a large permanent staff and acting company and maintains an active repertory. There is no compromise in physical production, casting, or rehearsal time, and by that I mean to distinguish the production from anything I have seen on Broadway. This is polish as opposed to slickness. My Broadway enthusiasms tend to be conditional: considering the limitations of the system, I think, it's amazing how well they did. There's nothing wrong with that—e.g., considering that he only had fourteen lines, he wrote a tremendous sonnet.

The Theater am Schiffbauerdamm, home of the Berliner Ensemble since 1954, is an ornate neo-Baroque 700-seat theatre of classical European design, with boxes where we would have balconies. It is not the theatre you expect, nor the sort of theatre that seems to lend itself to experimentation. But the stage has been transformed. Instead of the great gold front curtain, a flat white traveler extends across the stage on a wire, leaving a large open space above it. An ornately framed, curtained orchestra stand, visible over the curtain at the rear of the stage, echoes the rococo manner of the auditorium. The low white curtain parts, and the play is played. It's like that: quick, brisk, almost mechanical at times. It is given humanity by the level of craftsmanship. Nothing is left unconsidered, no prop, no piece of business, no unemployed instant of the most minor character role. The style forbids any back-and-forth with the audience: the songs are shot at us like tear-gas. When it's time for a song, the singer steps to the front of the stage into a bright amber spotlight, the bandstand curtains snap open, the band starts playing, the song is sung, the curtains snap shut, and the singer steps back into action. The songs are not staged. Nothing is made smooth, there is no lead-in, no subtlety. Here is the song: now it is over. Look, Jenny betrayed Mackie. This is the happy ending.

It is theatre without pretense. There is no need to suspend disbelief (isn't that a Romantic concept?), the audience is not being tricked or misled. All the well-known, ill-comprehended dicta of Brechtian theatre fall into place in action, making most American theatre look small-scale, tentative, introspective to the point of self-indulgence by comparison. The audience is not allowed the passive ease of voyeuristic naturalism; the actors do not seek to be liked or identified with or recognized as egos; instead doers and watchers engage each other as team to team in pursuit of comprehension, of how life is.

The current production of "Die Dreigroschenoper," which dates from 1960, was designed by Karl von Appen and directed by Erich Engel, who directed the original production in 1928 in this same theatre. Wolf Kaiser is a mature and complete Mackie Messer, unforgettable in stance and gesture. Peter Kalisch and Carola Braunbock are Peachum and his wife, conducting detailed, established lives in their bizarre establishment. Christine Gloger is a delicate, blonde Polly Peachum, radiantly beautiful in her bridal gown and a strong gang-leader when Mack goes off to jail. Siegfried Killian blends the funny and sad aspects of Tiger-Brown perfectly; his "Army Song" duet with Macheath is raucous and hilarious. Felicitas Ritsch in Lotte Lenya's role of Jenny is a major discovery. Right down the line to the smallest parts, the production is rich with enthusiastically dedicated, completely realized performances.   8/1/63

Polish Lab Theatre

The most impressive and inspiring experimental theatre I have ever seen is in Wroclaw, a depressing city in southwestern Poland, where I just spent several days in order to see Jerzy Grotowski's Teatr Laboratorium "13 Rzedow"— known as the Polish Lab Theatre. Their production of Calderón's "The Constant Prince" traveled in June to Paris and was the sensation of the Théâtre des Nations festival. After so many disappointments I am wary of big reputations, and Grotowski's theatre is suddenly legendary; but this time the reality is stronger than the legend. "The Constant Prince" was a revelation.

Grotowski founded his Lab in 1959, and it is supported by the Polish government. Its purpose is "to study technical and creative problems of the theatre by practical experimentation, with special attention to the art of acting." The project is tiny. The company consists of six actors plus, at present, six students; the theatre in its present configuration accommodates about forty spectators. But Grotowski's artistic ambitions are immense: to create a new technique of acting, develop a new method of training, and, evidently, to redefine the form of theatre. The emphasis of the work is on rehearsals, training sessions, and workshops rather than productions. Only one play at a time is produced, by contrast with most of the world's other important theatres; "The Constant Prince" has been performed more than 170 times, and there are no definite plans for a new production.

I don't know if I can describe the Lab's work in a way that will be useful to people who haven't seen it. Its force is partly the product of special circumstances: the subsidy, which permits its artists full, uninterrupted devotion to the work; its isolation, which reduces the distractions of competition; and especially the historical situation of Poland, communist and officially revolutionary, still a shambles from the war, its traditions lost or outmoded or discarded but still honored with nationalistic fervor. Art assumes a peculiar importance in these conditions. Wroclaw is bustling with activity but offers little diversion. Everything is drab and shoddy and out of date. The street scenes are gray, the food is heavy and monotonous, the fruit on the stands is bruised and pitiful. For all its energy, Wroclaw has no style.

But the Lab Theatre is a masterpiece of style, incredibly refined, exquisitely realized, indelibly original. What is most striking is how far each impulse is carried, the seriousness with which ideas are pursued in practice—until the idea is not only fully embodied but transcended. It is not the theory but the performance that astonished and exalted me. After attending one performance and two workshops and talking with Ryszard Cieslak, the leading actor, I could only conclude that the magic ingredient is work. The inspiration for this work and its aesthetic is provided by Jerzy Grotowski.

Grotowski redefines the physical form of the theatre.

In pace of decor, each production has a unique architecture that encompasses the audience as well as the performers. Grotowski emphasizes actor and audience as the essential ingredients of theatre and believes in close physical proximity between them. The tight rectangular playing area for "The Constant Prince" perhaps fifteen by twenty-five feet is enclosed by six-foot-high walls of wood. It is empty save for a low wooden platform about the size of a double bed. Two bright white spotlights at opposite corners, the only lighting, are already on when the audience enters. The spectators sit on a single row of raised benches looking down on the stage over the top of the wall. The arrangement evokes a gladiatorial arena, an operating theatre, a bull ring. The outside door is shut, an electric bell rings, the actors enter, the play begins.

The actors, practically within arm's reach, play continually at an ecstatic level of energy, they are sometimes all but naked, their concentration is perfect. The sounds and movements they make are indescribably extravagant; the extravagance is given force by impeccable discipline and control. Looking down at them from very close range, one might be examining them under a microscope—but they are full-size, human, alive. Grotowski says the spectator must see the beads of sweat on the actor's face. The experience is enthralling, too much to take in. The involvement between audience and actors is not intellectual or sentimental but overpoweringly physical and direct.

Grotowski takes a unique approach to the text. Calderon's "The Constant Prince" is a full-scale historical tragedy from Spain's Golden Age. Starting from a Polish translation by Slowacki, Grotowski has cut away most of the plot and most of the words; the program says, "Scenario and Direction by Jerzy Grotowski." What remains is Grotowski's idea of the essence of the play, which runs about an hour and is performed by six actors. Three of them play the principals; the other three sometimes fill subsidiary roles but more often act as expressive decor, establishing the context, reinforcing or ironically commenting on the action. There is not much dialogue; what remains is usually delivered at maximum speed in an incantatory monotone. Most of the time the actors make other sounds: chirps, screams, whistles, moans, chants—an uninterrupted nonverbal music. This is the first foreign-language theatre in which I have not felt handicapped.

It would be easy but inexact to describe the approach as nonliterary or even antiliterary. But Grotowski's involvement with the text is deeply literary and intellectual. His radical approach to it is meant to circumvent our habitual modes of response to literature, which are a frequent obstacle to the theatrical experience. Language is stale. Grotowski creates a fresh language of sound and gesture to renew our response to literature.

Direct physical action supplants psychological acting and imitative behaviorism in Grotowski's theatre. The actors' skin becomes intensely expressive; verbal communication is replaced by physical contact. The performance is austere and ceremonial yet violently sensual. I am told that the movement of "The Constant Prince" was created before the actors spoke the words. The movement vocabulary includes stylized pantomime and quotations from Catholic ritual but is never naturalistic. The mode of action is gesture. The gestures do not reproduce events but state them in heightened terms, express the experiential level, or comment upon meanings.

The action of the play has been reduced to a single line. A Spanish prince, captured by the Moors, is taunted and tormented but remains "constant" until death: he does not resist his captors but faces them with heroic passivity, accepting his fate ecstatically. To their furious rigidity, he opposes a noble yielding, transcendently confident and joyous; he is beyond their reach. He is humiliated and beaten, mocked, insulted, he is stripped and his body probed and finally he dies. Always he carries the play toward ecstasy. Halfway through, Ryszard Cieslak as the Prince reached an unmistakably ecstatic level which he sustained and further heightened until his death. The play ends abruptly, shockingly, while in full flow, the lights are switched out. They switch on again, and the stage is bare except for Cieslak lying on the platform shrouded in red; the audience files out stunned. I was stunned. I stood in the street outside for a long time unable to speak or move or think.

The discipline of Grotowski's theatre is total. "The Constant Prince" is performed at breakneck speed. Its physical and vocal demands on the actors are extreme and relentless. The complexity and technical difficulty of what they do on the stage requires maximum energy and concentration: it derives power from its physical danger and their complete and necessary absorption. The performance is like an athletic event; these actors must be athletes of the voice, mind, spirit, and entire body. One reason most theatre is dull is that it is too easy: the actors can't concentrate because they have too little to concentrate on. (Consider the American actor's idea that he should be "comfortable" in his role.) Grotowski makes the performance almost impossibly exacting: the actors must concentrate fully in order to get through it at all.

This concentration fills the actors' lives. They attend work sessions all day six days a week, and they have developed extraordinary technical resources. When I interviewed Cieslak, he emphasized the point that the technical training is not meant to enlarge the actor's repertory of "tricks" but to ease the limitations of not being able to do whatever he wants to do. The performance I saw proved the efficacy of the approach: it was flawless. Cieslak is one of the most beautiful actors I've ever seen. The entire company achieves discipline with no visible sacrifice of spontaneity or personal vitality. I came away from "The Constant Prince" with an enlarged sense of what actors can do and a new vision of the power of theatre.

Grotowski is no less demanding with himself as the director. His work is sensationally inventive, every element rigorously disciplined to the purposes of the play as a whole. The performance, though often wordless, is as richly detailed as Calderón's original text. It has the exfoliating, excessive beauty of Spanish Baroque architecture, implying the same fanaticism or faith translated into aesthetic terms. From the program: "Grotowski recognizes the primacy of the spiritual over the physical expression. In the play of the body he sees only a manifestation of its own destruction, the elimination of obstacles raised by the organism against the smooth expression of inner impulses. Detached acting assumes the supremacy of intellectual reasoning, the supremacy of the discursive layers of the actor's personality over the rest. Grotowski, on the other hand, probes the layers of spontaneity which lie deeply concealed, regarding the intellect as a tool of false rationalization and an excuse for half-hearted participating in the game." 11/3/66

Rome & Paris

Before memory fades entirely, I want to write about two curiosities I saw in Rome and Paris. Both were choices by default. This whole trip has been frustrating professionally.

The "new theatre" I'm looking for is, apart from the Living Theatre and the Polish Lab, virtually nonexistent. More is happening in New York than in any European city I have visited.

In Rome I had bad luck. The one theatre reputed to be worth seeing, that of Carmilo Bene, had just closed when I arrived. There just isn't much theatre in Italy—apart from the opera and the Church. I went to St. Peter's for a papal appearance. The Pope made a stately entrance, carried up the nave on a throne, acknowledging the crowd's applause with smoothly choreographed arm gestures and stylized, understated signs of the cross. Despite the grandiose dimensions of the setting and the role, the man was impeccably dignified, coolly at ease, even modest within the limits of the form.

Independent filmmaking is the new thing in Rome, and I saw some examples at a Communist cultural club. (Communism and Fascism are the political alternatives in Italy.) The films were of no interest, no more than first steps, which is odd in view of the Italian films being made and released commercially. Or not so odd: where would the American underground be without Hollywood's slickness and tight grip on distribution to oppose?

On Sunday afternoon I was taken to the Teatro Borgo Santo Spirito in something resembling a church basement not far from St. Peter's. This is the home of La Compagnia di Prosa D'Origila-l'Almi, which is as old-fashioned as my dream theatre is new. The company maintains a large, permanent repertory of plays on classical themes, which it has been performing for many years. The large audience consisted of nuns, elderly devotees, and a scattering of smartly dressed young intellectual types: this is a genuinely popular theatre and also something of a camp delicacy. At some moments the audience broke into factions: a laughing minority was quickly shushed while a woman near me was moved to tears.

The play was "Glocasta," by Ignazio Meo, a retelling of Oedipus's story with emphasis on his mother-wife. The text eluded my tourist Italian, but the events were familiar (apart from an interpolated second lost son). What interested me about the theatre was its ingenuously antiquated style. The action was framed by those painted drops cut out in leafy patterns that have elsewhere receded into history. The costumes were classical, the staging heroic, formal, and static, the tone earnest and appropriately grandiloquent. The performances were like high-school acting weighted but not refined by repetition. From the point of view of serious professional theatre, the production is terrible; but that's the wrong point of view. This is popular theatre, and in its context it is excellent, its style unmistakably theatrical and perfectly transparent, enabling its audience to focus on the timeless, magnificent story it tells.

"Glocasta" is built on the sturdy talents of Bianca D'Origlia, the company's co-director and star, an elderly actress carrying on an elderly and grand tradition. For most of the play she sits on a raised bench stage center; to stand and move she now requires a staff or supporting arm. She wears many jewels and a gown that shimmers hypnotically. Her bearing is stately, her dignity unshakable although she must know that to unnostalgic modern eyes she is often ridiculous. When she speaks it is as if the romance of poetry lives again, homage to the shape of words and sound of the voice. In her big moments (about four in the play) she pours on the passion, stage passion expressed in the face and voice—not insight or characterization or reality but *passion*. Her climaxes are stupendous, preposterous, thrilling tours de force. The one actress I can think of comparing her to is the French tragedienne Marie Bell, whom I've only seen in the colder world of Racine. This is the way I imagine Duse acted. It is a dead style but should not be forgotten. Its lesson is theatricality.

Then the floods came, I had just come from Venice via Florence. Venice is another century's dream, stone dissolving into postcards, blind to all but its own reflection, crumbling, magnificent, ravished but untouchable. While I was there the morning high tides half covered the Piazza San Marco. Temporary wooden walkways were set up, and people looked like interlopers in the water's city. The disaster at Florence is unthinkable. Apart from its beauty and treasures and tourist shrines, Florence is a living city, with the seductive, invigorating vitality of all the old Italian cities. Particularly in Italy one senses the precariousness and durability of civilization.

No trains were running north from Rome so I flew to Paris. Rainy, cold, beautiful, supercilious Paris. The theatres are filled with "boulevard" (read "Broadway") comedies. A French company playing the "Marat/Sade" has been legally enjoined by the Comte de Sade; the marquee of the Sarah Bernhardt Theatre reads "Marat/X."

The only theatre I could bring myself to go to was the tiny Théâtre de la Huchette, where the more or less original productions of Ionesco's "The Bald Soprano" and "The Lesson" have been running for nearly ten years. I saw them three years ago and wondered how they and I had changed. Happily, they or I have improved with age. What a wonderful play "The Bald Soprano" is! In Nicolas Batallie's essentially perfect production it is played with extreme precision and complete detachment, a kind of flat melodramatic acting that is as playfully objective in style as the script. Micheline Bona and Claude Mansard are glorious as Mme. and M. Smith, and the company plays with an enviable easy unity. "The Lesson" is an easier, less rambunctious play which I like mainly for its language. (It was good to hear both of them in French, poor as mine is.) Marcel Cuvelier's staging of "The Lesson" is sure-footed, but the actors were a bit shaky. The Student (Françoise Vaiel) at some point lost the rhythm, undermining what might have been a terrific performance by Yves Peneau as the Professor. The production is a classic of the free-swinging modern theatre; its style is technically adroit and rigorously disciplined. The combination is worth thinking about.

Now I am in comfortable London sating myself on English theatre and accelerating homeward as the money runs out. The plays I'm seeing are the equivalent of Broadway, since there's nothing else happening. 12/1/66

Peter Brook's US

Early last summer the Royal Shakespeare Company began work on an ambitious project. In open, unrestricted collaboration, the members of the company set about creating a theatre piece on the Vietnam War. They started without script or structure or any clear image of their destination. All they had was their individual and collective concern and conviction that the theatre could and should say something about the Vietnam situation and its implications. All hail!

In addition to twenty-five actors and director Peter Brook, the participants included a composer, a designer, and several writers. Over a period of months they studied Vietnamese history and the events leading to the present horror, reading widely and watching documentary films. Eyewitness observers including journalists and Vietnamese

Buddhists came to rehearsals and spoke to the company. The initial impulse was a general moral outrage and opposition to American actions in Vietnam, feelings colored by their experiences in New York when the company played "Marat/ Sade" here last season. They exposed themselves to a wide range of points of view and sought an understanding that would be coherent, factually accurate, and relevant to England—which is not a direct participant but has grudgingly supported American policy.

The formal demands of the project were a special challenge to this classical repertory company. Much of the work was necessarily improvisational. Joseph Chaikin of the Open Theatre came from New York to work with Brook for six weeks, sharing the techniques developed in his workshop and providing an American perspective on the subject. Jerzy Grotowski of the Polish Lab Theatre came with his leading actor, Ryszard Cieslak, to give the actors special training. In short, extraordinary efforts were made to reach an informed, committed point of view and to evolve a theatrical form that would convey the Vietnam reality with maximum urgency.

I applaud the attempt, not only because of my own convictions about America vs. Vietnam, but because of its potential value in a theatre that is dying of triviality and irrelevance. Even more promising than direct engagement with contemporary public issues is the idea of the actor's personal involvement in what he does on stage—the idea that he himself is actually present in his work, not just as an actor but as a man. This impulse, central to the work of the Living Theatre, happens spontaneously in much of the informal or anti-formal work now being done experimentally in New York. In the big-time context of the Royal Shakespeare Company it is startling, a radical questioning of the basic idea of professionalism. By exposing himself, not just his art, the actor evokes an extra level of identification and urges the spectator to respond directly and personally.

The project was similar in some ways to Megan Terry's "Viet Rock." But the Royal Shakespeare Company has greater resources than the Open Theatre. The tangible ones are its government subsidy, its big, well-equipped theatre, and the training and ensemble experience of its well-supported acting company. The intangible one, which really counts this time, is the RSC's location in the center of the British theatre Establishment; it is a major cultural institution in England, publicly supported, publicly responsible, and it has an international reputation as an outstanding theatre institution. All this guarantees that what the RSC does gets plenty of attention and is taken very seriously.

The result is "US" (unpunctuated to mean both "U.S." and "us"), which is the most talked-about production of the current London season. It has been lavishly praised and passionately condemned. It has been righteously censured for using public funds to criticize a British ally. It has positioned itself as part of a European "movement" called "theatre of fact." Before seeing "US" I went to a symposium on "Theatre of Fact" sponsored by the RSC, with Brook and others of the "US team" participating. Despite much articulate earnestness, it was obvious that "theatre of fact" is a non-category; the British are as concerned and confused as Americans about how to reach the audience, how to make the theatre matter. "US" is making people think about the theatrical use of Vietnam, not about Vietnam itself.

"US" is played on an open stage. In the center is a large "junk" sculpture of war materiel. Above the proscenium hangs a huge effigy of an American soldier, grotesque, obscene, reminiscent of Peter Schumann's peace-parade masterpieces, cigar-smoking and bloody-handed, with arrows in his eye and a rocket for a cock. The actors, dressed casually, as if in rehearsal clothes, enter and behave casually, as if gathering for a study session or, possibly, a protest demonstration.

The basic image of "US" is self-immolation. At the very beginning an actor drapes a yellow length of cloth over his shoulder, sits cross-legged downstage center, and pantomimes death in flames while the rest of the company soberly looks on. (Another actor handled the "gasoline" and matches, which confused me.) After this comes a long series of varied episodes including several songs. Documents relating to the war are read and sometimes staged, including a letter by the American Quaker Norman Morrison, who burned himself to death outside the Pentagon to protest the war. The history of Vietnam is told by means of fast-moving, flashy tableaux vivantes; the physical shape of Vietnam is represented by a skinny man in swimming trunks who is manipulated, mauled, painted different colors, eventually used as the rope in a tug-of-war. American soldiers are caricatured by means of quotations and descriptions from (I think) *Newsweek* in crisp, dehumanizing mass-media prose. The sexuality of the war (any war) is shown in a rock and roll number. And so on. The first act lasts two hours, most of it passionately anti-American, outraged, aggressively forthright, barely under control. In the original act ending, the actors, with paper bags over their heads as the war's helpless victims, blindly groped their way off the stage through the audience to the exits. From what I've heard, this made the audience very uptight; at the performance I saw it was omitted.

The second act consists mostly of a long dialogue between a calm young man who is about to set himself on fire and an angry, cynical young British liberal woman. The rest of the company sits about the stage watching. She struggles to get him to admit that what he is doing is pointless, that there is nothing to be done, particularly by the British, that the only response to the situation is despair. The scene was written by Denis Cannan, and it is intense, pointed, and engaging. It is played by Mark Jones with fine, simple directness and by Glenda Jackson with a brilliant drivenness, though I thought her near-catatonic rigidity tiresome and limiting. At its climax the scene rises to a new and astonishing level. The death of war in Vietnam is linked to death of the spirit in the materialistic, bourgeois West; the agony of conscience over the war is linked to the anguish of individual alienation. We want and make the war, the woman says, because our lives are intolerable: we are blinded by our pain and enraged by our frustration and self-disgust. Finally she demands that the war destroy her too, she wants it to get worse, she wants to see napalm on an English lawn.

"US" ends then with one final image. A man in black, gloved and quiet, brings out a small box. From it he releases a yellow butterfly, then another, and they flutter delicately up into the auditorium. He takes another butterfly, holds it up between thumb and forefinger, and sets it afire with a cigarette lighter. The actors freeze wherever they are on the stage and wait impassively for the audience to go home.

At the final moment of the performance I saw, just before the butterfly burning, two women stood up in the front row and cried "No!" One of them clambered onto the stage, took the butterfly from the actor's hand, released the butterflies remaining in the box, pocketed the lighter, turned to the audience, and said, "You see, you can do something." The scale of this action and its sentimentality were trivial in relation to Vietnam, but this was the most dramatic, authentic, and communicative event of the evening. On the whole, I found "US" to be inadequate and useless both theatrically

and as political action—a doubly dulling experience. I have thought about it for several weeks without reaching a unified vision of what went wrong: I have too many ideas, not too few.
    The easiest thing to talk about is the failure of style. "US" looks unauthentic, pretentious, and self-righteous. I don't suggest for a minute that the "US" company is not sincerely concerned with the Vietnam War, but sincerity is a virtue irrelevant to art, and concern can be the enemy of form. The problem is that the style the RSC is attempting in "US" is foreign to the actors and inaccessible to their technique. Their training for the great dramatic literature only hangs them up. Experts at playing characters, in playing themselves they can only characterize and thereby falsify themselves. (When they do play characters, they often assume American accents, which I disbelieved as an American, not a critic.) The play attempts to look unstaged, just as the actors attempt not to act; the result is a pervasive feel of pseudo-artlessness. It is staged, of course, and they are acting; instead of pretending to an artificial reality, "US" pretends to a lack of artifice, which is no better and hardly any different. Similarly, the evening's looseness of shape—the gangling, overlong, episodic first act, the second act's shift of technique—is not a new approach to form but a failure of form. "US" is not formless, it is crude. (Not always: sometimes Brook's skill shows. The tableaux vivantes are an example, although I thought them simplistic history; the tug-of-war in particular is a vivid but false image. Who are the opposing teams? Capitalism and communism? The USA and China? No good.)
    In sacrificing the standard formal artifices of theatre, from decor to plot, "US" means to break down the barrier between play and audience. Ironically, it erects a new and

higher one. Its aggressive experimentalism calls attention away from the content to the form, whereas the conventions are relatively transparent. Those artifices are not a barrier but a strategy for catching, holding, structuring, and intensifying the audience's attention. "US" disdains them willy-nilly (apparently confusing artlessness with honesty). Its insistence on factual reality appeals only to the political consciousness, neglecting every other response—the eye, the imagination, the personal sympathies. As a theatrical experience, it is incomplete and often dull.

One more formal note. I don't believe self-immolation is accessible to pantomime. The act itself is an essentially abstract gesture; its force and meaning derive entirely from its being real—an actual person actually dies. Pretending to do it is not doing it at all; if it is not real it is nothing. Its imitation in "US" seems to me cheap, easy, meaningless, and vulgar.

Charles Marowitz has criticized "US" for political inadequacy: he wants "answers." I share his wish that "US" were less balanced and more decisive; its audiences might be inspired to demand British renunciation of America's Vietnam policy. Beyond that, though, "US" can hope for no direct effect. My concern is more basic. "US" is a violent and aggressive play. It embodies a war-like state of mind, and I suspect it tends to promote war. If art is to propose an alternative, it must do so in aesthetic terms. Art can be political without ceasing to be art, without becoming politics. You can't fight violence, because fighting *is* violence. What we need is not to hate war but to love peace. It is on this level that art might hope to change the world. 12/15/66

Off-Broadway
1964

In the Summer House

A play by Jane Bowles, directed by Alfred Ryder, presented by Peter Goldfarb at the Little Fox Theatre.

This review would be easier to write if "In the Summer House" were a new play instead of one dating from 1953. I would then be able to say that Jane Bowles has taken a genre—the psychological mood play epitomized in early Tennessee Williams, Carson McCullers, and to a lesser extent William Inge—and turned it to subtler uses. The play was written in the thick of that historical moment, but I will act as if it hadn't been.

Mrs. Bowles's play begins with an interminable monologue that is well written but so familiar, so mannered as to make us despair of the evening. Then it explodes. After opening in Williams's sun-drenched-neurotic manner, the play bursts suddenly into a frenzy that brings the entire large cast of characters before us, and battle lines are swiftly drawn. Before the first scene is over, we realize that the author knows the tradition too well to imitate it accidentally, that she is kidding the techniques even as she is exploiting them, that the play is moving—brilliantly—on an entirely different level.

The action—it can't be called a plot—follows Gertrude Eastman-Cuevas, a widow living on a hot coast, and her daughter Molly into their marriages. Gertrude marries Mr.

Solares, a joyful, irrepressible Mexican, while Molly marries Lionel, a gloomy, none-too-bright American. Gertrude is obsessed with memory; Molly, for reasons unknown, withdraws into the summer house.

After the double wedding, Gertrude and Mr. Solares go off to Mexico on their honeymoon. A seafood restaurant takes over Gertrude's garden and Molly's summer house; Lionel works there. After a year Gertrude returns having been driven almost mad by the abundance of life around her ("There were four beds in every room"). Lionel asks Molly to go away to St. Louis and start a new life, unshadowed by the memory or fact of her mother. The play ends in a confrontation: Molly chooses her husband over her mother as Gertrude reaches the anguished core of her neurotic obsession with her father.

Rhe subplot brings on Mrs. Constable and her daughter Vivia, come to vacation. Vivian is almost hysterically alive; she uses no "controls." Her mother worries about her daughter dreadfully; Vivian banishes her to a hotel and takes up residence in Gertrude's house. Walking along the cliffs with Molly, Vivian falls or is pushed into the ocean to her death. Mrs. Constable takes to drink and reaches a state of ghastly cheerfulness in which she can say, not unbelievably, "My life is beginning."

The play presents itself as a study in destructive parent-child relationships; in reality it hardly cares. The author works like an Impressionist painter; as the Impressionists were damned by the standards of realism, "In the Summer House" has been criticized for its failure as a psychological mood play. Both psychology and mood are drawn in bright, broad strokes so no one can miss them. Psychology and mood are where the play begins, not its end.

The actual issue is the Freudian conflict between

civilization and life. Gertrude is farthest from participation in life. "I've always hated everything larger than life-size," she says. "I don't like pleasures." "I've never shown my feelings in my life. I don't know what you're talking about." And, coming back from Mexico: "I didn't like anything. It wasn't even civilized." Mr. Solares and his relatives, if "uncivilized," are certainly alive but seem to lack substance, refusing to be pinned down and defined. Mrs. Constable is more civilized than anyone, but her civilized manner drops away sharply when her daughter dies. "It hardly seems worthwhile to keep oneself clean after one has looked into the black pit," she says—ironically, but she means it.

You take your pick, civilization or "life"; the play's main characters are all trapped in between. They flutter frantically as things get "more and more unbearable." Unable to choose which way to move, they can do nothing, not even take their misery quite seriously, accepting it as a condition within which they operate and mostly manage to remain quite chipper, almost happy. Molly hates her life but can't stand for anything to change. If the characters are neurotic, the play itself (or is it the author?) is manic-depressive (manic most of the time), which is more interesting.

The effect is fascinating and peculiarly realistic. The characters talk out their neuroses like hip people we all know who joke about being in analysis. The point of interest is not the neurosis but one's attitude toward it, the way one "plays" it. In Albee, the characters are self-aware; here it is the author who knows her references. In this sense the play seems to be kidding itself as it goes along, which undermines its first level of emotion; but the ironic detachment of being unable to feel one's own pain is both more painful and more real.

This is dubious post-facto criticism: it is more than possible that Mrs. Bowles really meant all the psychology and exposed suffering to be the heart of her play. Whatever the intention, "In the Summer House" seems perfectly contemporary while the classics of its apparent genre, "The Glass Menagerie" and "The Member of the Wedding," are left behind it in history.

Alfred Ryder's production has a fluency and brightess of color that serve the play wonderfully. Estelle Parsons as Gertrude Eastman-Cuevas captures the complacent flatness of this woman who has resolutely faced away from life; her terrible breakdown at the end of the play is most eloquent. Susan Tyrrell is exactly right as Molly, all heaviness at the core. Leora Dana as Mrs. Constable makes the full swing from civilization to "life," and admirably maintains the play's diffidence about judging: who's to say that she is worse off drunk than living in constant fear of a disobedient, hateful, beloved daughter? Who's to say whether that look into the "black pit" hasn't brightened her existence? The rest of the cast also make valuable contributions to what is an exceptionally well focused, rhythmically precise production.

Tom Skelton's imaginative lighting carries the play outdoors where it belongs and bathes it in the hot, bright colors it requires. The lighting is the strongest visual factor in the production and makes it look marvelous in the odd new Little Fox Theatre. Oliver Smith and Ann Roth are responsible for the sets and excellent costumes.   4/2/64

The Slave
The Toilet

Two plays by LeRoi Jones, directed by Leo Garen, at the St. Mark's Playhouse.

LeRoi Jones's two new plays are personal, almost private works. Even so, they are being taken as political statements, public pronouncements, position papers on advanced intellectual, left-wing Negro thinking. "Dutchman," which last year brought Jones his first attention in the theatre, in one scarifying speech established him as an important Negro spokesman. His new plays—and other plays he has written—have little to do with race problems except on the surface.

Both of these plays are highly romantic. "The Toilet" tells a simple, slight, rather obvious story about the odds against love. "The Slave" is a more ambitious, complex, and original rumination on Jones's own position as poet-revolutionary. In each Jones has displaced emphasis, distracting from the actual content.

"The Toilet" is easily misread. It is devoted almost entirely to violence, much of it between the races. Jones is certainly not advocating this violence; if as playwright he has a position, it is that he deplores it.

Set in a high school men's room, the story details a beating administered, almost as a ritual, to a boy who has written a love letter to another boy. The lines of antagonism are implicitly drawn in terms of race, with almost no verbal reference to it. Karolis, the letter writer, is played as a Puerto Rican; Foots, the boy he loves, is an intellectual Negro whose honor is being defended by other Negroes; Karolis is futilely defended by a white boy. The play uses race for clarification, as boxers wear black and white trunks. The subject of the play is communication. Its desperately inarticulate characters communicate only within a formula so strict that almost all feeling is excluded. The characters who break through this formula and become individuals are punished.

The topic of the fight is made explicit by Karolis, who says that the boy the others call "Foots" is really named "Ray": there is a real person there as well as the formula. He loves Ray, and must fight Foots. "You stupid bastards," he says to the other boys, who are beating him, "I love somebody you don't even know." The play could be describing Jones's feelings, or anyone's—the depressing necessity of confronting social reality in terms of formulas, masks, pseudonyms, pseudo-selves: Foots triumphant.

In this hyper-realistic production the play is superbly exciting—the by-play and violence throb with energy and sweep the audience into their wild rushing rhythm. But the play is out of control: the hostility is so engrossing on stage that the softer center of the play seems hollow. The final moment, too, denies the clarity of Jones's vision: ending on an up-beat gesture of tenderness seems to say, "No, it's not really so bad after all." Leo Garen's direction is marvelous, although I wonder why he has changed the script's final pure gesture of love into a gesture of tender nursing. The cast is thrilling to watch: James Spruill, Gary Haynes, Norman Bush, Gary Bolling, Jaime Sanchez, Hampton Clanton are outstanding.

"The Toilet" is overwhelming. "The Slave" is dull. Designated a "fable," the play takes place during a future revolution in which Negroes and whites are fighting full-scale war. The play's central character is Walker Vessels, the Negro poet-revolutionary who has been the intellectual inspiration and phrasemaker of the revolution. He comes to the house where his former, white wife, Grace, lives with her second, white husband, Easley, and the two daughters she had with Vessels. The three of them engage in a long rumination, mostly about Vessels's contradictory roles as humanist intellectual and revolutionary extremist, and about the failure of intelligence. Vessels knocks Easley down and insults them both, often and violently. Vessels wants to take the two girls away with him; Grace pleads with him not to. Eventually Vessels shoots and kills Easley, who has tried to overpower him. Then an explosion knocks the house down, killing Grace. Vessels leaves.

The play is full of despair. Vessels has turned himself into a monster to serve a revolution that is pointless and doomed. His liberal antagonists—former allies—have been wholly ineffectual. There is little communication back and forth. When the talk is substantive, about the Negro-white conflict, both sides speak in clichés, irrelevant accusations and counter-accusations. They spell out the logic of disaster, they know how it happened, but none of them can break the paralyzing circle of his own thinking. The play's ethical vision is bleak: both sides are right—or at least wrong for the right reasons—and the result is still chaos, savagery, destruction.

Only when the play addresses Vessels's inner experience does it ring true, He still loves his daughters, he says—"In spite of all the people I've killed. No, better, in spite of the fact that I, Walter Vessels, single-handedly, and with no other advisor except my own ego, promoted a bloody situation where white and black people are killing each other; despite the fact that I know that this is at best a war that will only change, ha, the complexion of tyranny; in spite of the fact that I have killed for all time any creative impulse I will ever have by the depravity of my murderous philosophies; despite the fact that I am being killed in my head each day and by now have no soul or heart or warmth, even in my long killer fingers; despite the fact that I have no other thing in the universe that I love or trust, but myself..." This is the authentic voice. This is the voice of Ray, whom we met in "The Toilet"; but here too the action is dominated by Foots—Jones at his balancing act again.

This may be the play's trouble, for it is in trouble and doesn't work at all on the stage: the drama and conflict are within Vessels, and the interaction with others is trumped up. The impulse has not found direct outlet but leaks from the form every which way. Again Jones has embodied his statements about man in a form that splits his audience into black and white, that accepts blacks as allies and threatens whites, although this is not what either play is about.

Both plays express a conflict between love and hate, between an affirmative romantic humanism and a passionate, irrational rage against oppression. Jones is wrestling with the conflict of levels of duty—to self, to tribe, to mankind—a problem that is today graphically focused in the Negro artist. In "The Toilet" personal love is opposed to group violence; in "The Slave" poetry is opposed to war. It is stated in "The Slave." Easley: "Now, in whatever cruel...political synapse you're taken with or anyone else is taken with, with sufficient power I, any individual, any person who thinks of life as a purely anarchic relationship between man and God...or man and his work...any consciousness like that is destroyed... along with your enemies." Vessels: "Remember the time... in the old bar when you and Louie Rino were arguing with me, and Louie said then that he hated people who wanted to change the world... Yes, well, I knew I think then that none of you would write any poetry either. I knew that you had moved too far away from the actual meaning of life...into some lifeless cocoon of pretended intellectual and emotional achievement, to really be able to see the world again."

"The Slave" is clumsy and unsuccessful in writing and design. Despite the explosions, flashing of lights, and deaths, the play is actionless and static: the conflicts are explored but do not develop, and the deaths are almost accidental. Vessels, lacking motivation, attempts several times to explain his presence; he always fails. His repeated intention of taking his daughters away does not sound true—the naturalistic level of the action is unconvincing. The final moments of narrative are unclear. Further, the play seems badly edited; everything is evenly emphasized, as if everything were equally important—or equally unimportant.

Nan Martin finds many shadings within Grace but never has time enough to fit them in. Jerome Raphael is solid as Easley. He is repeatedly called a "faggot" and "closet queen" by Vessels—ritual insults—and sensibly plays entirely against this image. Al Freeman Jr. is taut and tormented but unclear as Vessels. He seems to have no middle voice, studding his speech at odd intervals with sharp modulations of emphasis that often hide the meaning. The vocal mannerisms limit his effectiveness. "The Slave" too is directed by Leo Garen, not so well. Before and between its moments of extravagant action, the play comes to rest; it is sorely short of pacing.

Larry Rivers designed the sets. The one for "The Toilet" is very good; the one for "The Slave" is attractive and functional, inexplicably decorated with two large imitation Franz Klines.

It is a misfortune when Jones's work is scrutinized for what it says about "the Negro situation" and overlooked when it speaks of experience on a subcutaneous level. If the plays are flawed, they are nonetheless greatly more stimulating than their competition. Jones is a victim of the new status of art as a public utility. Having reached, from its origin as public ritual, a point of utter privateness and individuality, the theatre is ironically caught up in a sudden and unprecedented distribution of art works, a "culture explosion" that is changing the use of art without yet changing its nature. The result may eventually be that the arts again become public in fact. In the meantime Jones is misunderstood. *Time* says his plays are "one-act spasms of fury." In reality they are cries of disillusionment. These two tell us that Jones is too aware of himself, too aware of level upon level of implication in every act, the infinite shadings of value and relativity of truth, to argue well for any single answer or be an effective spokesman for any group larger than himself and smaller than mankind. 12/31/64

Poets in the Theatre
1963–67

Diane di Prima
George Dennison

"*Murder Cake,*" *by Diane di Prima, directed by James Waring, and "The Service for Joseph Axminster," by George Dennison, directed by Lawrence Kornfeld, presented by Judson Poets' Theatre in the choir loft of Judson Memorial Church.*

The double bill at Judson Church begins with an elegant production by James Waring of Diane di Prima's abstract verse comedy "Murder Cake." The play combines sweetness with an antic manner into a most attractive entertainment. The privacy of its symbols does not hide emotions but makes them more poignant; the language is clean and fresh. Waring serves the play beautifully, endowing every moment with a radiant, exquisite grace, and his cast is marvelous: Garnett Smith, Shelly Burton, Kenneth Hill, James Jennings, Joanna Vischer, and especially Valda Setterfield.

George Dennison's "The Service for Joseph Axminster," which follows, is more straightforward, approaching its emotions directly in the action and situation. Three bums walking the rails near Wichita come upon the corpse of Joseph Axminster. None of them liked him, but he shared their manner of life and thus earned their respect. The paradoxical feelings are perfectly balanced, They are joined by a middle-aged woman whose man fails to escape from the nearby state prison. She is courted by each of the men in terms of his point of view toward life, each beautifully realized by the poet-author.

What we see is a reenactment for the benefit of two onstage onlookers who knew the deceased. A Mistress of Ceremonies narrates, embodies the dead man, and from time to time joins in the action. A train passes several times. Under Lawrence Kornfeld's direction, these devices fuse with the material inseparably. The most affecting performance is by Katherine Litz as the Lady, ably supported by Jerome Raphael, Peter Boyle, Al Carmines, Michelle Roseman, and Douglas Sheer. 3/14/63

LeRoi Jones

"The Eighth Ditch," a play by LeRoi Jones, directed by Alan S. Marlowe, presented by the American Theatre for Poets (New York Poets' Theatre) at the New Bowery Theatre.

LeRoi Jones's brief, lyrical, biting play "The Eighth Ditch" has been revived by the New York Poets' Theatre on the weekend bill at the New Bowery Theatre. The result has been a furor over its alleged obscenity. This is ridiculous. Although the action of the play includes sodomy performed on stage (with the lights out), the play is neither obscene nor pornographic. The sexual act is almost incidental to its actual content— innocence betrayed by experience. The play is certainly less prurient in tone and effect than a routine Broadway comedy like "Under the Yum-Yum Tree," less sexually provocative than much advertising.

"The Eighth Ditch" is written in verse and very deliberately keeps its distance. The sex act is visually referred to but hardly flaunted at the audience. The play is performed with taste, control, and considerable skill. Its fault is that it pursues its theme with honest directness, and this apparently threatens some people's psychic comfort. Such an effect is desirable in this age of indifference. Those who would declare sex or any other subject out of bounds in the theatre are senselessly limiting themselves.

Rufus Collins is stunning in the lead role of the seducer, with a firm sense of the play's rhythms and a sound command of its difficult, sometimes awkward language. Frank Cotner as his opposite number is less successful at encompassing the lines, and John Vaccaro as the narrator sounds more pretentious than necessary. Handsomely set by Robert Morris, the production is vivid, poignant, and exceptionally interesting. 3/19/64

Frank O'Hara
LeRoi Jones

"The General Returns from One Place to Another," by Frank O'Hara, and "The Baptism," by LeRoi Jones, both directed by Jerry Benjamin, at the Writers Stage Theatre.

For one more Monday a fabulous evening of theatre will be given at Writers Stage, and if you like fun, I recommend that you not miss it. It represents the first venture of Present Stages, a new group that financed the production with a series of poetry readings this winter at the Five Spot. What with Judson Poets' Theatre, the Hardware Poets Playhouse (constrained to make no public announcement of their plays), the New York Poets' Theatre (side victims of the recent film crackdown and temporarily homeless), and now Present Stages, New York theatre is being lavishly fertilized by poets, if only it would notice.

Frank O'Hara's "The General Returns from One Place to Another" is a wildly romantic chronicle of a semi-mythical, cartoonishly MacArthurish general's meander all over the South Pacific, trailing two aides and a collection of enamored women. O'Hara also finds room to bring Chiang Kai-Shek and Franco together in the Spanish hills. The play makes at least nineteen stopovers, some of them allowing only one or two lines, others prompting extensive monologues that are the evening's choicest morsels, a textbook of coolness in a hot and bothered world. The poet says of poems that it is "pleasant to leaf through a volume of them without paying any attention." The general appreciates flowers because they decay faster than people and are only knee high. An orchard reminds him of a seed catalogue. Such a world, where subjectivity is constantly drained away, takes a great deal of handling; "handling"— the kind of handling that would have made Marion Davies a bigger star than Norma Shearer—is "taking an optimistic view of reality and making it stick." The play is sparklingly camp, eccentric, severely understated, oddly touching, hilarious— and O'Hara makes it stick.

Taylor Mead is sui generis as the general, a masterpiece of miscasting. His screen performances are as nothing compared to his presence on a stage, rolling his eyes, twisting his mouth, waving his hands in the air before him like damp cloths. He reveals an exceptional talent for vocal characterization as well. The entire performance is a single paroxysm of hilarity. The play has been staged impeccably by Jerry Benjamin and is studded with delightful performances—notably by Veronica Castang, Loren Bivens, Jarrett Spruill, Russell Turman, John Worden, and Jeffrey Reiss.

"The Baptism" reveals LeRoi Jones in a new mode. I cannot convey the extent of the outrage it commits, the unrestrained blasphemous travesty it perpetrates on a flock of sacred subjects.

Some of them are literally sacred, like Christ—"that thin Jewish cowboy"—and others are merely delicate—like black-white relations and several departments of sex: masturbation, frustration, adolescent seduction, all scrambled up together. It has the further temerity not even to take its outrages seriously but persists in being outrageously funny all the while.

The plot involves a fruity priest, an irrepressibly homosexual young man who drops into the church on a lark, another young man who comes to be baptized because he has "sinned"—he says, "Thinking of God always gives me a hardon"—a spinsterish woman who has witnessed his sin and is furious with desire—"You spilled your seed in God's name," she screams, pulling up her skirt—and a flock of girls he has seduced by telling them he is Jesus returned. When he says he isn't really Jesus after all, they try to destroy him; he sorrowfully draws a golden sword and slays them.

I will not spoil the continuing twists of this plot, which go much further. I was glad to discover that Jones has, in addition to his strength as a playwright, a wild satirical sense of humor. The play seemed to me almost perfect in structure; it also manages a good measure of pathos and wistfulness and so transcends the simply comic.

Although some moments of the staging looked chaotic and makeshift, there are some superb performances. Russell Turman as the boy makes exact transitions from the sublime to the ridiculous and back again. Taylor Mead is very funny as the homosexual (although something of a scene-grabber). Jarrett Spruill, Beverly Grant, and Mark Duffy are also excellent.

Both plays benefit from strong, witty sets by Joe Brainard.

3/26/64

Peter Hartman
Wallace Stevens

"*Vistas of the Heart Unveiled,*" *by Peter Hartman, and* "*Carlos Among the Candles,*" *by Wallace Stevens, directed by James Waring, at the Caffè Cino.*

The two poetic monologues at the Cino are full of friends of mine. I was reluctant to go for fear I might not like their work. But the plays are delightful: I went back a second time purely for pleasure.

Peter Hartman's "Vistas of the Heart Unveiled" is a richly romantic succession of images in the mind of an old, elegant International Set lady, looking back over her life as she looks forward to death. Hartman concentrates on the sounds and nuances of words, seeking to convey a flavor of period and social milieu rather than a particular meaning, story, or drama. The play is profoundly silly but also profoundly pretty, strewn with euphonious references like dropped names: Melachrinos, Vanity Fair, Grand Corniche, Mainbocher, the Promenade des Anglaises. The play is thick with nostalgia, and Charles Stanley performs it strikingly, setting off his full black beard with a white turban and white floor-length gown. It is the most authoritative and fully realized of his several performances as women in recent café productions.

In "Carlos Among the Candles," written by Wallace Stevens in 1917, stage directions call for the actor to light and extinguish twenty-four candles. Director James Waring dealt with the action abstractly: the audience's mind supplies the literal level. Deborah Lee, blonde and glamorous in white tie and tails, plays Carlos, sometimes dancing (to Mozart), sometimes moving with the words, sometimes simply speaking, and the performance contains several moments of startling lyricism. Its climactic sequence about "the extinguishing of light" is the soul of beautiful simplicity, beautifully performed.

John P. Dodd did the lighting for both plays, in separate styles. Their abstract character left him limitless possibilities; spectacular effects are balanced and controlled by a fine sensitivity to phrasing, dynamics, and the flexibility of theatrical time. 3/24/66

The Beard

A play by Michael McClure, directed by Rip Torn, at the Evergreen Theatre.

Michael McClure's "The Beard" is a perversely elegant meditation on the man-woman pair stripped down to post-mythical, narcissistic essentials. Man is Billy the Kid, Woman is Jean Harlow—a clean pop selection—and they are located in "eternity," two fancy chairs flanking a table centered on the curvy plush stage, surrounded by "blue velvet."

Before they appear, the stage and entire auditorium of the new Evergreen Theatre (formerly the Renata) have been engulfed in an multimedia collage of projected slides, movies, and lights, like the sleekest of discotheques. A trio of tribal-looking musicians sit on the stage in candlelight, playing and singing along with a sound collage that includes McClure speaking his "beast language" with a group of lions. As they exit up the aisle, the environment melts into a recognizable dark theatre, and Billy the Kid and Jean Harlow materialize on the stage, idly beautiful in the two chairs.

"Before you can pry any secrets from me, you must

first find the real me," Harlow intones. "Which one will you pursue?" So begins the litany. He says she is "meat." She says he envies her beauty. He wants her to sit on his lap and lick his boots and touch his cock. These are the basic ingredients. Sometimes they get up, occasionally they do something; the action is in the words. Harlow and the Kid tease, taunt, put each other down, and outcool each other. This is eternity, timeless, beyond psychology; they are "divine," solitary as gods, not emotional but impersonally, imperiously desirous. Being archetypes they do what they exist to do. In eternity it doesn't matter when anything happens—instead of drama we observe the way the inevitable is danced.

These are not persons, but they do have personalities. McClure isn't a bit interested in the "real" Kid and "real" Harlow; he uses them clinically as masculine and feminine images. He takes a meaty, mean, cheerfully simple view of his subject. Each sex is essential to the other's sexuality, hence identity, and they both know it. They fight it in a self-indulgent yearning for narcissistic self-sufficiency. They resist the coming capitulation largely to make it more interesting, to come together not dutifully but with style: what's at stake is ecstasy. They don't "play games," rather the "whole thing" is a game in a sense too broad to kid around with. This is serious play.

The words dance. Theme and variations: the opening line (quoted above) repeated periodically, countless times, triggering a sequence in constant variation, inversions, syncopations, interchanges, reversals, leading anywhere and back. Other themes are gradually woven in; the line of action traces itself without haste. The Kid is lyrical about his boots; then admits that when he says boots he means cock, and scorns to speak of boots again. He tells Harlow to take off her pants; she does. He takes them, smells them, rips them in two. After that there's no question. Before long she finally does sit on his lap and does what he wants, boots forgotten; then he gets down to it, attentive and deliberate, and she cries, "Stars, stars..." as the stage dissolves into whirling flecks of light silhouetting them, "Stars, stars..." to the Hallelujah Chorus, believe it or not.

It's a specialized taste, I suppose, but I love a good dance of words, and McClure's is wonderfully clear, elegant, and lively. He uses today's gritty urban words distilled, without the dramatical sentiment that makes them emotionally overwrought and shrilly literal. His language is raunchy and unflinchingly direct, rich in four-letter words-as-words, shamelessly self-romanticizing, unillusioned, spare. The play is witty rather than clever, profoundly silly without being camp. It's all a camp as it's all a game, and offers no vantage for that vulgarizing outside view. From the inside it's all there is.

The audience, accustomed to plays, has some trouble with "The Beard." If it is poetry, they think they should take it seriously. As drama it's thin sludge. It isn't pornographic despite being saturated in sex and graphic to the point of literalness at the climax. It's a short play, even with the electric prologue, and people have questioned the money's-worth. I can barely think about that, since I never pay for theatre.

Certainly it's unique—and uniqueness per se is to be valued and cherished. The entire evening is organized into theatre poetry, with a formal unity encompassing the reconstructed auditorium as well as the play. The media-mix prologue is a contentless, neutral decompression chamber; it brings the audience bodily into the "eternity" of "blue velvet." If the audience refuses to go with it they're fools.

The performance is brilliant and indelible, a masterpiece

of style. Rip Torn directed an immaculate economy of gesture, keeping the pace stately the better to relish the words. Billie Dixon as Harlow is beautiful and ugly, vulgar and disdainful, petulant and vicious, without sign of strain or effort, with perfect control. Richard Bright as Billy the Kid is beautiful and ugly, foppish, repulsively confident, eloquently graceful, virile beyond virile mannerisms. Both are called upon to embody the myth, not enact or present it: the distancing is built-in. In their auras of irreproachable tinsel divineness, they look entirely at ease within the superrefined style, playing with the words with solemn delight, giving each its full weight; they play together like fine chamber musicians.

All of it is elegant, from the tasteful extravagance of the prologue (by USCO) to the astronomical cunnilingus. This is Rip Torn's professional debut as a director, amazing for the sheer care that has been applied everywhere, in concept and execution. The costumes by Ann Roth fit the legends and actors; the stage lighting by C. Murawski is subtle and beautiful. What a treat! 11/2/67

Repertory Theatre of Lincoln Center 1964–65

After the Fall

A play by Arthur Miller, directed by Elia Kazan, presented by the Repertory Theatre of Lincoln Center at the ANTA Washington Square Theatre.

Under that flat, drab, unexpressive yellow metal shed on Fourth Street east of the Square is a theatre that is beautifully alive. The audience sits on a slope carved down into the ground like one-third of a giant bowl, and the stage thrusts out to meet them. The audience is wrapped around the play, giving physical form to the mental act of focusing. It is a theatre cleared for great actions: one can imagine Sophocles played here, or "King Lear"—I have seen "Uncle Vanya" played with superb effect on a similar stage.

This thrilling instrument is being misused by Arthur Miller—and, to a lesser extent, Elia Kazan—as a confessional in which the act of telling gives absolution. In a key line of "After the Fall" Miller writes: "I hate what I did. But I think I've explained it."

Miller does not invoke the ceremony of religious confession. Instead he has his stand-in hero, Quentin, confide in the "Listener," an imaginary creature poised halfway between the edge of the stage and the first row of audience. This Listener is, specifically, a psychoanalyst whom Quentin or his first wife Louise or his second wife Maggie seems to have visited two or more years earlier. Quentin comes back, now that Louise is divorced and Maggie is dead, for advice on whether to take a third wife. In Miller's theatre the audience is the author's psychoanalyst. Ironically it is we who have to pay (both in ticket money and tax abatements) as Quentin relives the key incidents of his life before us. They are:

—His powerful father's fall into bankruptcy; Quentin's childhood discovery that his mother considers his father to be an "idiot."

—The failure of his first marriage because he is not in touch with his own feelings. (His wife Louise calls him an "idiot.")

—The collapse of a valuable friendship when his friend goes before an unnamed "Committee" to "tell the truth" about his Communist past and "name names"—thus becoming a "moral idiot." Another friend, caught between the Committee and a driving wife, throws himself under a subway train, thus lifting from Quentin the "burden" of being his only friend and engendering in him a feeling of "joy."

—His meeting with and marriage to Maggie, the fabulously beautiful and sexy pop singer who is "all love," whose ignorance and complete lack of pretense to "innocence" seems to Quentin the truest innocence of all, who is driven by guilt and terror to the barbiturate suicide that Quentin has finally come to desire.

—The death of his mother, for which he feels guilt apparently because as a child he once hated her for betraying him.

—His discovery of hope in Holga, the German woman ("girl") he visits a gas chamber with, the anthropologist who lived through the war and learned in the Third Reich that "good faith is never sure." She teaches him that despite the gas chambers, despite the deaths, one must embrace one's life, embrace even the wish to kill, "and with a stroke of love—as to an idiot in the house—forgive it; again and again...forever." In the final stage direction: "A whispering goes up from all his people. He straightens against it and walks toward her, holding out his hand."

Unlike Quentin, Arthur Miller cannot seem to straighten against his people; in fact all he hears is their muddled whispering. I have gone into so much detail about the content and concerns of "After the Fall"—certainly there is rich material here—to reveal what process is going on. It seems evident to me that the play is not an act of imagination but a case history in which a few cursory details have been altered. Miller is tragically embedded in his own past images and unable to see or feel any reality.

As for the play's "Committee": Miller has a well-known history in relation to the House Committee on Un-American Activities. In 1952 Elia Kazan, who had directed "Death of a Salesman" and brought Miller to fame, publicly confessed to having been a Communist and gave the names of several former comrades. Miller, not subpoenaed by HUAC at that time, dissociated himself from Kazan for a number of years and wrote "The Crucible," a play about an accused man who dies rather than name his accomplices in guilt.

It is common knowledge that Arthur Miller was subsequently married to Marilyn Monroe, who died of an overdose of barbiturates in 1962 after being divorced from Miller. Much of their life together was reported in the press, and most of those incidents are referred to in the play. There are references to Lee Strasberg—as "Ludwig Reiner," a famous vocal coach who "won't even take opera singers unless they're, you know, like artists." Strasberg and Kazan were co-directors of the Actors' Studio (where Marilyn Monroe came to audit) until Kazan quit to lead the Lincoln Center theatre.

(The fact that Miller's present wife is the Austrian photographer Inge Morath might be irrelevant, except that Salome Jens, playing the German anthropologist Holga, persists in carrying what looks like a camera bag.)

In short, the chain of correspondences is so complete as to overpower the illusion of characters and drama. Quentin at all times remains Arthur Miller questing among memories, fumbling through his moral flash-cards, muscling his way toward the perfect analysis. The men who face the Committee remain amalgams of Kazan, Odets, Philip Loeb, John Garfield, and the others (it is hard to make sense of their section of the play without matching back to the facts). Most obtrusively of all, Maggie remains Marilyn: all the scenes between Quentin and Maggie come across as scenes between Miller and Monroe: we are treated to the insidest, most uncensored, most teasingly intimate view possible.

All of it is filtered through the mind of Arthur Miller—and that mind, for all its earnestness and unsparing effort, for all its depth of experience, remains disconcertingly naïve and, finally, square. The play has the unprocessed, untransformed, of-itself-uninteresting sound of a patient on a couch. It plays to the audience's curiosity. The spectacle of Kazan directing Miller's confession which includes Kazan's confession is more a voyeur's dream than it is art.

Miller's attempts at form would be touching in a novice author, but in one of America's major playwrights they are appalling. The devices of the Listener and of the psychoanalytic ramble through the "mind, thought, and memory" of the hero were described by Miller in *Show* magazine recently as a "new form"; they are a gimmicky frame for the play and a way of avoiding formal construction. The intracranial setting permits Miller to begin and break scenes at random, to pop one-line significances out of the darkness at will, to speak more or less directly to the audience—in short, to be formless. (This lack of clarity forces the interested spectator to the printed text, now available in the *Saturday Evening Post*.) Further evidence of Miller's craft-consciousness is provided by the chiming repetition of key words: "innocence," "truth," "bless," "idiot."

Miller is a talented and sometimes skillful writer, and a number of his scenes, for all the inadequacy of their framework, are strong and convincing. I cannot think this is a good play—but neither can I deny the shock of seeing, time and again, that this man Quentin's mind is my mind. Such a stab into reality, if not sufficient, is a marvelous and rare thing in the theatre. The mind I recognize, however, is my mind at its most hung-up, self-involved, self-tormenting, self-defeating, selfish. It is real but dead. For all the play's talk of love, there is no love in it and little evidence of human contact. This is its sadness and real hopelessness.

Kazan is surprisingly uncertain in his use of the new stage, surprising especially because he was involved in its design. (The present, temporary theatre has entries for the actors onto the stage only from the back, necessitating entrances and exits over an awkward distance; the permanent theatre under construction at Lincoln Center will have downstage tunnels as well—like its ancestors at Stratford, Ontario, and Chichester in England.) Miller's script calls for the "instantaneous" appearance and disappearance of the characters who come and go in Quentin's mind; Kazan has found no solution but to have the actors walk on and off, more or less carrying their characters with them. It is a lame, distracting answer that cannot provide the flashes of association Miller intends. Kazan also has failed to establish a coherent style. Into the front of the otherwise abstract stage, for example, there is built an ashtray for Quentin to tip his cigarettes into. Quentin's father makes his first call on a real telephone, thereafter mimes an imaginary one. At first there is an imaginary glass; then Maggie takes pills from a real bottle while lying on an abstract bed and drinks from a real but obviously empty bottle. These details are distracting. It is more crucial that Kazan and Miller repeatedly fail to establish locations, sequences, and contexts. Much of the play is vague and therefore unengaging. Miller's word-association game is imprecise in the first place, and Kazan softens it further.

Jason Robards, Jr., who plays the marathon role of Quentin, is the ideal actor to represent Miller, perfectly embodying the script's hard-working, slow-witted dullness and doing so with considerable skill and charm. Robards maintains his concentration in a role that makes it very difficult and maneuvers through the whims of form with an admirable attention to detail. I thought as I watched him that he was making the lines very clear—he seems maddeningly reasonable—but I find on reading the play that I missed or half-heard a number of key speeches. Like the script, his performance is believable but without fire.

Barbara Loden rises to the challenge with a splashy, persuasive performance as Maggie, and there is superior work by a number of other members of this promising company—particularly Mariclare Costello, Zohra Lampert, Miss Jens, and Ralph Meeker. 1/30/64

Marco Millions

A play by Eugene O'Neill, directed by José Quintero, presented by the Repertory Theatre of Lincoln Center at the ANTA Washington Square Theatre.

The Repertory Theatre of Lincoln Center, on which for the past two years have been pinned so many hopes for restoring professional theatre in New York to some sort of creative life, this week leaps into repertory. Alternating with a clumsy, pretentious, self-involved Arthur Miller play is now "Marco Millions," one of Eugene O'Neill's most difficult and unrewarding works and, in its production by José Quintero, a deadly bore.

With two productions in view, it becomes possible to get some idea of the Lincoln Center repertory concept. The most disturbing discovery is the fact that the theatre's directors, Elia Kazan and Robert Whitehead, have been deceiving the public, their actors, and presumably themselves about the nature of the acting company they have formed.

A number of young actors were assembled two years ago, given a long, intensive, exclusive period of training under Robert Lewis (much of the time receiving no pay), and through a rigorous process of elimination pared down to a select group that was to comprise the new theatre's acting company. Many of these actors were highly accomplished before the training period began, but all the truisms about the superiority of a unified company's acting were trotted out to whet the public's expectations and convince the chosen actors that their sacrifice would prove worthwhile. There would be no stars at Lincoln Center; famous and unknown alike would alternate in small parts and large. Fine.

Then, this past fall, when the plays had been selected,

the real actors were hired. Just like Broadway, the new theatre went out and hired name actors to fill the major roles. Jason Robards Jr., David Wayne, Hal Holbrook, Ralph Meeker, Salome Jens, David J. Stewart, Michael Strong, Zohra Lampert are among those who were brought in. The pretense of a starless company is maintained: all are listed in alphabetical order. But the same actors play the leads that would play them anyplace, the same unknowns get their big breaks as would get them elsewhere, and those well-trained kids are kept busy in bit parts or as extras. Like the Actors Studio Theatre, which in theory had a built-in head start toward an acting company, Lincoln Center challenges Broadway in Broadway's own impoverished terms.

O'Neill's play, written in 1928, tells of Marco Polo's visit to the court of Kublai, the Great Kaan; of the Princess Kukachin's love for him and his boisterous, self-confident, materialistic blindness to it; of his success in making millions and her death from unrequited love. Marco and the West triumph for all the wrong reasons; Kublai, Kukachin, and the East are exploited despite all the right ones. It is a thoroughly American play. O'Neill is sentimental, insecure, and wise enough to mistrust materialism and long for a mystic serenity; at the same time he is the self-congratulating realist who knows that gunpowder, once invented, has to be used. He deplores Marco's manners, methods, and morality but believes they will prevail and is glad, essentially, to be on the winning side.

All this produces a wobbly and unconvincing tone, which is further aggravated by O'Neill's customary trouble with the language. Kukachin's poetic orientalia is about what you'd expect and fits awkwardly with Marco's brashness, a satirical swipe at the American salesman of O'Neill's own time. The play is beset by problems of style and technique that O'Neill did not manage to solve which, although it remains a literary curiosity, render it dubious at best for major production. David Wayne gives an admirable performance as Kublai, a role that leaves little impression, but the praise stops there. Hal Holbrook gives Marco a flat, false boyishness that dominates the evening with its dullness. It is true that the written character has no inside, but that is no reason its performance should stay so resolutely on the surface. Zohra Lampert is choked, self-conscious, and disappointing as a misconceived Kukachin. Joseph Wiseman is a catalogue of old-fashioned acting mannerisms as the sage Chu-Yin. The rest of the actors give styleless, ill-matching, mostly anonymous performances of familiar spottiness.

The cast has been lavishly costumed by Beni Montresor. This material extravagance is the production's strongest distinguishing feature. David Hays's sets are sometimes pretty, sometimes clumsy. Quintero's direction has the on-and-on-ness we remember from "Strange Interlude," without the moments of good acting.

Quintero staged the play symmetrically, organizing the action on an axis straight up the middle of the stage. Throne room scenes are always difficult to block, since everybody is upstaged by the ruler. Their failure on this occasion leads to questions about the new stage. At Quintero's former home theatre, the Circle in the Square, an actor all the way downstage facing upstage is visible to half the audience; at Lincoln Center he is visible to almost no one. If he turns downstage, he is facing away not only from the action but from a considerable part of the wrap-around audience. In short, there seems to be a nearly useless playing area downstage center on the new stage. The first two directors have treated this stage, which does not thrust out far enough for arena staging, as if it had a proscenium, and side-seat viewers of their productions are cheated. The new stage requires new techniques of staging—centrifugal or diagonal patterns, perhaps. If the present trend holds true, as manifested in choice of scripts, management, casting, and direction, the opportunity will continue to be wasted.

2/27/64

Tartuffe

A play by Molière, directed by William Ball, presented by the Repertory Theatre of Lincoln Center at the ANTA Washington Square Theatre.

Exquisite irony. The Repertory Theatre of Lincoln Center, in the very moment it is felled by bureaucratic apoplexy and gout, does its first good work.

In six productions the company has selected only two worthwhile scripts—"Tartuffe" and "The Changeling"— and the latter was massacred in production. All but the two Arthur Miller plays, which could easily have been produced on Broadway, have been withdrawn because of audience indifference. At this point one might sympathize with Robert Whitehead, whose resignation because of cavalier treatment by the theatre's board of directors and the Lincoln Center administration has left the theatre without a leader. The debacle was foreshadowed and partially caused by indecision on all levels. Evidently Whitehead was expected to run the Lincoln Center theatre with a commercial producer's eye on the balance sheet, although the other Lincoln Center constituents—ballet, philharmonic, opera— are institutionalized as deficit operations. If it is true that Whitehead was selected to run the company because of his experience in the commercial end of theatre, then I'll concede it's not much of my business: I am not a critic of commerce. This is the heart of the confusion. The Lincoln Center theatre company was founded to attract large audiences to work of the highest caliber and has so far failed at both sides of its task. As culture becomes increasingly institutionalized and established—"culture" being a generalization in which the nature of the particular art is not so important—the artist and businessman are more and more allied, largely by the artist's wish to survive. It is questionable how healthy the relationship is for either. Businesses buy paintings as wall decorations and tax deductions. Actors sign contracts with Lincoln Center and, in exchange for financial security, let their talents go to waste. The Repertory Theatre has never used its company of actors decently—it was a mismatched and almost unusable company to begin with; none of the leaders had any experience in forming companies. Now there is no leadership, the next production has been canceled, no future plans have been announced; work continues on a stunning new theatre up in Lincoln Center proper, with a second, experimental theatre downstairs. It is an epic in the history of art by board of directors—it takes three program pages to list them all—and the result is real estate.

Meanwhile the "Tartuffe" is brilliant, a joyous occasion. Director William Ball brought in a handful of outside actors to fill the principal roles, and it is these outsiders who set the style of the production, not the company who have been in training for this very task for a couple of years. The play itself is a masterpiece—richly comic, profusely active, fervently moral; Richard Wilbur's translation, in rhymed couplets, is fast-moving, light, and witty. The tale unfolds with that perfect assurance that marks a classic—it never occurs to us that the author might make a mistake, that we might be let down, that this or that improbable device is anything but a daredevil feat of virtuosity.

Michael O'Sullivan as Tartuffe gives an extravagant, daring, fully realized performance that radiates energy into every part of the production. It is acting of a kind we see too seldom, in which the actor uses every expressive means at his disposal, face, voice, body, entire space. He is intricately in motion at almost every instant. The crossing of a leg is as integral to the characterization as the calculated smile, the oily smirk of righteousness, the panting lust, the pounce, the proud strut, the body twisted as grotesquely as the mind and as agonized in failure. It is complete acting.

Ball's concept of the play emphasizes its moral intensity. Instead of making Orgon the laughably gullible, pitiable victim of Tartuffe, he makes him a full and decent man whom we can respect. Orgon is the victim of his own virtue, trust; otherwise he is admirable—what we feel for him is not pity or disdain but concern. The entire family has a fine solidity of emotion among its members. These are not caricatures but persons firmly set in time and place; all the production's high spirits and hilarity express this reality. Always we are aware of Molière's radiant moral vision, and it is this confidence in virtue that validates the play's action.

This is the inside of the play. Ball has also done a spectacular job with its outside, using the actors' moves to comment upon the words, to make a series of verbal-visual puns that flow together as convincingly as the writing itself. The stage picture is prettily composed at every moment—something that many contemporary directors apparently forget altogether—without unintended jolts, without self-consciousness. It is the characters' pleasure to look their best at all times; the actors are remarkably at ease in their seventeenth-century clothes and manners.

It addition to O'Sullivan's masterful Tartuffe, there are other fine performances. Sada Thompson as the maid Dorine carries much of the first act with high spirits and bubbling good will. Claude Woolman, Laurence Luckinbill, Joyce Ebert, and Salome Jens are excellent as various members of Orgon's family, and Larry Gates brings just the right shadings to Orgon himself, keeping the man's goodness strong beneath the evil obsession. Hal Holbrook contributes a fine crotchety characterization of the bailiff, M. Loyal (his curtain calls are an occasion in themselves). Jane Greenwood has done everybody up in lavish and beautiful costumes.

This is a production that could not have been done on any other New York stage—or certainly would not have been done. It is a welcome contribution of pleasure to the season.

1/21/65

Shakespeare
1964-68

Burton's Hamlet

Richard Burton's portrayal of Hamlet (*at the Lunt-Fontanne*) is memorable and beautiful. Burton defines Hamlet so thoroughly, with such apparent ease, so clearly and eloquently, that he becomes my very image of Hamlet. He makes Hamlet's fascination and mystery perfectly apparent: he suggests no "theory" of Hamlet, presenting the so-called enigmas of the character not as unanswered questions but as legitimate complexities. Most Shakespearean performances are pale images of the literature, which they diminish; Burton augments it.

The essential quality of this Hamlet is self-awareness. Hamlet refuses to comfort himself with deceptions or to be so comforted. His is an unremitting intelligence—a mind that will not stop questioning, eyes that demand to see—and he is faced with an unaccountable situation. He is not driven mad; he is not neurotically blocked. He hesitates—that centuries-long hesitation—because the moral problem he faces is complicated and the evidence uncertain; because he is as much a man as Claudius and can therefore trust himself as little; because the ghost of his father is even less a man, perhaps not to be trusted at all; because if there is anything outside him that he can cling to it is the women, his mother and Ophelia, and they both betray him. He cannot solve the problem because he is too honest, too aware of his oneness with the problem, too clear-headed to stupefy himself and simplify his moral life. The "disorder" in this Hamlet's mind is not pathology; it is a true reflection of the tragic sense of life.

Who is brave enough to believe his entire world wrong and himself right? Such men are judged mad. But Hamlet, after all, is right; Claudius really did murder his father. Burton gives us the incredible flashes of bravery in which Hamlet achieves self-trust and becomes a tragic hero, only to lose it again to his humanness.

He also discovers the humor. Hamlet knows himself—inexorably, wearily knows himself—and so cannot entirely take himself seriously. He sees through himself as he sees through everyone else—catches himself in heroic and tragic poses, mocks himself. The result of this is to set up the shield Walter Kerr (in the *Herald-Tribune*) mistook for lack of emotion. When Hamlet's focus wanders elsewhere and the emotion breaches that dam—in the graveyard scene, for example—feeling is raised to a higher level than in a more obviously "sensitive" Hamlet. Burton's Hamlet is not concerned with his emotions: he is driven by them to a draining concern with truth.

It would be reasonable to call this an existential Hamlet, but such a term suggests that Burton has imposed some modernizing concept on the role, which is not the case. He has found what in the role is timeless, periodless, what is most essentially human. He has not imposed himself on Hamlet but has taken Hamlet into himself. Hamlet seems to fit easily, almost comfortably within him; and with perfect tact he permits that in him which is Hamlet to reveal itself.

There is no surface evidence of calculation in Burton's performance, no deliberateness. And yet it is fantastically detailed. The sense of each speech emerges as if it could be stated no other way. For him, like few other actors, poetry is the natural mode of expression; he does not toss it off but hears and ironically relishes his own wit, or deflates himself halfway through a grandiose phrase. Simultaneously the performance has a shape. The drooping, laconic, sad youth of the first scene springs to life when he hears of the ghost, hot on the trail of what is distracting him. Then he loses it. Thus the energy level rises and falls in structured measure through the play. He returns from England to the deceptive lightness of the graveyard scene, glibly spinning skeins of images about death, the subject hovering over all the play. But grief overflows in him and sweeps him into Ophelia's very grave. He is numb then, without will, and accepts Laertes's fatal challenge quite casually. It is perfect.

There is no nonsense about the performance, no tricks in evidence, no mannerisms other than simple manly directness. Burton doesn't exactly impersonate Hamlet; he doesn't try to fool us, to pretend that he really is Hamlet; instead he shows Hamlet to us, demonstrates the nature of the character, lets us in on his vision. The acting approach could be called Brechtian, but doesn't call attention to itself. Burton's Hamlet is a complete man.

The rest of the production, which was directed by John Gielgud, seemed to me rather stupid. It pretends to be a rehearsal rather than a performance, which leads among other things to its being played against a fake brick rear theatre wall. Such heavy-handed attempts at illusion are hopelessly outdated and serve no purpose today. Every aspect of the physical production is equally false and distracting in its pretense of naturalness and informality. Only Burton is at ease in his so-called rehearsal clothes on the make-believe preliminary set.

He is surrounded by performances of no better than dull competence. Hume Cronyn's Polonius rises above the swamp to provide some penetratingly funny ironies in the first act, and George Rose makes a briefly engaging Gravedigger in the second. The rest are submerged. When Hamlet goes to England in the second act, the stage becomes less interesting than the ceiling of the theatre.

It is Burton you must see. You must see him. We are threatened with mediocrity from all sides, and mediocrity leads to indifference. Burton proves it can be overstepped.

4/23/64

Othello in Central Park

The play by William Shakespeare, directed by Gladys Vaughan, presented by the New York Shakespeare Festival at the Delacorte Theatre in Central Park.

The special problem facing a director of "Othello" is how to balance the play's climaxes and maintain a coherent emotional movement. By contrast with the other major Shakespeare tragedies, "Othello" is simple in design. Its initial impulse establishes Othello's overwhelming, almost unbearable love for Desdemona. At its height this love is abruptly undermined by Iago's villainy. And from that moment until Othello's murder of his beloved, jealousy runs its course at a measured pace. There are few hesitations in the development of Othello's detested passion, few moments of emotional release; there is little clowning and no major comic interlude. All the subsidiary events of the play feed directly into the central dramatic action.

"Hamlet" develops obliquely, through a series of separate incidents with no immediate connection to each other. The basic scheme of "King Lear" consists of parallels and giant metaphors—Lear and Gloucester, Edmund and Edgar, the bad sisters and Cordelia, the king and the kingdom, the mind and the universe. "Macbeth" is crammed with exciting action, a tragedy of regicide as melodramatic as the histories. But "Othello" has only its single story of a single emotion, jealousy fed by Iago and eating away at Othello, one long emotional line, and the action of the play lies entirely within the modulations and development of that line.

Gladys Vaughan's production in Central Park is a good one, with numerous strong characterizations and vigorous staging that thoroughly animates the script. Yet the central emotional line remains unarticulated. The production focuses unremittingly, as it should, on the cancer of Othello's suspicion; but it is allowed to grow as uncontrolled in the play as in the character. The climax of love between Othello and Desdemona comes too early; we are already in a cooler zone by the time Iago plants the first rank seeds. Othello rises to his highest pitch of torment too soon, so that the critical scene in which he determines to kill Desdemona and orders Iago to kill Cassio is not the high explosion of his madness but a second height.

As Othello, James Earl Jones, an actor of exceptional articulation and intelligence, finds so many levels and shifts within each scene that the over-all development is further obscured. The sharpness of his rediscovery of love each time he sees Desdemona throws us off the track of what is happening in the play, although the moment's insight is valuable.

Many elements of the performances are superb. Jones's strong but subdued presence in the opening scenes gives a clear picture of his authority. Many moments with Desdemona are exquisitely tender. As he approached the great tragic moments of the play, it struck me how much he looks like Orson Welles: he has the same kind of presence before an audience. He maintains a fierce individuality of gesture, a style of physical movement that is his alone. Often it produces revelations, as in the final moments of the murder scene, in the kinetic force of the murder as he makes us see it. His great strides and monumental postures achieve a size quite out of the ordinary.

Julienne Marie is a fine Desdemona. After beginning somewhat too bubbly, too playful with Othello, she settles into a radiant simplicity that encompasses and makes sense of her passivity in the face of falsehood. I have always felt surprised that, although she stoutly maintains her innocence, Desdemona never turns against Othello for his credulity. Sada Thompson is a strong, convincing Emilia, and James Antonio a lively, suitably amusing Rodrigo.

Mitchell Ryan gives us an Iago seeming bare of interpretation, an Iago of surfaces, an Iago entirely defined by what he says and does. We sense nothing hidden in him, no buried springs leaking poison. Is Iago really, as he tells Rodrigo, motivated by vengeful ambition, his hatred of Othello based on the promotion of Othello over him—or is he evil by nature? This Iago is blunt and "honest" in manner at all times, whether he is planting further deceit or speaking from his heart in soliloquy; no distinction is made between the outward Iago and the inward. Apart from the words themselves, there is no indication of the true sources of his perfidy: that he himself is obsessed with jealous imaginings, seeing his own wife seduced by Othello, by Cassio, seeing the "daily beauty" of Cassio's life, seeing Othello, the converted heathen, displaying the nobility of spirit that Iago himself lacks, lusting after Desdemona to repay imagined cuckoldry in kind. Iago need not be a mere plotter.

At moments the production comes to rest in static tableaux with all the faults of recent Central Park productions: too much set, too much costuming, too many extras standing around. But this "Othello" sticks to the point and at times proceeds with great vitality, on its own straightforward terms a comprehensible reading of the tragedy. 7/23/64

A Midsummer Night's Dream

The play by William Shakespeare, directed by John Hancock, presented by Theodore Mann and Paul Libin at the Theatre de Lys.

John Hancock's brilliant off-Broadway production of "A Midsummer Night's Dream" is a tour de force of imagination. Hancock takes a jarringly modern, aggressively inventive approach to the play, tipping its familiar balances every which way, reinterpreting it in detail and in general. The production has been coldly received by the critics. I can only attribute their response to outrage at its irreverence. I would hardly promote it as the definitive version, but it seems pointless and irrelevant to ask that it should be. Maybe they just didn't like it: the interpretation is sardonic, super-sophisticated, and sick, certainly less pleasant than the usual production. Outrageous it sometimes is, but it held my attention to the play as much as to itself. It was witty, lively fun, and it made the particulars of character and action immediate, accessible, and recognizably real without destroying the play's oddities of form and dense moral ambiguity. Taste aside, the production is important for sheer imagination and style in a time when much that is being done desperately lacks those qualities.

There is always a disturbing aspect to this play, a manipulative cold-bloodedness in the characters' treatment of one another (and Shakespeare's treatment of them). The literal inhumanity of Oberon and Titania infects the whole play, and the final resolution is too pat, too formally hedged, to seem more than a patronizing, even sarcastic ceremonial gesture. If you let Shakespeare get away with saying it was all a dream, you reduce the play to a flashy, empty trick, inspired but frivolous fantastication—which is to miss its resonance and deny its passion. I love this play, partly for its inexhaustible strangeness. I was thrilled by Hancock's strange production.

It would take a scholar to sort out all the reasons and meanings in Hancock's interpretation. Instead of digging for a unifying rationale, let me simply describe some of it. The tone is set from the beginning, when an old-fashioned jukebox is revealed, lighted and bubbling, and begins playing the familiar Mendelssohn music. Down a sweeping spiral ramp within high black plastic walls comes a grim procession with a cart of corpses: the whole play is haunted by plague. In the Athenian court, Theseus has his bride Hippolyta caged and closely guarded; she is ferocious, brooding, dressed in leopard skins, an image of Diana. The two unhappy pairs of young lovers are introduced: Hermia is a teenybopper; Helena is played by a tall transvestite.

Visually, the production is based on drawings by Jim Dine. The scenes at court are mostly black and gray. The sub-plot—Nick Bottom and the other rude players—is drab in brown. All this is conventional enough. Then we enter the forest kingdom of the fairies—a few trees on a turntable within the ramp—and ultraviolet lights flood on. Puck is painted in wide horizontal bands of dayglo colors. Oberon is a shimmering silver cape and one striped hand, the rest of him invisible, a menacing shadow. Titania has pop target tits and a pale dress slashed high, flashing colors from inside. Her attendant fairies are fluorescent tweakies manipulated on poles and strings by figures invisible in black. The effect is supernatural: they are playing with electricity.

In the court the mood is tense, enclosed; people breathe through cloths against the unmentioned plague. Theseus plans festive nuptials in fierce defiance of the morbid atmosphere around him, applies the law as harshly as it's written, and revels in his cruel conquest of his Amazon bride. Decadence is palpable. Among the rough workmen comically preparing their play, the feeling is much like rehearsals I've actually been in. The fairy king and queen, having total magic power, are driven by absolutes, beyond human restraint. They are played by the same actors who appear as Theseus and Hippolyta, raising decadence to a higher plane. Oberon uses his magic casually to meddle in the human lives that chance before him. Once Puck has muddled the potions, Oberon is in action; with an off-hand wave he enchants the young lovers, Strauss is heard, and they move in slow motion through their arbitrary torment. Puck enjoys their squirming: "What fools these mortals be."

The overriding wisdom, the sense of rectitude of Oberon and Theseus, is not compassionate but coldly knowing. These mortal fools are contemptible. The lovers' feelings are measures of a dance. The amateur actors are not merely ridiculous, they are crass and grasping: after performing they clamor to be paid and are driven out contemptuously by the guards. The background of this "Dream" is a diseased, demonic world, against which the action has a grotesquely practical logic.

This interpretation is defensible, if not necessarily desirable, and Hancock has set it forth with bold authority. Some of his ideas are dazzling. Resexing Helena destroys the lovers' symmetry but provides a telling context for her distrust and sense of being mocked. Identifying the magical and earthly rulers resolves the contrast but suggests a mysterious, unified conspiracy. There are frequent implications of sinister perverted sexuality. Together with the modernistic visual style, this gives the play an implied metaphorical relationship to our present world—possibly an examination on a pin.

The more I think about it, the more unsettling it becomes. At the time, though, my principal feeling, nearly till the end, was intrigued delight at the fresh, free-wheeling invention, the wit, the rich, extravagant play of imagination and intelligence. My emphasis of the quirks of concept is probably misleading. Hancock has not sacrificed the play to his interpretation but has created the full life of the play within it. Moment by moment the characters live, feel, and interact, the different worlds are distinctly contrasted and intermixed, the action develops a momentum strong enough to hurt. Shakespeare speaks with uncommon clarity and precision of meaning. This is not a bunch of flashy ideas but a complete conception; not a flourish of theatrical tricks but a fully realized production, with an original and coherent style and point of view. Hancock's work is enormously impressive.

The cast are remarkable in their disciplined respect for the production's style. The strongest of the actors is Alvin Epstein, whose ease and assurance give Theseus and Oberon their authority. He is beautiful speaking Shakespeare, conveying the meaning in impeccable detail and sharing his appreciation of the style. Gloria Foster is intense and statuesque as Titania and gives Hippolyta a wonderful roughness and burning sensuality. Robert Benson plays Helena with Kim Novak dignity; Susan Anspach as Hermia is weepy, willful, irritating, and convincing. The nuances of their twisted romances are developed in remarkable detail.

Bottom and his mates are more real than usual, less the

coyly dumb buffoons, therefore funny on a more interesting level. Barton Heyman brings out the thug and bully in Puck, contributing a coarse, mocking low-comedy tone that won't tolerate pretension.

This "Midsummer Night's Dream" is an extraordinary event, and anyone interested in or susceptible to theatrical style should make an effort not to miss it. 7/6/67

Papp's Hamlet

The play by William Shakespeare, adapted and directed by Joseph Papp, presented by the New York Shakespeare Festival at the Public Theatre.

Anybody who has worked on a play knows the intensity of concentration that goes into every choice, the infinite rational subtlety with which the creators' minds grope for each decision, the proliferation of considerations until, in the actual creative leap, reason (but not intelligence) must be left behind. The critic, seeing the results once, can have only the most superficial impression of what is happening on stage; he too may elaborate subtleties, but they are rarely those of the event itself. Everyone knows, anyway, that the essential theatrical experience is not reasonable, controllable, or explainable—certainly not if it aspires to being art. Creator and critic are stuck with their feelings of the moment, subcategorized respectively as inspiration and taste, taking reason seriously only before the fact, to make it possible, and afterwards, for coherence.

"Hamlet" has probably inspired more analysis than any other literary work but the Bible; it's barely possible to be other than theoretical in producing or criticizing it. Either you smother it with respect or you dry it out with interpretation.

Now Joseph Papp, whose Shakespeare festival in Central Park owes a certain obligation to the Bard's ingenuity, has directed a production of "Hamlet" at his more intimate Public Theatre on Lafayette Street. He has shaken the daylights out of Shakespeare and turned "Hamlet" upside down, scrambled it, pared it down, pasted it back together all out of order. As it is generally thought to be in the first place, it's a hallucinatory "Hamlet," with the clashing styles, jagged emotional tone, and image overload of specifically the 1960s. It is not a "modern-dress" "Hamlet," but a new "Hamlet" with attention to the full range of attitudes that beset the modern mind. The theatrics owe less to the Shakespeare tradition than to the circus, the movies, vaudeville, and Olsen and Johnson.

Let me not go into more detail than it takes to tantalize. Claudius is a crude, practical military dictator, a parody of the classic model, South American or South Vietnamese; Gertrude is his pitiful and contemptible hennaed floozy; the hipster Hamlet sleeps in a coffin at the foot of their bed. Horatio is an unaccounted-for convict in prison stripes and handcuffs; the Ghost is a flesh-and-blood farceur in long johns; Polonius is a suave, pompous fathead; Laertes an elegant, snooty collegian; Ophelia a dithery teenybopper caught between Hamlet and the generation gap. The action, crammed into one fast act, takes place on a three-story steel set under the menacing eye of Claudius's tough palace guards. The climactic dueling scene is abstracted into a ritualized game of Russian roulette. The whole play is permeated, sometimes penetrated, by a rock score by Galt MacDermot.

It would be silly to complain that Papp's production makes a mockery of "Hamlet"—though it does. So what? Papp has acted, forcefully and in his own fashion, on Artaud's cry, "No more masterpieces!" The point as I take it is not that there are no masterpieces or that masterpieces should be destroyed, but that masterpieces are tough, they don't need coddling, they'll go the distance and give as good as they get. In a program note Papp quotes the Polish critic Jan Kott: "One can perform only one of several Hamlets potentially existing in this arch play. It will always be a poorer Hamlet than Shakespeare's Hamlet; but it may also be a Hamlet enriched by being of our time." Kott inspired Peter Brook's famous "King Lear" a few seasons back, a bare-bones intellectual approach that left me cold. Papp goes too far, but in the opposite direction, Dionysian rather than Apollonian, you might say, which appeals to me far more.

The production's justification is not to be found in theories but in its life on the stage. You'd have to be sadly uptight about Shakespeare not to get great fun out of it. Further, the interpretation works to some depth. In place of the usual Freudian hangups and egg-head equivocations, the hinge of action here is a matter of realities. The status quo at Elsinore has changed abruptly and under dubious circumstances, and everybody but Hamlet is trying hard to adapt to the new facts of power. Everybody but Hamlet (and the outsider Horatio) is pragmatic, opportunistic, "realistic." Hamlet alone can't or won't accept the change, recognize Claudius as the "real" king, yield to the situation. The conflict is between his reality and theirs; his motives—whether moral, political, sentimental, or Oedipal—are beside the point. The play becomes a resonant spectacle of chaos as the two irreconcilable realities destroy those who have simply been trying to live within them.

The production is largely comic, to be applauded for achieving depth and seriousness without coming on that way. It is fast-moving, packed with changes, fanciful, free, and frivolous; the content is there for the taking, not imposed.

The performances are wonderful. The play is acted in an outgoing, vivid, energetic style that is meant to be enjoyed and consistently succeeds. Martin Sheen plays Hamlet with a low-key self-mockery that declares his utter alienation from the scene around him. He is marvelously energetic and has a fine comic sense; the "To be or not to be" soliloquy, mumbled in cornball Mexican dialect, is inspired. To praise the deserving performers, I'd have to list virtually all of them, which would make dull reading. Go see for yourself.

1/4/68

Theatre Genesis
1964–68

Cowboys
The Rock Garden

Two plays by Sam Shepard, directed by Ralph Cook, presented by Theatre Genesis at St. Mark's Church in-the-Bouwerie.

It sounds pretentious—Theatre Genesis at St. Mark's Church in-the-Bouwerie, dedicated to the new playwright—but they have actually found a new playwright, which is more than you can often say for Broadway or Off-Broadway. The playwright's name is Sam Shepard, and I know nothing about him except that he has written a couple of provocative and genuinely original plays.

The plays are difficult to categorize, and I'm not sure it would be valuable to try. Shepard is feeling his way, working with an intuitive approach to language and dramatic structure and moving into an area between ritual and naturalism, where character transcends psychology, fantasy breaks down literalism, and the patterns of ordinariness have their own lives. His is a gestalt theatre that evokes the existence behind behavior. Shepard clearly is aware of previous work in this mode, mostly by Europeans, but his voice is distinctly American and his own.

The first play, "Cowboys," introduces two young men attempting to deny the external world and live in terms of specific small remembered physical realities and various simple heroic myths. Their basic mood is exhaustion bordering on despair, but from it they rouse themselves into bursts of wild energy, alternately joyous and desperate, as they channel Wild West heroes surrounded by marauding Indians and relish in memory the sensate details of breakfast, among many things. The play's prime virtue is the author's self-trust. The language and form have a questing air of spontaneity that is perfectly appropriate to the content. The language is vital and engaging, the characters not less convincing for being stranded in no-space. The play has flaws: occasional flashes of defensiveness and second-hand hostility toward convention, an insufficient attachment to the level of fact, a conclusion that is too vague and too easy. One comes away feeling that the playwright has kept some of his secrets, perhaps kept them from himself. At least he has secrets to keep.

"The Rock Garden" is a more schematic play. A boy serves without comment a demanding, nagging, boring bedridden woman; then in a separate scene sits passively, falling asleep while listening to a beer-drinking man make inane and endless plans for building rock gardens. One marvels at the boy's self-containment, his not needing to fight back, until his focus finally is revealed in a single quiet, specific speech about sex that ends the play. The writing is beautifully controlled and conveys the overpowering boredom of the situation without being boring for a second.

The production of "Cowboys" is excellent. Robert F. Lyons and Kevin O'Connor, the two actors, animate the writing with extraordinary energy and attention to specifics. The play is done on a bare stage as it should be, directed with subtlety and precision by Ralph Cook.

"The Rock Garden" is not so convincingly staged. Its physical setting attempts realism with inadequate means, and there is room for further exploration of the two talkative characters. Stephanie Gordon as the nagging woman neglects to define a tone early enough and leaves us thinking we are watching dull naturalism until the play's structure takes over. Kevin O'Connor as the rock garden man stays on the same note too long and resorts to excessive mugging. The central figure of the play, although he has the fewest lines, is the boy, who is played with exact understatement by Lee Kissman. He manages some remarkably precise physical acting and oversteps all the dangers in the final speech. Again the work of director Cook is unusually responsive to the play's intent.

Theatre Genesis intends to continue finding and producing the work of new playwrights. Already we have reason to be grateful. The project deserves all the encouragement we can give it. 10/22/64

Chicago

A one-act play by Sam Shepard, directed by Ralph Cook, presented by Theatre Genesis at St. Mark's Church in-the-Bouwerie.

Another delightful play from Sam Shepard. If you have not yet seen his work, this is a good occasion. "Chicago" is the extremely cheerful lament of a young man whose girl is going out of town on a job. Stu is in a bathtub throughout the play, waterless, wearing pants, and most of the play is devoted to his rambling fantasies. He talks about biscuits, fishing, train travel, and a vision of free life and love on a beach. Other actors come to visit Joy as she is packing—all the real action of the play occurs off stage. When she leaves, they line up along the front of the stage with fishing rods, as if the audience is the lake. At the end all join in a rhythmic breathing involvement with the "neat air."

Shepard's vision is clear and precise, his writing original

and particular, his plays ebullient in their sense of life's fullness. "Chicago" seems to be more poem than play, a personal statement of feeling rather than a drama. Its imagistic method and structure are related to happenings, its images often pictorial. The play exists as a cunningly wrought object which we appreciate from outside, not a dramatic event which draws us to its heart.

Kevin O'Connor is superb as Stu. His ecstatic plunges into the rich language are breathtaking. He is unfalteringly attuned to the play's impulsive, fragmented rhythms. Under Ralph Cook's direction the whole cast is unified and effective, the play as refreshing as a dip in the sea. 5/13/65

The Hawk

A play collectively created by the Keystone Company, written by Murray Mednick, directed by Tony Barsha, presented by Theatre Genesis at St. Mark's Church in-the-Bouwerie.

Take "The Hawk" as a play like any other and in many ways better than most: it holds your attention, it is about interesting people doing interesting things, it is convincingly detailed yet mysterious, the point of view is sharply contemporary, the form strange but not obstructive; it is performed with exceptional immediacy and authority; its ultimate intent remains veiled or vague but the other levels are so rich it doesn't matter.

The play is about a heroin retailer, the Hawk, to whose unsettling blue apartment come a series of female Victims, each of whom reveals herself too directly before receiving a fatal overdose; and two men, a comic raving Inspector out of Burroughs and a manic raving Dealer, who replenishes the drug supply before the play ends.

Next layer: the Hawk has a Double with whom he chants a ritual invocation of the hawk ("He kills because he's hungry") between callers, who otherwise silently observes and serves, who at the end gets the super-O.D. operatic death flash. The play is preceded by a formal Invocation in the form of Chinese dance.

Next layer: the first visitor is imaginary, a girl invented, altered, killed in the imagination(s) of Hawk and Double, remaining as an imaginary corpse to haunt the whole play; suggesting that the four embodied girls who follow are extensions and repetitions of the first and precisely as real; locking into the basic staging convention, which on a bare stage specifies a detailed naturalistic environment and sustains it until it is more real, more present to the spectator, than anything visible; until we are willingly and equally bewitched by several kinds of realness in the magic theatre.

The musical interludes of metaphoric ritual that punctuate the play are evocative but obscure when in the foreground; then with a flicker of figure-ground reversal establish context and order for the action. The first Victim has just left home (Brooklyn), covets the racing romantic new life of her best friend, who she won't believe is a lesbian (although "we do everything together"), only wants warm communication, "That's what matters." The second is a flower child in a psychedelic jump suit fleeing into a private game world of magical richness and pitiful solitude. The third is an aging spiritualist of British pretensions who abdicates all decision to her spirit voices, which she can't hear without junk. The fourth is a hooker who images herself Harlow and dreams her own sordid lonely tragedy in the flesh. The Inspector comes in halfway through for a long solo reconstruction of the first (imaginary?) crime in parody, establishing all the invisible things we already know in such profusion that they farcically come to life and multiply. The Dealer, before giving Hawk the stuff, recapitulates the entire play, raving about Dream-Orgasm-Death in the Now.

This would be quite enough without the rest—hawk image, ritual, formal filigree, God knows what intimations. As a play like any other, "The Hawk" goes too far in pursuit of meanings and wanders into a house of mirrors, leaving those living dying women to choose significances they alone could yield. Plays are first of all about people in action and move not between particular and general but from one particular to another, actor to spectator. "The Hawk" is too strong a play to explain itself, and unconvincing when it does. Emphasis, balance, proportion are off here and there; that's life.

Now the story of how the play came into being and why it is actually not like any other. Theatre Genesis rented a farm in Pennsylvania for the month of August, and Murray Mednick and Tony Barsha, writer and director, lived and worked there with the cast of this play. Mednick provided a bare scenario to start, and from that the group communally made "The Hawk." The actors' involvement in creating their roles helps explain the special quality of the acting, which approaches documentary realism within the austere stylization of the form; it also lets them improvise in performance: the work goes on. Mednick's effort, I'd guess, shows in the nearly faultless tone of the language, despite its range; in the avoidance or reanimation of cliché, the direct, honest precision of what is told; and in the freedom of imagination behind the play's richness and density. Barsha must be credited at least with the immaculate staging, which establishes the form and gives the play unity and momentum; and the clarity, lightness, and economy of transitions. Eddie Hicks plays guitar and sings. The actors are Ching Yeh, Tony Serchio, Lee Kissman, Sally Sommer, O-Lan Johnson, Walter Hadler, Scarlett Johnson, and Barbara Young. Individually and collectively their work is beautiful.

Several groups have recently begun developing communal methods of creating theatre, abandoning the rigid separation of author, director, actors. The Living Theatre's "Frankenstein" was the breakthrough. It is an inefficient, terribly difficult method, exacting a mutual trust and sacrifice of ego rare in the theatre. "The Hawk" is a daring experiment that succeeds. 10/26/67

Willie the Germ

A play by Murray Mednick, directed by Ralph Cook, presented by Theatre Genesis at St. Mark's Church in-the-Bouwerie.

"Willie the Germ" is a testament to how bad life feels to one individual. Murray Mednick pictures America as a freak show funhouse carny trap. Mama is a spider, papa is a bully, daughter is a teenybopper, sonny goes to college. Willie is trapped, their slave and victim, eternally watched by the Button-Pusher, rudely cut off by Dr. Sam. Willie is a gentle loser and all he wants is out; he has to dance or be castrated. Eventually he is castrated.

The play is a single cry of pain. It would be easy to fault it for paranoia or stridency or overstatement—Willie is passive, almost professionally a victim, his tormentors caricatures—but the pain is convincing, and the play expresses it with energy and ingenuity. I found it grating only to the extent that Mednick is uncompromisingly hostile toward his audience and indulgent toward Willie.

Ralph Cook's production is superb, with a clean, clear, imaginative use of space and a vivid declarative style. Victor Eschbach is resourceful, persuasive, and affecting as Willie, and well supported by Michele Collison, Delia Duke, Gene Elman, and Tom Lillard. John P. Dodd did the lighting, which greatly helps define the moods and structure of the play. Dominick Capobianco contributed zapping sounds and a grisly statue of poor Willie's doom.   5/16/68

Notable Playwrights
1964–68

Terrence McNally

"...And Things That Go Bump in the Night," a play by Terrence McNally, directed by Lawrence Kornfeld, at the Tyrone Guthrie Theatre in Minneapolis.

Despite the squabbling that surrounded its premiere at the Tyrone Guthrie Theatre in Minneapolis, "...And Things That Go Bump in the Night" opened on schedule and was revealed as the most impressive new American play I have seen this season. Terrence McNally has written a drama which, without violating naturalism, incorporates an exceptional range of theatrical effects and earnestly attempts a final transformation into ritual. While the play is not wholly effective, it is the work of an unusually gifted writer who has the courage to attempt a direct confrontation with real issues of our time, both personal and global.

The action is set in a luxurious bomb shelter where the family have been living for some time. Ruby is the mother, Sigfrid and Lakme the operatically named son and daughter. Grandfa, confined to a wheelchair, is preparing for departure to the loony bin: "I'm a loon," he says. Fa sits through the play almost invisible in an armchair, gloomily reading bad news in the papers, sometimes snoring, ready to die.

Outside, something, some danger, some *It* is moving west. ("We're the west," says Grandfa.) No one knows what it is: no one who has seen it has survived. It is considered safe to go outside during the day, but after dark, after curfew, everyone moves into sanctuary. This family's situation is even more desperate. In order to protect themselves from one another, every night they bring in a victim from outside: every day Sigfrid and Lakme go out and find a guest to bring home for the night to distract and amuse the family.

Tonight's guest is Clarence, a meek, earnest, probably homosexual peace marcher whom the handsome Sigfrid has lured away from his protest march. In the course of the evening Clarence is destroyed, and the family is left alone to chant its litany of strength and brute survival.

Beneath the surface the play is more complex. Beneath fear of the bomb or of the outside world, McNally is writing about a deeper fear of self, fear of life, fear of innocence. It is his people's own hearts that go bump in the night and terrorize them; their only answer to this terrible sound is to drown it out. The play describes a world in which God is dead but Satan lives; in which the meek shall not inherit the earth but be destroyed by the strong; in which purity, honesty, and goodness are not just worthless but liabilities. The play's statement is devastatingly dark, the author's attitude toward it disturbingly uncertain.

The three acts do not hold together very well. The first, devoted to the family at home, is full of irony and painful thrusts of humor. The long second act, with its earnest attention to Clarence, includes a campy sequence of Ruby impersonating an opera queen. The third act, which begins after Clarence has been disposed of—that is, after the plot tension has been released—finds its way to the demonic final ritual with considerable difficulty. And yet there is so much going for it, so much in both content and execution, that much of the experience is electrifying.

The production under Lawrence Kornfeld's direction was somewhat uneven, ranging from brilliance to mere adequacy. Joseph Chaikin gave an extraordinary, definitive performance of

Clarence, and Leueen MacGrath was splendid in the somewhat unwieldy role of Ruby. There was also good work done by Ferdi Hoffman, Robert Drivas, and Lois Unger. 2/20/64

Lanford Wilson

"Ludlow Fair," directed by Neil Flanagan, at the Caffè Cino; "Balm in Gilead," directed by Marshall W. Mason, at Café La Mama.

Off-Off-Broadway has been turning into a Lanford Wilson festival. His "Ludlow Fair" is currently running at the Caffè Cino; "Balm in Gilead," Wilson's first full-length play, just ended a week at Café La Mama; "No Trespassing" was revived in a Theatre 1965 workshop production at the Village South Theatre; "Home Free!," veteran of two iterations at the Cino, is one of the three plays on the New Playwrights bill opening this week at the Cherry Lane.

It is rare to have available such a range of any playwright's work, much less that of an "unknown." (The Cherry Lane production is his "professional" debut.) Wilson's talent is unmistakable; it remains uncertain what he will do with it. All the plays are distinguished by flexible naturalistic speech that establishes relatable characters expertly and precisely and lends itself to the monologues by which they like to reveal themselves. His works deal mostly in character rather than idea or image and are similar in impulse, if not in style, to plays of Tennessee Williams. Wilson is deft at controlling mood and tends toward clarity and simplicity of structure.

"Ludlow Fair," a bedtime conversation between two girls who live together, is ostensibly about the latest romantic disappointment of Rachel, who is pretty, takes herself seriously, and constantly falls in love. As it proceeds, the emphasis delicately shifts onto Agnes, her wise-cracking roommate. Lonely, plain, and normally more realistic, Agnes permits herself to look forward to the fantasy of romance at her coming lunch with her boss's skinny son.

The material of the play is conventional, its development straightforward. Wilson combines precision with emotional discernment and makes his familiar characters particular. The play is funny and entirely enjoyable, especially Jennie Ventriss as Agnes. Neil Flanagan's direction is witty and full of movement.

"Balm in Gilead," seen at Café La Mama two weeks ago, is Wilson's most ambitious play to date. The play occurs over two nights in an all-night coffee shop on the West Side of Manhattan. The personnel are homosexuals of both sexes, drug people of various persuasions, prostitutes, pimps, and others more or less cut off from conventional settled society. The play's concern is their solitude and the various means by which they express and cope with it; its statement is bleak but charged with energy.

Wilson's kaleidoscopic technique frees him from the obligation to show these characters in dramatic confrontations. Instead the stage is occupied by fifteen or twenty characters at once, each of them sharply defined, and attention roves among them. The texture is further complicated by shifts out of documentary realism when a few of the characters, ostensibly emerging from the coffee house into the night outside, turn to the audience and speak directly, describe their hang-ups, entertain with an ironic song or anecdote, clarify "in" references.

The play is given shape—not quite successfully—by its focus on one story, the encounter between Joe Conroy, a boy on the make who has slipped into the clutches of a dope pusher, and Darlene, a new girl in town who lacks the words for feelings. Against the constantly shifting background of the coffee shop, plus one scene in Darlene's hotel room, their fitful, fragmentary liaison is followed to its violent end.

Much of the play is brilliant and all of it is entertaining. At times the intricate technique gets out of control, and the author resorts to melodramatic cliché action to solve his problems. The story of Conroy's involvement with the gangsters is unconvincing, not because it seems to distort reality, but because it is too familiar. Darlene's monologue about her love life in Chicago, on the other hand, delineates a fresh, startlingly recognizable self-awareness.

Marshall W. Mason did a fine job of staging the play, keeping its moving focus clear and the relationship between its many elements alive and persuasive. The large cast included a number of excellent performances, notably Avra Petrides, Gregory Rozakis, Neil Flanagan, Mary Tahmin, Dennis Tate, and Michael Warren Powell. 2/11/65

Ronald Ribman

"The Journey of the Fifth Horse," a play by Ronald Ribman, directed by Larry Arrick, presented by the American Place Theatre at St. Clement's Church.

I enjoyed and admired Ronald Ribman's "The Journey of the Fifth Horse," a work of literary theatre, an unfashionable mode among younger American playwrights. (Ribman's play has this in common with Robert Lowell's "The Old Glory.") "The Journey of the Fifth Horse" is an intellectual play, demanding a certain sophistication about form on the part of its audience. It is also somewhat undramatic, its charms closer to those one anticipates from solitary reading. The play has an air of privacy which I appreciated for possibly nontheatrical reasons: it is intricate and cunningly fashioned, not assertive or directly communicative.

The play is "drawn in part" from a story by Ivan Turgenev. Its form is extraordinarily tricky—Pirandellian, you might say. An old woman submits the manuscript of a diary for possible publication. The diary is the work of the woman's recently deceased employer. The head of the publishing house has likewise just died, and the publisher's "first reader" takes the manuscript home. As he reads it, the diarist appears and relives certain of the events described, with other characters acted by figures from the reader's real life. The reading is interrupted by events and fantasies in his own life and mind, a coarser version of the contents of the diary, which reveals an exquisitely developed sensibility.

The theme is loneliness and isolation. Two love stories unfold side by side, one the epitome of romance, the other a madman's vulgar fantasy, both leading through foolishness to rejection. One is subtle and tragic, the other gross and farcical, yet both end the same way.

It is striking how Russian the play seems—how foreign and old-fashioned. The diarist sounds a lot like Turgenev, frequently evoking *A Month in the Country*. The reader, by contrast, sounds like darkest Dostoevsky jazzed up with flashes of black humor. Ribman's bravura technique shows in his handling of the structure, absorbing in its pure virtuosity. Ribman is a very talented writer (it was apparent in his first play, "Harry, Noon and Night"). This play keeps something in reserve, withholds some contact: one admires it and delights in it, but from a distance; I would like to be let in on its secrets. I'm glad it has secrets; I'm glad it is too complex and subtle to be comprehensible, rather than too simple and obvious to be worth attention. I like the inspired craziness that breaks through from time to time.

The American Place Theatre production is a little heavy, a little too literal for the play. It keeps facing all the way into Turgenev, where some acknowledgement of present-day consciousness is the play's only chance for immediacy. When it gets too smooth, too well worked out, the two stories slide into the same level of reality, and the play loses some of its formality.

Dustin Hoffman is superb as Zoditch, the reader, furiously caught up in a comedy of madness, becoming hateful, loathsome, Hitlerian, grotesque, and simultaneously funny and unexpectedly human. Michael Tolan is very good as the materialized diarist, encompassing the bursts of lyricism and unabashed romantic sincerity without strain. Hoffman and Tolan are at pains to make the language clear, which I greatly appreciated. Larry Arrick's direction is excellent on this score, with good performances by many others in the large cast. I think the play calls for a simpler setting. Perhaps not. I seem to be weighing old-fashioned pleasures against new-fangled ones, forgetting to enjoy them both.

4/28/66

George Birimisa

"Daddy Violet" and "How Come You Don't Dig Chicks?," two plays by George Birimisa, directed by the author, at the Troupe Theatre Club.

George Birimisa's "Daddy Violet" is a genuinely strange little play that uses a variety of tricks to confuse the boundaries between life and art—pseudo-improvisation, real ad libs, excursions into the audience, actors' real names, etc.—combined into a disconcertingly tight formlessness.

Instead of the usual easy tidy-up, Birimisa pushes steadily into abstraction. For all its gimmickry, his play is effective on a mysterious, unfamiliar, oddly provocative level. The play begins unobtrusively as the three actors wander onto the stage and do a few relaxation exercises. One of them explains the particular acting exercises they are working on: the idea of the actor's "center," which can be moved about (from chest to mouth—or crotch); and a dangerously foolish set of flower impersonations. This might be an acting class (school of Michael Chekhov) or three actor friends working together informally or a demonstration of curious acting techniques. It looks nothing like a play.

The girl, who is working on becoming a violet, finds her way into a vapid little song about blooming on a mountainside and looking down on the cloud-covered...Mekong Delta—she shies right away from it. Interlude of bickering, playing with the audience, etc., then back to violets. Becoming a violet apparently feels wonderful. Eventually all three of them are tender violets on the mountainside singing above the clouds, which now part and reveal the war going on below in close, horrifying detail, which is too much for the fragile flowers. They panic, they are hysterical—until the "leader" abruptly changes the Mekong into the Salinas Valley ("Steinbeck country"). Whew! The violets are safe, sweet, and happy again—and the play is brought to a swift, graceful end.

Without characters, plot, or setting, Birimisa has shaped a seductive experience that looks into a particular kind of contemporary consciousness in relation to the actual world. As violets the actors embody the love-oriented, passive, wide-open state of the acid generation, grooving, which leaves them so vulnerable that they are unable to face external reality and switch it off—the drop-out's cop-out. It's a theme that needs exploring, and Birimisa's odd enterprise succeeds in getting at it more concisely and pointedly than any straightforward approach I can imagine. This is a small, slight play—its imagery is too frail and frivolous to support much weight—but surprisingly forceful and genuinely original. The play's tendency to mock itself and thus limit itself is one of Birimisa's close-woven ironies: it is this ironic self-consciousness that produces the improbable contrast between the play's form and function and its silly ingredients. It is certainly a far-fetched way to write a play, but it came alive in performance, drew me into its off-hand, undefined world, and took me through a provocative adventure.

Birimisa directed and acted in his own play, which turns out to have been a good idea. I doubt if any other director could have grasped his elusive intent well enough to hit the right levels of naturalness, tomfoolery, virtuosity, and regular acting. He is extravagant, impulsively daring, taut with restrained force. His triple function puts him farther outside the play than the others, which fits well enough but—with no character to hide behind—leaves him exposed in his own fierce vision. Dan Leach is fine and funny as his prize pupil, giving us a couple of flashy demonstrations of preposterous acting stunts. Sylvia Strauss, playing a beginning student, is acceptably inept and touchy without losing her sense of the ensemble, which is precise, coherent, and quick. What a curious and cunning thing Birimisa has made!

"Daddy Violet" was preceded by "How Come You Don't Dig Chicks?," a shorter play by the same author. A seedy, vaguely aging, faintly pathetic homosexual brings a butch, naturally surly trick up to his apartment and goes smoothly, rather likably into the ritual of seduction. The hustler, condescending but curious, finds his questions answered with surprising self-accepting dignity. Phase two: the hustler turns thief and bully; the man unexpectedly stands up to him, then helps him save face and lets him go without rancor. Left alone, he is only briefly blue before realizing what a charmingly concise, even funny incident he's just been through, and ends up laughing.

This is standard stuff. The distinction is its tone, low-key, understated, almost undramatic, and its respectful, loving attitude toward the characters, who abandon melodrama in order to stay real people. The hustler is flat, but the homosexual emerges as a dignified, honest, impressive character—perhaps the first such to disdain self-pity unequivocally.

The play is somewhat sketchily written: the words are an exoskeleton; the play goes on between and behind them, in the subtext, in the things unsaid. Again directing his own play, Birimisa holds it way down, generally to the level of casual conversation, keeping the pace leisurely enough to let the silences be heard. Any other approach would have led to mawkishness and fakery. Claude Barbazon is excellent as the homosexual, too knowing for explanations or excuses. Don Barshay is good as the hustler, ill at ease with real human behavior, suddenly feeling exposed, shocked to find his tough-guy mask is transparent. The play is no more than an anecdote, but its delicacy and honesty are special.

6/15/67

Rochelle Owens

"Istanboul," a play by Rochelle Owens, directed by Don Signore, at the Playbox.

When Rochelle Owen's play "Istanboul" was done by the Judson Poets' Theatre a few years back, I thought they overdid it. Reading the script confirmed my impression that Miss Owens had written a more serious and interesting play than had reached the stage. Flashy performances and production values obscured its peculiar brooding, obsessed tone; its oddly deep historical and geometrical resonances were sacrificed to boisterous humor. Now "Istanbuol" has been revived at the Playbox, where I found it bewitching, even thrilling. The production is more modest than Judson's, but the play is all there, and it is brilliant.

Unfolding in Constantinople in the thirteenth century, the play's preoccupations are religiosexual. A Crusader named Godfrigh (because he "frigs God") has bought a shrine on the road to Jerusalem. All the place needs to make him a killing is a resident holy personage. In a native café he meets St. Mary of Egypt, who raves that "Saracen never touched me," among other things; whether she is divinely inspired or plain crazy is not to be asked. Godfrigh's cross and glory is a fetishistic obsession with hairy women, and praise be, St. Mary is hairy beyond imagining; since he is no infidel, she is not defiled by his touch (in fact she loves it). Godfrigh is ecstatic. His gleaming, hairless wife, Alice, meanwhile, is sleeping with Leo, the stud dancer from the very same café, adored by Turkish and European women alike, who may or may not be a Westerner in native guise. The atmosphere is drenched in exotic sexuality, and the Westerners are spellbound. They think they are raping the East; in reality it is raping them. Ultimately St. Mary of Egypt has a hashish vision in which God directs her to cut off Godfrigh's leg, and he dies. But it doesn't really matter, it even makes sense as the ultimate fulfillment of his obsession, and with stoned Levantine cruelty, life goes on

The play's fascination is its extraordinary density; a plot synopsis cannot convey that or its uniquely pungent atmosphere. The basic situation shows East and West, reciprocally awed and contemptuous, weirdly embraced in an ecstasy of destruction. As history "Istanboul" is fanciful and romantic, but it isn't frivolous: the Crusades are hard history to swallow, but they really did happen. Miss Owens snags into her play all the threads of thought that converged in this special time and place and knotted forever. The climactic but unresolved confrontation between East and West might be a mythical exemplar of duality, or of inevitable deadly conflict based on irreconcilable contrast. (It has nothing to do with Vietnam, by the way. Miss Owens is dealing with historical consciousness, not current events; hers is an Orient of the mind.) The play's dynamic springs from opposing pairs—East vs. West, Christian vs. infidel, dark skin vs. light, purity vs. defilement, body vs. spirit, and so on. (The characters come in pairs too: Godfrigh and Alice both have confidants; two women pine over Leo's dances; and a mysterious Robed Man, silent and expressionless, constantly watches St. Mary as well as Leo, paired with neither, either, or both.)

Miss Owens's characters are formed by the irrevocable abstractions of myth and history on one hand and immediate physical needs on the other. She celebrates lusts not directly but in the amplifying perversity of their conjunctions with mind and spirit; even Leo's sensuality is complicated (or decorated) by a dangerous edge, a glint of drivenness. The characteristic modes of feeling are obsession, fetishism, bemusement, frustration, madness, and a desperate blind groping for satisfaction, often literally orgasmic. Isolation is breached only in chance realizations of fantasy, as in Godfrigh's apocalyptic, fatal meeting with St. Mary, and perhaps in such fantastic social enterprises as the Crusades themselves. Godfrigh's hair hang-up is no more freaky than the compulsion that brought them all so far east.

These windy reflections are not meant to sum up the play's meanings, God forbid, only to suggest its richness of texture and fabulous intricacy of allusion and connotation. I hope I haven't made it sound intellectual and pretentious, because it's not. The story is told simply, almost crudely; the play realistically catches the hypnotic rhythms of cannabis cultures and their stupor of will. The shining energy, music, grandeur are in the writing itself, at once hysterical and obsessed, vagrant and knowing, flamboyant and concise. What is indescribable is the personal vision manifest in every line, every leap and flash of imagination. Owens's work is stubbornly eccentric and unaccountable but insistent in its honesty, integrity, and rooted strength.

Despite some technical shakes on opening night, Don Signore's production was obviously sturdy, accurate, and airworthy, and it's probably flying by now. Jean David was magnificent in St. Mary's climactic monologue, which reaches the sublime. Richard Dow had physical attributes and nerve enough to be sexy as Leo; most actors would flirt and camp and preen. Irene Schaeffer was a potentially wonderful Alice, surely realized by now. Lewis Jacobson, miscast as Godfrigh, looked like a vacationing student, not a crusading knight; by the discretion and focus of his acting he brought Godfrigh to life anyway. Miss Owens herself, in the bit part of Gertrude, was charmingly real. The lighting by Donald L. Brooks helped greatly in setting locales, controlling transitions, and sustaining the flow, and the use of music was superb. 3/7/68

H. M. Koutoukas
1965–67

Only a Countess May Dance When She's Crazy

A one-act play by H. M. Koutoukas, directed by the author, at the Caffè Cino.

H. M. Koutoukas's "Only a Countess May Dance When She's Crazy" is an intriguing if overwrought exercise in expressionism. In circumstances both dire and extravagant, a countess goes crazy in monologue form. She talks to herself, to the walls, to the furniture, to the sole survivors of a "mushrooming catastrophe" on the earth, and to her employer, the mysterious Dr. Till, who keeps his medieval laboratory atop a tower and is running short of victim-specimens for his experiments. The countess sings poignant, painful songs—she is in the final stages of desperation.

Carole Griffith plays her with remarkable daring and unfailing concentration. The script has an angular expressiveness and highly personal style. The failures are on the side of intensity and strict devotion to the choices made; both author and actress are impressively gifted. The production is a technical extravaganza, given the limitations of the room, with complex, evocative lighting by Denis Parichy and harshly stylized direction by the author. Koutoukas is a strong addition to the Caffè Cino's roster of talented young dramatists. 1/14/65

Medea

A "ritualistic camp" by H. M. Koutoukas, directed by the author, at Café La Mama.

H. M. Koutoukas's new version of "Medea" is so eccentric as to be nearly unthinkable. His play is a straightforward enactment of the final terrible scene when Medea murders her children to avenge herself on Jason. The language is high-flown as befits tragedy, the tragic impulse is pursued without deviation, and Koutoukas has injected a philosophical content of evident seriousness—the play is violently anti-logic, anti-Greek. Medea is the very heroine of old—fantastical, hideously wronged, ecstatically suffering.

But the action is set in a laundromat. The children are killed by being thrown into an automatic washing machine. The nurse is a Red Cross nurse. Jason is a drab nonentity. Medea herself is played by a six-foot-three man!

I don't know what to make of it. Some of the language is beautiful, some of it is unintelligible. Sometimes the lines have the force of passion, sometimes they sound arbitrary. At times the tone of the language is so uncertain as to create unintentional comedy, but the comic effect of the setting is certainly not unintended. What are we to make of that?

Much of the production is barely competent, but then come flashes of an inner design. Charles Stanley is a grotesque Medea in not quite the same way that Medea was a grotesque woman, but as the play goes on he becomes invidiously convincing. His ambition overstrains his acting ability; choreographic movements and modulations of intensity remain intentions, without the organic unity a more experienced actor could accomplish. One can see his mind working, and it is distracting. But he is an astonishing apparition when Medea sheds her despised Greek garments and steps forth in the dress of her native Colchis. Pat Holland is properly furious as the nurse. The musical score by Robert Cosmos Savage contributes strongly to the tragic tone. Koutoukas's "Medea" is appalling. For all its obvious faults, I can't swear that the quality is wrong for the subject.

10/21/65

All Day for a Dollar

A play by H. M. Koutoukas, directed by Deborah Lee, at the Caffè Cino.

"All Day for a Dollar," H. M. Koutoukas's made-to-measure "divine Christmas ecstasy" at the Caffè Cino, was entirely fantastic, entirely detached from reality. Koutoukas set his play in the limbo of broken wind-up toys and peopled it with exiled stars. The conceit grew cumbersome and even tiresome at times, but the final moments had a sweetness and naïve simplicity that I found charming. Deborah Lee staged the play in its revival last week and scattered the action all over the café, which was decorated throughout with Christmas trees, painted stars, and objects reflecting Koutoukas's predilection for glitter. Surrounded by the actors, engulfed in their fanciful environment, I was delighted by the high moments in the production: a faded star's reminiscences of Flo Ziegfeld, the creation of the waltz, an unexpected, touchingly sincere rendition of "Silent Night." Koutoukas's script badly needed editing, but the warm-heartedness of the ending made the earlier excesses worth enduring. Robert Dahdah as Sascha Stavrapoulos and Charles Stanley as Young Becoming gave imaginative, convinced performances, and Joseph Cino, the café's proprietor, made a spectacular appearance as St. Peter of the Golden Keys. The play was an intimate event, no more to be judged in a broad artistic context than any family's Christmas carols—a perfect meeting of event and place, and a special pleasure. 1/13/66

When Clowns Play Hamlet

A play by H. M. Koutoukas, directed by the author, at La Mama Experimental Theatre Club.

"When Clowns Play Hamlet," the current event in the Ruth Yorck Golden Series at La Mama, is H. M. Koutoukas's best play. Koutoukas has a deserved reputation, based on numerous off-off-Broadway productions, for his camp extravagance and unique personal style. It's a lush jumble of romantic poesy, boisterously eclectic theatrics, vivid, eccentric imagination, a gift for aphorism, and a shy but considerable depth of feeling. His previous plays have been so badly muddled, cluttered, overripe—usually in production as well as writing—that it was all but impossible to see them. Shaky in style, ramshackle in structure, and altogether unlikely, they seemed preposterous, self-parodying: one could not quite mistake ineptitude for irony. There were no terms in which to take Koutoukas seriously, yet it was unthinkable to dismiss him. He called his early plays "camps," as if they really were as frivolous as they looked. But under the glitter was honest sentiment, an impulse toward tragic grandeur, an intense compassion. The plays' grotesquerie masked Koutoukas's unfashionable, uncool, possibly embarrassing romanticism.

In "When Clowns Play Hamlet" Koutoukas seems for the first time to be catching up with his talent and impulses. All the Koutoukas flash and madness is there, but the play is comparatively coherent, direct, and accessible.

The setting is backstage at a circus. The characters are three sad clowns—Pancho, a hermaphrodite, Berliner, an old gypsy woman, and Gamina, a young blind girl— all victims of fate, alumnae of the freak show. They commiserate, reminisce, sing a few songs, and rehearse their act. Meanwhile, the plot. The circus elephant, Gamina's sole protector against her arch-enemy the panther-gorilla, has died. Pancho and Berliner are trying to keep this alarming news from her, though the elephant lies rotting nearby and Gamina periodically asks, "Would somebody be kind enough to tell me what that stench is?" Soon after Gamina learns of her loss, the panther-gorilla breaks loose, terrorizes the circus and destroys most of it, eats a quantity of babies, and starts closing in on Gamina. Pancho and Berliner resolve to sacrifice themselves to protect her; they go forth to meet the beast, return fatally wounded, and die; the helpless, terrified blind girl is alone.

This is a notion of imaginative writing that went out with Maeterlinck, and more's the pity. Reality and abstraction are in, imagination and the picturesque are out. Tennessee Williams has always had a fecund, expressive, colorful imagination; Paul Foster has an unusual feeling for milieu; but most other contemporary playwrights settle for either a rarefied locale of the mind or a recognizably "real," more or less ordinary corner of direct experience. What's become of the joy of making things up, the delight of unfettered invention, the exhilaration of creating a world? Koutoukas has it. It makes his plays look extremely strange, even silly; but that's just the surface put there to amuse—it's worth looking beneath to the feeling that animates and authenticates the plays. Koutoukas writes with real compassion for the creatures of his imagination, who in turn face a cruel world open, fragile, sensitive, and oddly heroic: they are imaginary but their experience is real. The plays express a knowing, melancholy vision of life that is convincing and affecting.

Jeff Weiss, Mary Boylan, and Beverly Grant bring three colorful, distinctive personalities to their roles; as director, Koutoukas has led them to a blended style of playing that serves his intentions. They are effective individually and together. Robert Cosmos Savage has written incidental music that is exquisitely responsive and helpful to the play's moods. The physical production has the slightly moldy, thrift-shop air familiar from previous Koutoukas ecstasies. It presumably happens by default, but maybe it's just right for these curious plays.

The second act was much too long on opening night, urgently calling for more work; I hope Koutoukas has done it by now. My one serious disappointment was the elephant, an impressive theatrical symbol reduced to dull paint on a flat surface. There are other gauche moments, but they seem superficial when one tunes in to Koutoukas's imagination. He is special and worth cherishing. In who else's play could a character say, urgently and with poignant adult directness, "Oh, if we only had an elephant!" 2/23/67

Caffè Cino II
1965–68

Directing Icarus's Mother

A play by Sam Shepard, directed by Michael Smith, at the Caffè Cino.

I thought Edward Albee's review of "Icarus's Mother" (in *The Voice* last week) was just in its overall estimation of what he saw, but I won't resist the temptation to reply on a few details. Albee wrote: "[Smith] knows it is the function of the director to illuminate the playwright's intention, and I would imagine that he and Shepard worked together on the project and are convinced that the wattage is fine." I am not sure a director's function is so simply defined. I tried, in this instance, to work closely with Shepard and produce the play as exactly the way he wanted it as possible, choosing to believe that he knew what his intention was and to some extent how to achieve it. But there are alternative approaches. I would prefer to say that the director's function is to illuminate the play's intention, not the playwright's. The director may see intention more clearly or deeply than the playwright does, or may imagine a stage action more appropriate than the stage directions indicate. (I considered using untrained performers in "Icarus's Mother," for example, but finally bowed to Shepard's casting. With due respect to the actors, I'm still not sure I was wrong. Shepard himself replaced an actor who got sick for the final eight performances and brought a fresh, loose, light quality to the production that it had previously lacked.) I did not change a single line of Shepard's play and followed the stage directions as best I could; but I cannot accept as a general principle the director's subordination to the playwright. Everyone is in service to the play, which is an event before an audience.

And of course, neither Shepard nor I thought the "wattage" was anywhere near right. Albee is not a critic and cannot be expected to distinguish the director's hand from the author's, and so I mean this as no slight. But his review blamed Shepard's play for characteristics that existed specifically, and only, in my production of it. It was exciting to diagnose and cure some of them during the course of the run and to see the play itself emerge. Close attention to "Icarus's Mother" has confirmed my belief that Sam Shepard is an extraordinarily promising playwright, and working on the play was a privilege and a painful pleasure. 12/2/65

Moon

A play by Robert Heide, directed by the author, at the Caffè Cino.

"Moon" is Robert Heide's new play. What a week! The one-act is set in a vinyl-mod apartment where a boy and a girl are trying to get over whatever happened last night when they got so drunk at that party. Trying to calm themselves, they smoke a joint, put on Indian music, and sit down to meditate. Enter couple two, strangers from the party whom they seem to have drunkenly invited over. Boy two is a taciturn, guilt-ridden, explosive ex-Marine; girl two is an unhappy bitch out to break his balls. The social scene is strained enough, and then the second couple get into a fight beyond manners. Girl one flees, boy one asks the unwanted guests to leave and they do. A young homosexual painter, who has just moved in upstairs with his lover, brings a fresh loaf of bread as a get-acquainted present and doesn't stay long. When he's gone the girl returns. Finally just short of despair they hold each other tight in melancholy affirmation.

As in his earlier play "The Bed," Heide shows himself perceptive, intelligent, and a peculiar dramatist. His worst fault is a penchant for psychoanalytic jargon, which leads him to a mechanistic view of human nature. The clinical words the characters use make them sound alternately like detached scientists and pretentious fools. They wind up feeling unreal to themselves and to the audience; those real feelings of unreality are the subject of the play.

The best moments are the play's flights into fancy, although it's disconcerting that Heide looks for his fancies to the movies. The painter's brief visit seems random but adds something essential—I know not what or why. Two brief sequences are genuinely theatrical, realized thanks to the lighting by Donald L. Brooks. Victor LiPari in the main role tends to overstate and illustrate his anger, almost as if parodying it. In quieter moments he is fine, as are John Gilman, Jacque Lynn Colton, Jim Jennings, and Jane Buchanan. 2/23/67

News report:
Death of Joe Cino

Joseph Cino committed suicide early Friday. He survived for a couple of days in critical condition and died Sunday evening in St. Vincent's Hospital. He always told people: "Do what you have to do." Nothing can be said about his death except that he did what he had to do.

Joe Cino's death is unthinkable because he was always a creator of life. In 1958 he opened the Caffè Cino at 31

Cornelia Street and the fun began. Painter friends hung their work on his walls. Poets came in and he let them read. Actors came in and he let them act. Playwrights came in and he let them put on their plays. At first the plays got simple readings. For the past six years, the Caffè Cino was presenting a full production of a new play practically every week. Joe Cino had created the prototype for Off-Off-Broadway.

Hundreds of plays and dozens of playwrights had their first encounters with big-city audiences at the Caffè Cino. Countless actors, directors, designers, and technical people had their first chance to make real theatre there.

What Joe Cino did has the air of historical necessity. By the early 1960s Off-Broadway had become too expensive to be of much use to unknown playwrights, especially if they had unconventional ideas, and with little prospect of production it seemed pointless for young writers to write plays. When the Caffè Cino started putting on new plays, a dam broke. The results are still incalculable. Playwrights appeared from everywhere, unimagined numbers of them, far more than could be scheduled at the Cino. Actors and directors arrived eager to work. Café La Mama, Judson Poets' Theatre, and Theatre Genesis came into being, all doing new plays, followed by many more cafés, bars, lofts, workshops, church groups. Off-Off-Broadway was born. In the past year or two it has spread far afield, with successful European tours by La Mama troupes and others, publication and commercial production of plays by several of the new playwrights, foundation grants, publicity. The American theatre hasn't had so much fresh vitality in years. An essential part of the spirit behind Off-Off-Broadway springs from the initiative and example of Joe Cino.

Cino's allegiance was to personal necessity in himself and those around him. His own necessity was to make things possible. He had no aesthetic theories, no pretensions, no impulse toward selfless service, nothing to prove. He seldom involved himself as a theatrical producer and insisted he was running a café, not a theatre. (His weekly ad in *The Village Voice* appeared, not in the theatre section, but under Cafés and Coffee Houses.) He provided space, equipment, and an audience and did whatever was necessary to make it all happen. It was his café and had his personality, but the plays belonged to the people who were doing them. There wasn't much money, but people were doing what they had to do, and that was what mattered. He chose plays by choosing people, and asserted his vision by leaving them scrupulously free.

What he demanded of a play and production was that it come to life; when it didn't he could drive people to hysteria trying to kindle the spark he believed in. He had little patience with limitations of nerve, passion, or energy. He despised ego games when they detracted from the work. If he was sometimes impossible, it was because he was sometimes bitterly disappointed.

Joe Cino loved people for their uniqueness. He loved the energy that flows from people doing what they love to do. Best of all he loved "magic time," that moment of infinite possibility when the lights dim and an unknown world miraculously comes alive. 4/6/67

The Clown

A play by Claris Nelson, directed by Marshall W. Mason, at the Caffè Cino.

The Caffè Cino is continuing under the management of Charles Stanley. Last week it presented Claris Nelson's brief, light fantasy "The Clown." I found it charming. The play is about decadence, and most of the cast appeared to know what they were talking about. Marshall W. Mason's staging was showy and frivolous. The glory of the production was the costumes, great elegant elaborate capes and drapes, tights, veils, jewels, and other improbable courtly elegances, the work of Michael Warren Powell. 4/20/67

This Is the Rill Speaking

A play by Lanford Wilson, directed by the author, at the Caffè Cino.

"This Is the Rill Speaking" is Lanford Wilson's most beautiful play so far. It is similar in form to Dylan Thomas's "Under Milk Wood" and in language to Thornton Wilder's "Our Town," and still it succeeds on its own terms. With six actors and forty minutes of playing time, Wilson portrays a complete day in a small town in the Middle West—three generations, a catalogue of relationships, a cross-section of incidents. It's all typical and familiar and corny; it's all convincing. Whether you've been there or not, Wilson, who grew up in the Ozarks, takes you there now. It could be anyplace but it's not, it's here, it's where you are while it's happening. It's hometown USA, the archetype, the American dream of innocence. This isn't how it was, this is how it must have been, the voices, the banalities, the sameness and change, the desires and frustrations, simple and seeded with complexity, the hope, the loss, the rhythms of sentiment and season, light and dark, the myth behind memory. This is home again, where you can't go, because it isn't what you want it to have been. The play is nostalgic, melancholy, beautiful like the fall of leaves in a windless autumn of the mind.

Original or not, the play is perfectly written. The Caffè Cino revival, directed by the author, ingeniously makes it all look easy. The acting by the entire cast is fine—Tanya Berezin, Philip Clark, Jacque Lynn Colton, Fred Forrest, Marvin Peisner, especially Mae Durnhelm. All but Forrest have trouble with the regional accent, but no matter, they make music together, and that's what Wilson clearly has in mind. Charles Stanley's evocative, responsive, imaginative lighting contributes a bonus of beauty. Altogether it's a gem.

5/4/67

The Brown Crown

A play by Haal Borske, directed by Neil Flanagan, at the Caffè Cino.

"The Brown Crown" is a first play by Haal Borske, who also acts the leading role. It's hard to imagine where else but the Caffè Cino this play would find a welcome.

Borske plays Zephyrus, god of the west wind, who was banished by Zeus because of the Hyacinthus affair and has languished for sleepless aeons in this tiny, tacky circus ring. The worst of his curses is that Helios the sun no longer shines on him; even his friends the hyenas have died. He is visited by a scientist, who falls in love with him, and by the Sandman, who charms him to sleep. He speaks on the phone to Echo and learns that all the gods have fallen on hard times. The chariot of the sun is now driven not by Helios but by a mortal (Marlene Dietrich, apparently). The curse is lifted and seems to fall again. Finally the Sandman is transformed into Beauty, which will give him enough to think about for all eternity.

It is a weird, even unaccountable subject for a play, and

the style is equally weird—campy, downbeat, sarcastic, often funny. The play continually puts itself down and refuses to be taken seriously; together with the shifty tone of Borske's performance, this is its peculiar charm. He is assisted by Irving Metzman, hilarious as the scientist, and Walter Harris, sweet and simple as the Sandman. Although the writing is clumsy, the plot snarled, and the play too long, it's worth noting that Borske is an original and already, apart from echoes of Koutoukas, speaks with his own voice. The rest can be learned. 12/13/67

News report:
Caffè Cino Closes

Joe Cino died on April 2, 1967. This week, just less than a year later, the Caffè Cino has closed, probably forever. I am inarticulate with too many, too mixed emotions—sorrow, anger, outrage, frustration, civic despair—and would rather turn them off, if I could, than act them out in public. I am much too involved to be objective: I have loved the Caffè Cino for years, personally and theatrically, for what it represents and what it made possible; and since New Year's I have been its co-director, working to renew its life..

Shortly before Christmas, three months ago, it became apparent that the Cino was near collapse. Charles Stanley, who had managed to keep it going since Joe's death, realized the task was consuming him and, for his own survival, had to bail. I suggested to Wolfgang Zuckermann, with whom I've run two good seasons at Sundance, a summer festival in Pennsylvania, that we take over and try to inject some new life into the situation. Wolfgang was enthusiastic, and Charles abdicated to us with dispatch and obvious relief. I was just leaving to spend Christmas in California. Before I left we made plans to close on New Year's for two or three weeks of urgently needed rejuvenation. I left New York feeling, for a change, eager to come back.

While I was away, an event quietly happened that was eventually to do us in. The MacDougal Area Neighbors Association (MANA), a body dedicated to cleaning up the "mess on MacDougal Street" on behalf of local residents, brought suit against the Mayor and the Police Commissioner and obtained a court order requiring the authorities to enforce the administrative code regarding "coffee house" licenses. The day after this judgment was reported in the *Times*, the Caffè Cino received a summons, charged with "operating a coffee house without a license," for which the fine is, since 1965, a mandatory $250.

Joe Cino had periodically received such summonses during his eight and a half years at 31 Cornelia Street—nowhere near MacDougal Street but close enough to get singed when the heat was on. Joe would explain to the judge that he wasn't on that scene, wasn't bothering the neighbors, wasn't running the kind of commercial operation the coffeehouse law was meant to regulate, and he'd get a $25 fine or a dismissal. Knowing this we paid little attention. Off-Off-Broadway is chronically in trouble over technical illegalities, and this looked like just one more. We went on with the work, closing for the first three weeks in January, rebuilding the kitchen, replacing much of the equipment, and repainting the walls. The Cino reopened on January 23 with a production of Tom LaBar's play "Empire State."

At that moment MANA had sought and won a confirmation of the previous court order and a demand that it be obeyed. Three days later two plainclothesmen watched a performance and had a surprise for us afterward. There was an eleven-year-old boy in "Empire State," along with a few four-letter words; not only did the cops write us another license violation, they arrested Wolfgang Zuckermann, as manager, and a member of the cast, the boy's uncle, charged them with endangering the welfare of a child, and kept them in jail for the night and most of the next day. (When the police delivered the boy to his mother, who had seen the play several times, her first question was, "What are you doing home so early?") That was the end of "Empire State." The trial is next week. At that time we'll find out if the charge was a technicality, in which event it will presumably be dismissed, or an example of police exercising moral judgment, which is censorship.

We were left alone for a while after that, scared but running, with others plays lined up, and the good Caffè Cino spirit began to revive. We got another summons after a week, another one ten days later; the pressure was mounting almost too slowly to feel. We hired a lawyer and found out all we could, talked to everybody who would listen. Then a License Department inspector began to haunt us, and we had to cancel performances to avoid getting more summonses. (It's the plays that are forbidden, not the café.)

By the end of last week we had accumulated seven more summonses, seven trials ahead, seven unavoidable fines, no end in sight. Nothing we tried seemed to protect us from this relentless drain, no one could suggest a practical answer to our problem, neither of us was willing to throw his whole life into the Caffè Cino, as Joe Cino had done, and we closed.

It's very undramatic, we're just another sad civilian victim. I ought to scream bloody murder and go to jail to save the Cino—but it wouldn't work. One difficulty that plagued us is the enemy's elusiveness. Everyone we talk to professes to value the Cino's existence, no one to desire its destruction, and still it is destroyed. It isn't persecution of artists or censorship or anything substantive. We are doubly caught in political crossfire and the clumsiness of the city's administrative code. There is no license that fits the Caffè Cino and there needn't be. We were trying to do something good, harming no one. Why should we ask the city's permission?

As I pieced it together, it happened like this. The present coffee-house law, with its vague wording and high fines, came out of another "mess on MacDougal Street" flap in 1965, meant to control the boisterous cafés that opened up to receive the flood of kids discovering Bohemia, on the odd theory that the cafés caused the crowds. The law was theoretically aimed at the big flamboyant places; because of poor wording it turned out that the few licenses granted went to the big ones, while the little ones got threatened with the inflated fines. The MacDougal residents had a genuine and obstinate problem: on weekends their sidewalks were a manic freakshow. (Then too, however, their very houses were supported by the high ground-floor rents brought by the crowds.) To represent them in municipal matters, Edward I. Koch, then Democratic district leader, now Councilman, formed MANA, with Emanuel Popolizio, a lawyer, at its head, clearly as Koch's liaison with the traditional, conservative Democratic, preponderantly Italian community of the Village south of Washington Square and west on Bleecker and Carmine Steets.

Now Koch wants to run for Congress, and he needs all the Village's Democratic votes, including those DeSapio won against him in the old days when people cared. The MacDougal Street clean-up didn't accomplish much, besides replacing a few unique places (like the Night Owl) with pizza stands and poster shops. Lindsay was cooling it until Popolizio, as chairman of MANA, made his move and incredibly won a writ of mandamus, launching the cops and license inspectors on their fearful rounds. I understand the intention—defending stable residents against rowdy commercialism—but the action has no value in solving the MacDougal Street problem, which mainly involves kids milling about on the sidewalks, not going into the coffee houses. (No one claims the coffee house law works, just that it's the only weapon at hand. Anyway, the kids are shifting east to St. Mark's Place, where nary a coffee house is seen.) Secondarily, it looses uncontrollable forces of destruction that specifically have destroyed the Caffè Cino even though nobody wants them to. Everyone is sympathetic but no one can stop the process, even those who started it. I can't help thinking that the Cino is somehow, indirectly, accidentally being sacrificed to Ed Koch's political ambitions.

I think it's shameful. I am offended in a sense of civic propriety I hadn't known I had. What I mind is not that politics are rough but the dishonesty that offers futile gestures and expects credit for them, not that the law is stern but its stupidity and coarsening generalizations, not that a swamped bureaucracy is rigid but its pride in detachment from individual human considerations, as if anything else mattered. It is sickening to be told by a smiling cop how much he enjoyed the show and what a nice place the Cino is while his amiable buddy writes out a summons meant to close the Cino down. It is sickening to find that everyone who has any power is paralyzed by his involvement in a system that is compulsively, profitlessly destructive even on so casual and everyday a level, sick of finding that even down here words are more respected than realities, sick of being forced to hide, to lie, to think on a level I despise, to fight. What we wanted was joy.

Our trials begin this week, and it's possible we'll get dismissals and be able to reopen; or we could organize a club of people interested in the Cino and open up to members only, as Ellen Stewart had to do at La Mama; or a zoning variance might let us be licensed. But our reserves of spirit as well as money are depleted; a few convictions and the Cino is gone for good. Personally, I would be relieved. I didn't question my motives at the start, but I suspect they're based in nostalgia. I am devoted to the place more than the plays; to some imaginary spirit life that lingers in the room and among the people there; to the good times and the truest remembered intentions of Joe Cino, not to any vision of my own. If the Cino is an anchor in the past, I'm better off without it.

The theatre is poorer, though, and here I can objectively lament. The Caffè Cino opened in 1958 and started presenting new plays as early as 1960, making possibilities that grew into Off-Off-Broadway and a whole new impetus in our torpid theatre. It is the oldest Off-Off-Broadway theatre and the only real café theatre surviving. It has given first productions to countless authors and hundreds of plays, enabled innumerable actors and directors to practice and show their work, yielded irreplaceable experience in the art and craft of making theatre in the presence of an audience. What's been done is only a beginning, and a whole new group of places are eager to take up the tradition, and maybe the Cino is tired. Maybe it's a relic of less up-tight Village days. Maybe what I loved was not the Cino but Joe, maybe his life was the life of the room, this new life artificial, backward facing, forced, the effort to live it cowardly, not brave. 3/14/68

Broadway
1966–67

Marat/Sade

The rambling title of Peter Weiss's play (*at the Martin Beck*) is a concise statement of what happens in it: "The Persecution and Assassination of Jean-Paul Marat as Performed by the Inmates of the Asylum of Charenton Under the Direction of the Marquis de Sade." But that's no more than the frame. The picture within has a two-layer subject: a view of the French Revolution with Marat in the foreground (as Danton is in the foreground of "Danton's Death"); and a philosophical dialogue between Marat, the idealistic revolutionary, and de Sade, the pessimistic individualist.

The play's impact has to do with its theatrical method, which is determinedly, extravagantly modern. The author and his director, Peter Brook, have given body to many ideas of Bertolt Brecht and Antonin Artaud, two great theorists of theatre in this century. And the production is top-quality throughout: Brook fulfills his intentions authoritatively, and the actors, members of the Royal Shakespeare Company, are superb. With all this before you—the French Revolution, a nineteenth-century madhouse, Marat, de Sade, philosophy, Brecht, Artaud, and solid theatrical know-how—you can hardly fail to be interested.

Still, I was disappointed by the experience of seeing the play, which makes me think. In Brecht's terms, this sounds like the right effect. (Artaud was more interested in visceral response.) But what I have been thinking *about* is less the content or meaning of the play than its technique. The author, brilliantly abetted by the director, has constructed a play so complicated, detailed, and bold as to be almost invisible. Its intricacies are wonderful for contemplation in the library, where the philosophical dialogues seem obviously to be its meat. It is not, however, intended as literature but as a work of theatre. I agree emphatically with the view that a production should not interpret a play but bring the play into being. The text is holy, but plays exist in performance.

I found the Brook-Weiss "Marat/Sade" elusive, confusing, and unengaging. The complexity of Weiss's metaphor—the device that lunatics are playing historical figures speaking words written by de Sade—makes it impossible to take any of the play's "content" literally. The conflict of philosophies may be legitimate and timely, but its grip is weakened at too many points, the opposing views confused by their context until they sound like word games.

The enterprise is commendable for its ambition and daring. Pursuing Artaud's "theatre of cruelty," it sets out to shock, horrify, and disturb the spectator, on a primary, pre-intellectual level. At the same time, faithful to Brecht's idea that the spectator should be forced to think about and draw conclusions from the events shown on stage, the play sets its events in relief, contriving a context and jagged rhythm that forbid sustained emotional engagement. This sounds as stimulating as being splashed alternately with hot and cold water. But as I sat in the theatre, it seemed to me that the waters mixed, that what reached me was only tepid. I watched the "shocking" moments of the play with a detached curiosity, wondering how they would be managed. I thought about its arguments in a state of confusion until my mind tired of the effort.

Ambivalence is the most striking characteristic of the

play on every level. The solution is consistent: if you can't decide between possibilities, use both. This irresolution, I believe, lies behind the attempt to employ both Brechtian and Artaudian techniques. Brecht justifies Weiss's refusal to take sides in the play's argument; Artaud excuses his failure to be more coherent. But the play cannot commit itself even to irresolution; it ends with a ringing challenge to the audience: "When will you learn to see! When will you learn to take sides!" The challenge may be legitimate, but in this context seems opportunistic, hollow, and presumptuous.

"Marat/Sade" is extraordinarily interesting theatre. Its interest lies, I think, in the quantity of ideas it puts on stage rather than their quality. Brecht's and Artaud's suggestions mostly seemed not to have their intended effect. I felt neither enlightened nor assaulted. The author's information about Marat, de Sade, and the French Revolution is extensive; he does not so much say something about the subject as deluge the audience with data. (The emotional tone leans heavily toward de Sade's black view—one perceives Weiss as a disenchanted social idealist; still, he cannot resist appending that final revolutionary shout.) His "Marat/Sade" strikes me as proof that the artist must "take sides," both in form and in content. Weiss has done so much, presented such a quantity of theatrical stimuli, that one feels impertinent in asking how well he has done it, or to what end.

"Marat/Sade" opens new areas of possibility. Its popularity should give other producers the courage to try more of the far-out ideas proposed a generation back. Artaud especially remains virtually untapped (although the Living Theatre's production of "The Brig" was more effective Artaudian theatre than "Marat/Sade"). It is as a demonstration of techniques, rather than as a work of art, that "Marat/Sade" must be seen. 1/13/66

The Homecoming

Harold Pinter's "The Homecoming" (*at the Music Box*) is a Broadway event for sheer integrity of writing—Pinter never breaks stride, never cheats or cheapens; it is a Pinter event for intensity and implicit theme. The setting is an old house in London where a retired butcher, a widower, lives with his two sons, one a pimp, the other a demolition worker and would-be boxer, and his bachelor brother. Home on an unannounced visit comes third son Teddy, a Ph.D. who teaches in America. With him into this house of men he brings a surprise, his wife. The fierce old father instantly attacks, the woman is baited and grossly insulted, then suddenly charmingly welcomed. One minute the play is broadly comic, the next minute grotesque, the next heavy with gloom or raucously vulgar or drenched in nameless fears. What's happening? It changes, changes, and every ambiguity is cause for alarm. Is it about men laying traps for a woman, their hated desire? Is it driven by febrile misogyny? Will evil win, and when it does will I believe it? Yes, yes.

It is a stunning play, and yet halfway through the second act it lost me, I stopped caring, I found myself numb to surprise or shock, tired of it, dulled. Apparently Pinter's technique is self-limiting. Once you realize that anything can happen, you're immunized against it when it does. If anything can happen, everything is the same—and sameness is death to drama. Still, I wouldn't have missed it; and it doesn't mean much that it lost me—I may have been lost alone.

The Royal Shakespeare Company production has a detailed, controlled ferocity that is a lesson in itself. Peter Hall's direction is so superbly done that it seems disrespectful to question its premises; yet I wonder if the play couldn't have been made more convincing and effective as a whole. Hall's staging, in a vast, sullen set by John Bury, emphasizes the patterns and groupings in space, isolates the meaningful gestures and stark vulgar threats where the play is dangerously mannered to begin with and seems to want an anchor in the ordinary. Who knows? Hall's extraordinary ability is not to be doubted. And the actors: Paul Rogers as the father, Ian Holm as the pimp, John Normington as the brother, Terence Rigby as the boxer, Vivien Merchant as the woman, Michael Craig as the professor—they are beyond criticism, or certainly beyond my desire to criticize. Their performances individually and as an ensemble looked definitive to me. 1/12/67

Rosencrantz and Guildenstern Are Dead

Tom Stoppard's "Rosencrantz and Guildenstern Are Dead" (*at the Alvin*) is an immensely witty and charming play, from the initial idea through virtually all its thorough elaboration. Rosencrantz and Guildenstern, in case you have forgotten, are minor characters in "Hamlet," plot functionaries Shakespeare didn't bother to account for, interchangeable, remarkable only for their names, gratuitous victims of the tragedy. Stoppard has written the play that happens to them; their moments in "Hamlet" are the high points, but the time between has to be lived as well.

The play's focus is their anguished helplessness. Having lost all will, fast losing their separate identities, they don't know why they are at Elsinore or what they are supposed to be doing or how to do it or what's happening. They have a premonition and then foreknowledge of their deaths but can't do anything but continue as directed, as written. Meanwhile the events of "Hamlet" pile up around them, king, court, and Hamlet himself appearing on stage for few, brief words with R. and G., other times glimpsed passing. They tangle independently with the elaborated players, but mostly they are left desperately alone. What they do is talk and wait. "Somebody might come in." They speculate and struggle to devise alternative actions. Mostly they divert themselves with words, scattering them with a crisp Elizabethan flourish, tossing and juggling them, twisting, teasing, tormenting them. Later on their situation is less funny and their thoughts turn more and more to death until finally they talk themselves out of existence.

The writing is brilliantly clever, the basic trick a tour de force, and the play is great fun. The drawback is Stoppard's attempt to push it to deeper significance. The play echoes "Waiting for Godot" in sound and situation but lacks its resonance: these "intimations of meaninglessness" are Shakespeare's doing, not the human condition. Death per se is not a dramatic event, and Stoppard's decision to have R. and G. see their execution order and dumbly accept it makes them fools. The feeling of being at the mercy of events is familiar and true, but this special instance doesn't illuminate it for me. Rosencrantz and Guildenstern and I have had certain of the same experiences but not remotely in the same way.

The production is handsome and large-scale, with an extensive "Hamlet" cast in full regalia only occasionally seen. Brian Murray and John Wood are delightful, expert, and often touching in the title roles. 10/26/67

The Ridiculous I
1966–67

The Life of Lady Godiva

A play by Ronald Tavel, directed by John Vaccaro, at the Playhouse of the Ridiculous.

Ronald Tavel's "The Life of Lady Godiva" is terrifically entertaining. Its flavor is inexpressible, almost unspeakable—imagine a combination of "Tom Jones" and "Flaming Creatures." Self-categorized as "an hysterical drama," the play is a true novelty among forms, a partly factual chronicle of Lady Godiva, set in her period and told in the ancient-Greek way, with chorus and fate; a mocking inquiry, in the form of a theatrical game, into the possibility of free will; a psychological satire on the subject of women castrating men, particularly mothers their sons; and a no-holds-barred, outrageous farce, its humor derived from the classic subjects of sex and religion. I've never seen anything like it.

As staged by John Vaccaro, it has a distinctive consistency of style. The writing, both broad and intensely witty, mixes vaudeville gags with verbal stunts—pun, innuendo, vulgarism: Tavel covers the whole range of humor. The conditions of production have a high-school feel, tacky, clumsy, but disarmingly unpretentious, direct, uninhibited. The surface is glazed with pure, pre-publicity camp—the camp of Jack Smith or H. M. Koutoukas, not of Serendipity or Rudi Gernreich. The "sick" content is balanced by a joyous if sometimes bogus naïveté, the bad taste by innocence; it is in these delicate balances that the work succeeds. This is a real play, solidly constructed and intelligently written; it has an emotional substructure I found strong and convincing, although barely under control. Frivolity is its manner but only part of its spirit.

The setting is a combination convent-brothel. The Nuns' Chorus enters followed by Mother Superviva (John Vaccaro), who turns to the audience and speaks the first words: "You will discover that from this point on, every line is better than the next." Lady Godiva arrives in the guise of a worn-out whore, demanding new soles; Sister Kasha Veronicas, a shoe fetishist, accepts the task with relish. Tom, the horse-taxi driver who brought Godiva, remains in the background stealing scenes. Thorold, Superviva's fat son the sheriff, arrives followed by Earl Leoffric, the local nobleman, an S&M type in black satin and bullwhip. After an orgy, Godiva agrees to ride naked through the streets if Leoffric will revoke the harsh new tax. Tom performs a divertissement.

In the second act, a quartet of angels (Superviva, Kasha Veronicas, Thorold, and Leoffric) gather to advise Godiva. It's uncertain just what their motives are, but they are obviously strong and sick. Godiva dons a long blond wig and doffs her clothes. After a musical number by the nuns, Superviva reappears as Delilah out for hair, and Leoffric announces he won't revoke the tax anyway. The play ends as Godiva rides off astride Mother Superviva, her shoes repaired, laughable and lovable, appalling and appealing to the end.

The play is being presented in dingy, makeshift premises on West Seventeenth Street. I hope this won't keep audiences away. The production's roughness fits here. The setting lets it be robust and hearty rather than effete and precious—it may be the ideal playhouse for this work. A key ingredient in the pleasures it provides is the stops-out brashness of performance, vigorous, inventive, infectiously enthusiastic. About two-thirds of the way through, Vaccaro seems to lose control; until then his work is excellent. (The second-act opening is a masterpiece of staging.) Vaccaro often coordinates all the elements and makes several things happen at once, filling the stage with action; periodically he stirs up a frenzy of activity, even an orgy. His work is never dull.

As Godiva, Dorothy Opalach is good over a wide range—from brassy bravado to demure confusion. Charles Ludlam is spectacularly active as Tom; Vaccaro is spectacularly mannered as Mother Superviva and Elsene Sorrentino convincing as the shoe-licker Kasha Veronicas. Dashwood von Blocksburg is funny as Thorold, and Tom Shiboca's unimpressiveness as the sadistic Earl lends the character a nice irony. The Nuns' Chorus consists of Regina Hirsch. Sister Flossie of the Cross, Mario Montez, Heller Grace, and Margit Winckler. Jack Smith designed the costumes, which are as remarkable as the nuns.

A man arriving close behind me asked the theatre manager, "Is this one of those way-out things, or can you have a good time?" The only answer is, "Both."   4/28/66

The Life of Juanita Castro
Kitchenette

Two plays by Ronald Tavel, directed by the author and Harvey Tavel, at the Play-house of the Ridiculous.

Ronald Tavel is back with two plays, old and new, at the Play-house of the Ridiculous. I am a Tavel fan. His plays—like those of Pinter or H. M. Koutoukas—have a unique personal style, persuasively suggesting an original and self-contained theatrical mind. What is unique is valuable. Tavel's mind slyly eludes me; I can follow him only so far and then have no idea what he's up to.

Tavel's "The Life of Juanita Castro," originally the script for an Andy Warhol movie, has been done before but I had never seen it. It was written around the time of the Cuban missile crisis using Juanita Castro's own words, and it is so preposterous that it must then have been appalling. Now any political meaning has faded, leaving behind a subtle, intriguing exercise in form. The play pretends to be a movie—it is addressed to an imaginary camera—and has five characters. Juanita is played by a man, Fidel, Che, and Raul by women. Behind them sits the director, played currently by the author. He holds a script and reads instructions to the actors ("Fidel, say, 'Puta'"), which they dutifully follow. The words and actions are chaotic, elusive, arbitrary, nasty, silly, and often very funny. The tricky technique with its double assertion of unreality has an almost hallucinatory effect. The sex reversals are so confusing that at first it's hard to remember who's who; then gradually the Castro family gathers unexpected reality and the casting ceases even to seem odd. Simultaneously the director, who speaks all the lines before the actors and commands every move without moving, seems to fade from view until his presence seems quite normal. By the end the only thing that seems improbable is poor Juanita's words. The sum is a modest and delightfully effective tour de force.

The performance I saw was marred by Grover Noel's behavior as Juanita, all self-indulgence and cute carrying-on, paraphrasing and parodying the actions—although the play can work only when the actors obey the director exactly. Mary Woronov, Diane Dorr Dorynek, and Maria Antinakes were excellent as Fidel, Che, and Raul, and so was Ronald

Tavel as the director.

"Kitchenette" is the larger work on the double bill. Another pseudo-movie, it is indescribably looser; I can't even guess what it is supposed to "mean" or be "about." Leggy, strikingly forceful Mary Woronov plays a wife and Eddie McCarty her exquisitely strange husband. They are in a kitchen and flash through various personalities—McCarty is especially flashy—in various abortive encounters, all sick, some obscene. Later they are joined by another couple with sex-reversed names, the man a rampant queen, the woman a shrieking bleached blonde played all-stops-out by Diane Dorr Dorynek. Harvey Tavel is the onstage but inactive director. The play gets wilder as it goes on, builds up a berserk hilarity and daredevil velocity, and seems in constant danger of flying apart entirely. It never quite does. Though I have no idea what holds it together, something does.   1/12/67

Gorilla Queen

A play by Ronald Tavel, directed by Lawrence Kornfeld, presented by Judson Poets' Theatre in the choir loft of Judson Memorial Church.

"Gorilla Queen" brings underground playwright Ronald Tavel into a known context for the first time. His previous plays have been done in out-of-the-way places including the Play-house of the Ridiculous, an awkward, under-equipped loft space, mostly under the idiosyncratic, in-your-face direction of John Vaccaro; and his film scripts for Andy Warhol have been obscured by Warhol's personality. Now Tavel is at Judson Poets' Theatre, where "Gorilla Queen" has been staged by Lawrence Kornfeld.

Still he eludes perspective. Like a few other young

playwrights (including Sam Shepard and H. M. Koutoukas), he has developed a style so unique that no known standards apply. I am tempted to cop out by saying it's a matter of taste, either you like it or you don't, there's no good or bad; or by reporting on audience response. I like Tavel's plays. I am mystified by his writing but convinced of its integrity; it really is what it is, whatever it is. Its peculiarities are necessary, even compulsive, not modish mannerism, not failed imitation. For all its silliness and sometimes nasty perversity, his writing is dense, felicitous, energetic, complex, and intelligent; his theatrical vision is not only outrageous but original.

"Gorilla Queen" is a long play with songs that mimics the corniest conventions of jungle movies. It is held together, more or less, by a ridiculous, impenetrable melodramatic plot: Claudette Colbert and Karma Miranda are scheduled for sacrifice to the gorilla god, Queen Kong; but Sister Carries, the witch doctress, preoccupied with air pollution, won't burn them until someone finds the Chimney Sweep, who is meanwhile being sexually devoured by Venus Fly Trap. Clyde Batty, stud animal trainer, undertakes the search in order to save Karma, with whom he has a frustrated tryst; and to avoid the lusts of Taharahnugi White Woman, a native boy in drag, and of Queen Kong himself; and so on and on. In the background throughout are the Glitz Ionas, a tribe of obscene gibbons. In the foreground is the language, an unbroken series of lewd remarks, salacious innuendoes, obvious and obscure puns—beyond wit, beyond self-indulgence, beyond belief. The language is distracting, nearly opaque, maddening. I'm not sure whether it destroys the play or is its glory. The language has an insane momentum all its own that gives the play a weird intensity and drivenness foreign to its campy, frivolous setting and action.

What it "means" I can't even guess—probably nothing.

What it does, however, is kid and beguile the spectator into a world where values are grotesquely vilified and mocked, taste is gratuitously outraged, behavior is vulgarized, reason itself is inbred unto idiocy. It's a camp, it's a trip, it's a nightmare. It is silly, exhausting, fun, disgusting, and disturbing because deep inside it's real. Tavel is really doing something.

On opening night the production was a shambles studded with inspirations. It seemed unfinished and will presumably get better as it runs. It seriously lacked clarity and focus and all blurred together, essential action and irrelevant diversion, and as a result became monotonous. It was played too slowly and emphatically and seemed labored at times, nagging, unfunny, and too long. The songs were a complete mess. Robert Cosmos Savage is listed as the composer, but Al Carmines wrote three of the songs (the best in the show), and many others are set to standard tunes. Rehearsal is needed.

Already, though, there is plenty to praise. The individual performances are fine. Eddie McCarty is astonishing and brilliant as Sister Carries, rambunctious, apparently out of control, but unerringly stylish. He alone knows exactly how to play Tavel, and while imitation is out of the question, the rest of the cast should learn from the spirit of his example. (McCarty was a late replacement in the cast: "Hastiness in creation is at the core of camp.") Quinn Halford is lovely as Taharahnugi White Woman, so persuasive that his climactic humiliation is touching. Norman Thomas Marshall is alternately ponderous and light, hulking and girlish as Queen Kong. Barbara Ann Camp, wisecracking in terror, is funny and winning as Claudette. Paula Shaw as Karma, James Hilbrandt as Clyde, George Harris II as Brute, Jo Ann Forman as Venus, and David Kerry Heefner as the Sweep are all surprisingly convincing—in brief, an excellent and interesting cast. John P. Dodd's lighting (which I helped set up) saturates the sprawling stage in tropically lush colors, helps pinpoint locales, ranges in mood from Broadway gaudiness to jungle night mystery, and theatricalizes the whole play. Jerry Joyner's set rambles about fulfilling its functions, which is an achievement. Kornfeld made it happen, and that's praise. He has done well by the characters and had several giddy flights of invention. His placement of the action often lacks focus, though, transitions are vague (that may improve by itself), and he hasn't found an entirely effective approach to the language. (These comments are suspect: I wanted to direct "Gorilla Queen" myself.) There is a question to be asked: whether the production should rattle along as boisterously as the play itself, matching madness for madness; or whether it should provide the structure and clarity the script so obviously lacks. Kornfeld has tended toward the former and pays a price in formlessness and incoherence; but the latter threatens a moldier doom, that of taming the play and muzzling its mayhem. You take your chances. 3/16/67

Conquest of the Universe

A play by Charles Ludlam, directed by John Vaccaro, presented by the Play-house of the Ridiculous Repertory Club and Wynn Chamberlain at the Bouwerie Lane Theatre.

I quote at length: "'Conquest of the Universe' is a paramoral study of these space-intoxicated times. Here 'camp' comes to its delirious climax—Adolph Hitler's writings mingle with the old movie scripts and TV ad libs in the dialogue. The dour pornography of daily Vietnam reports meets the screaming pornography of the truth.

"In 'Conquest of the Universe' the intergalactic

voyager meets in the kings and queens of far-flung planets doppelgangers of Earth's everyday psychoses. Here is the ambassador alone with his mistress, the National Leader alone with his Self. The prospect for human survival is no better than the secret lives of these remote creatures. 'Conquest of the Universe,' in its diabolic view, is a supreme comedy of The End. Aristophanes, Martial, Swift, Brecht—these viewed, through the prism of art, the incipient ruin of their respective times. Charles Ludlam's play, interpreted by John Vaccaro, aspires to a similar panorama."

I wish whoever wrote that press release would write the rest of this review as well. "Conquest of the Universe" is an explosion of talent that leaves the mind in tatters. Historical melodrama of a pop fantasy future, filth, climactic camp, allegory of Armageddon, Shakespearean parody, juggernaut vehicle for superstars—one interpretation is as good as another, if not better. See it all on stage at the Bouwerie Lane and shudder for the future of the theatre and the species.

Tamberlaine is conquering the solar system planet by planet, imprisoning and humiliating the kings and queens, between barbarities languishing with boredom over his heirless guerrilla queen and buggerous lust for Bajazeth, enslaved king of Mars. Bajazeth's own queen, Zabina, is betimes in contact with her brother Cosroe, who is planning restoration and revenge. Then there's a war of the worlds, which Tamberlaine wins, I think, and a banquet, which he loses. Oh, it's beyond me, it's ridiculous.

The Play-house of the Ridiculous strikes again. If this is about the ruin of our times, it is also a stunning example of it, and there's no way to take it but lightly, acknowledging the honesty and accepting the invitation to laugh. The core is a point of view that faces the horror of history, and personal horrors too, and somehow glories in them. The Play-house of the Ridiculous knows exactly where Nero was at while fiddling, and it's information worth having.

The central purveyor of decadent truth is Ridiculous director John Vaccaro, for whose strong, idiosyncratic work Charles Ludlam's scrappy, hysterical play is a fine occasion. Vaccaro's specialties include lewd revelry, crude frenzy, and moments of exquisitely outrageous theatrical corn. His style incorporates moldiness and tackiness into a grand design a la Radio City Music Hall, and he has managed to shape "Conquest of the Universe" into a coherent if staggering experience.

Vaccaro has assembled an astonishing cast, many of them ex-inmates of Andy Warhol movies, who produce countless flashes of brilliance. They don't, on the whole, know much about what is usually called acting, but this style doesn't call for much acting; instead they perform, presenting themselves with straightforward razzmatazz that should be the envy of many otherwise fine actors. Transvestism is a Theatre of the Ridiculous hallmark, and many of them appear, and are surprisingly convincing, in roles of the opposite sex. Mary Woronov is an authoritative Tamberlaine, mean and fierce, drawing his desperation with a taut line. Ondine as Zabina makes me feel I've seen something of Callas's Tosca; he is equally persuasive as the arch-conspirator Cosroe, always with incisive, surprising timing. Beverly Grant is comical and affecting as Tamberlaine's wife Alice; Ultra Violet is brilliantly funny as the Italianate Natolia; René Ricard is elegantly anguished as Magnavox; Patsy Lamers is adorable as Ebea—all of them performances of remarkable if unnameable reality and considerable pathos. Taylor Mead makes several impeccably pure appearances as a guest star, Francis Francine is among the chorus of Fire Women, director Vaccaro appears as the cringing but uncowed Bajazeth, and if that's not enough, there's also a rock and roll band, the Third Eye, as well as sets by Bill Walters and extravagantly imaginative costumes by Trina. If you can't go home again, go to the Bouwerie Lane. 11/30/67

Tom O'Horgan
1963–71

Love and Variations

At the Caffè Cino.

A program note describes Tom O'Horgan's diversion at the Cino as a "contemporary masque," but esoterica gives way to erotica when the lights go out. The theme of the work is stated in quick calculations based on average orgasm incidence multiplied by the population of New York City reduced to a per-hour basis, a snap-of-fingers basis—etc. The variations outdo one another in perversity, and the show skitters along the brink of appallingly bad taste. Still, despite errors in timing and a tendency to underkey the climaxes to the point of disappearance, the whole thing can be described as lewdly charming. The performers are adaptable, the costumes by Jim Feliciano are inventive, and John Dodd's lighting is effective and imaginative. 9/26/63

Futz

A play by Rochelle Owens, directed by Tom O'Horgan, presented by La Mama Troupe at La Mama Experimental Theatre Club.

Rochelle Owens asked me not to review her play "Futz." Fudging, I still want to talk about Tom O'Horgan's direction. It is fascinating to watch O'Horgan's development as a director. In the past two or three years, staging all the productions of Ellen Stewart's La Mama Repertory, which have toured Europe and played here at La Mama and the Martinique, he has been serving an intensive, high-pressure apprenticeship in directing, and learning fast.

Recently O'Horgan's work has begun to have a particular direction, and "Futz" is a blazing statement of it. The basis is distorted, exaggerated, often non-realistic sound and movement; it is the vocabulary of Jerzy Grotowski's Polish Lab Theatre and, recently, of the Living Theatre. It is an extravagant, genuinely experimental style, and it can have spectacular, life-giving results.

This production style gives the performance of "Futz" a life of its own, almost independent of the play—a dense, fierce continuity of energy, fearless physical vitality, expressive vocalization. The performance is dance and music as well as drama.

Members of La Mama Troupe studied in Sweden last fall with Eugenio Barba, a student of Jerzy Grotowski, and Grotowski exercises were used in working on "Futz." O'Horgan and company have just begun to explore the new style, and already the effect is startling, stirring, beautiful. The method is similar to Grotowski's, however, only in appearance. Basically O'Horgan is illustrating the text, by representing the images, underscoring the mood of the action, enlarging the action, stating attitudes. Grotowski by contrast creates a counter-text, an inner text, an alternative expression of the script in radically transformed terms. Grotowski's actors may speak the words and simultaneously express a wholly separate context and level of feeling. The Polish Lab Theatre's performance, for all its passion, is at heart an abstract, austere, formal event, a ceremony, serving the soul of the play by making an independent and equal statement of the same concern.

O'Horgan is working at a simpler level (which I may in fact prefer), using the technique to energize the text, to jazz it up, and his production of "Futz" tends to turn into a series of theatrical effects. They are uncommonly thrilling, but they seem at times to overstate, overdecorate, and obscure the play, and it's probably just as well that I'm not reviewing it.

3/9/67

Tom Paine

A play by Paul Foster, directed for La Mama Troupe by Tom O'Horgan, presented by William Derr and Michael White at Stage 73.

"Tom Paine" is where we go from "Futz." The play is a dazzling, strikingly original theatre experience. It demands attention as the utmost extension to date of the style being developed under Tom O'Horgan's direction by La Mama Troupe. "Futz" was its first appearance and decisive for the company: in the work of "Futz" they glimpsed an identity and a direction, and everything they've done since has built on that.

The climax of their European tour last summer came at the Edinburgh Festival, where the company premiered Paul Foster's "Tom Paine," the first play written specifically for its new-found capabilities. Between the innovative force of "Tom Paine" and the "filth" of "Futz," La Mama Troupe became the sensation of the festival.

The new La Mama style is current controversy in Britain but virtually unknown here; like the Living Theatre, they have had to do their pioneering work abroad. Isn't that strange and depressing? Now the work is on view off Broadway and must be seen. It's not that "Tom Paine" is entirely successful.

But the ideas behind it represent a major impulse in American theatre experiment, and this is the fullest, most convincing life they have yet achieved.

I don't want to finish off the new style by pinning it up for classification. It is less programmatic or even historical than it is personal—a particular point of view toward the interactions between and among the text, the director, the actors, the audience, and the various realities that are always involved. It amounts to a fresh vision of theatre, not a theory. Its basic ingredients are three:

—ideas about direct confrontation between actors and audience; about "transformation" as a convention for moving through space and time more freely than illusionistic realism allows; about physicalization rather than rational verbal exposition as the basic expressive mode; about onstage events themselves rather than underlying psychological causality as the basis of structure; and about ensemble—old ideas revived in various ways by Grotowski, the Becks, Joe Chaikin, among others, and the best going alternative to the Method within the theatre tradition;

—the skills and inclinations Tom O'Horgan brings from former lives as, among other things, a harpist accompanying Second City on their wildest flights of improvisation, in a nightclub, facing the toughest audience short of Italian opera; as occasional director of semi-private esoterica (including the best "Maids" I've ever seen); to say nothing of the personality that takes off from there and dominates the company's work. As a director he is no respecter of playwrights: the plays on stage are as much his as theirs; so actors are his instruments and he plays them for results; he is inventive, ironic, impish, ultra-knowing, and like his theatre, theatrical;

—the resources of the company, what the actors can do, which is necessarily ragtag for want of a living classical technique, an honorable tradition, a recognizable way out and forward; which makes the actors responsive to O'Horgan's leadership, especially now that it's leading somewhere, willing to get in deep and go far out. It also holds back their ability and sophistication, setting limits that partly define the style, which for unity must heed the range of even the weakest, deriving its force from such factors as involvement and dedication, not technique; the result of which isn't an ideal style, but real, a brilliant exploration of the possible.

I want to say something about "Tom Paine," but it isn't easy to see the play in all this. Paul Foster has written a large-scale historical narrative, almost a pageant, centered on the life story of Thomas Paine. Following Howard Fast's *Citizen Tom Paine*, the play picks him up leaving London for America, young but already a drunken wastrel; makes an agonized Atlantic crossing with him; records his authorship of "Common Sense" and other essential calls to Revolution, with illustrative side trips to the French and English courts; explores his drinking habits and the feedback from his conscience; takes him bodily to France for that Revolution, which he barely survives; thence, after years in jail, back to America, an old man, only to be disenfranchised by democracy's own little tyrants.

Political biography is the start; the play's scope is vast. Paine's life is not chronicled but referred to as if archetypal, as if we all know his story; but we don't, and the play stirs curiosity only to frustrate it. Nor is this Paine an individual. Nothing he does on stage makes us care about him or see how he wrote what he did; nor are his doctrines presented except in anarchic, egalitarian generalities and specifics lacking context..

That's just the beginning of what the play doesn't do, but I hesitate to criticize it for failing at undeclared aims. Who knows what Foster was after besides a performance vehicle for the company? He has made a huge success of that. Does it matter that Paine eludes him? That the narrative is incoherent, its point blunt? (Obviously this has some relevance to the present—Vietnam, urban riots, and all—but Foster doesn't say what it is.) Does it matter that we miss words' meaning, that they become background music? That the characters' emotions seem forced and gratuitous and our own are never stirred? That what keeps the play going is not the action it describes but the action that describes it, the action on stage? Does it count against Foster that we are not engaged by the drama—which if it has depths hides them—but diverted by the production? After all, the real play is what happens in the encounter of performance; Foster wrote the text that led there, and a reseparation is false on any grounds. Just don't look for the satisfaction normal in history plays.

When you get instead is so physical, so self-contained that I can only speak of fragments. The broad stage is bare except for low boxes, a high pedestal, and a big, long, curved structure of steel and wood. This turns into a wildly rocking boat, among other things, and the whole cast of eleven rides it across the ocean. Besides rocking it also spins, sometimes overhanging the audience; Paine's spasmodic seasickness is projected unforgettably. The basic costumes are black simply suggesting the period, with added fancies as required, variously decorated but mainly black and white—all but the French King's billowing crimson cloak, the queen's aquamarine. Paine, in a drunken fantasy, gets twisted and swaddled into kingly robes at the end of Act I, red for France and white for England, great wads of the stuff hobbling him up on the pedestal. (A later costume trick, nudity draped in filmy blue and green, looks ridiculous. Maybe these are the turtles, often mentioned but never seen.) Yet another episode of flimsy relevance dramatizes Paine's terror of the guillotine, with half a dozen hooded figures sharpening knives, sparks flashing from their grinders in the dark; this achieves the momentum and bravura of a good production number. The meaning or what-you-will is not in the discrete images nor in their bearing on Paine's progress; it's in their making on the stage, in their succession, above all in the ensemble transitions toward them and away again.

Individual performances are almost beside the point, though most have their showy moments. The roles, even Paine, are embedded in the play's texture and inextricable. "Tom Paine" relies on ensemble playing, and La Mama Troupe is remarkable in its sure, intricate coordination, often at high speed. Kevin O'Connor plays Paine and John Bakos his embodied Reputation, another foggy concept. The others, all in plural parts, are Mari-Claire Charba, Peter Craig, Jerry Cunliffe, Michael Miller, Sally Kirkland, Victor LiPari, Beth Porter, Marilyn Roberts, and Rob Thirkield. Michael Warren Powell made the many costumes, from the simple and serious to the extravagant and preposterous, and they are an active element in the play. John P. Dodd's meticulously detailed, tirelessly fluid lighting is not only beautiful looking, with maximum restraint in the use of color, but discloses the action with a structural clarity that helps where help matters.

Even with all this going for it, "Tom Paine" is too long by roughly ten minutes per act. But don't let that—or anything else I've said—keep you away. Go see yourself. You too may fail to make sense of it, but you won't have seen its like, and more plays make sense than I'll ever send you to see.

3/28/68

Hair

Instead of reviewing "Hair" (*at the Biltmore*) I should simply report that something downtown, dirty, ballsy, and outrageous has hit Broadway at last, and it's a smash, and Broadway will never be the same. "Hair" demonstrates that there's no need to be cautious, polite, and self-censoring, that you can get away with anything, that you can do your thing and win fame and fortune too. The Beatles have been saying it for years, and it's high time that liberating spirit hit the theatre. "Hair" on Broadway is a good start.

This authenticity is not built into the show but specifically added by Tom O'Horgan, the director of this new incarnation. "Hair" was a pushy, phony drag in its original version at Joseph Papp's Public Theatre. The basic idea was good—a rock musical about hippies—but it was hoked up and conventionally show-bizzed in the writing, acting, and staging to the point of betraying everything it was trying to represent. O'Horgan has not only recast and almost totally restaged the show, he has also virtually eliminated the book. Instead of a patronizing portrait of hippies, "Hair" is now a direct freak-out. O'Horgan pulls every trick in the book, old and new, and writes a second volume of tricks of his own. Never has a show been so chock full of shock effects, so manic in pursuit of novelty. Every mockable subject yields its moment of fun—flag, church, home, color line. Half-naked hippies roam the aisles waving at friends and passing out incense and flowers. Boys and girls alike strip and stand frontally exposed across the front of the stage (though not brightly lit). Where will it all end?

Except for the songs, set to rockish music by Galt MacDermot, what remains of the original "Hair" is a bit of a bring-down, but there's more than enough of the new to make it an overall ball to see. O'Horgan has put together a joyous cast who project fine-spirited physicality and togetherness. The principal roles are unsympathetic and virtually unplayable; Gerome Ragni and James Rado, the writers and leads, are not shown to advantage. The more likable and happily memorable performances are those of Steve Curry, Sally Eaton, Jonathan Kramer, Walter Harris, Paul Jabara, Shelley Plimpton, Melba Moore, and Ronald Dyson. The show periodically betrays some seriousness of intention, struggling to say something about the draft, the generation gap, drug revelations, and so on, which is generally unconvincing. Only at the end does it communicate real possibilities, in a movingly simple Shakespearean duet, "What a piece of work is man," and a stirring ensemble, "Let the sun shine in." Its importance is not anything it says about hippies, but the plain fact that O'Horgan has blown up Broadway. 5/2/68

Jesus Christ Superstar
Lenny
Inner City

Tom O'Horgan directed four of the shows currently lighting up Broadway—"Hair," "Lenny," "Jesus Christ Superstar," and "Inner City," which opens this week. I first met Tom a decade ago when I sublet an apartment from him in back of his loft on West Third Street. A night or two before moving in I dropped by to look it over. Tom was having a Halloween party, I think—the visions were fantastic, hallucinatory. Through my vacant, candlelit rooms, festooned with dirt and the remnants of a gaudy décor, flickered provocative androgynous creatures in amazing likenesses, pre-Cockette apparitions, visitors from a spirit world to unconditioned eyes. His guests? His creations?

At the time Tom was playing incidental music for "From the Second City" in a cabaret on Fourth Street. Tom played piano, harp, gong, and anything else that came to hand, including a hose-and-shower-nozzle apparatus he could blow like a bugle. Before that he had been a harpist, touring a solo nightclub act on something like the same circuit as Lenny Bruce.

The first version of O'Horgan's style emerged clearly in "Futz," Rochelle Owen's play, and was extended in Paul Foster's "Tom Paine." Sound and movement took over from drama. All kinds of sounds, human, instrumental, animal, percussive, underscored the words of the plays; realistic movement gave way to an acrobatic, hyper-expressive body language and spatial dynamic. The direction was toward spectacle. In this apprenticeship O'Horgan came to rely neither on good acting nor on a playwright's vision. In "Lenny," for instance, one is hardly aware of Julian Barry's play; the actors, except Cliff Gorman, are used as stand-up comics or as scenery.

Both "Futz" and "Tom Paine" were hits off-Broadway and abroad, and O'Horgan later directed a movie version of "Futz" with La Mama Troupe actors, the original cast. The movie was not a success, but O'Horgan's hunger for new forms to conquer was evident. In this period he also did "Changes," a participatory theatre piece based on a text by Megan Terry, the direct source of the Company Theatre's "Liquid Theatre."

That was after he had transformed "Hair" into an emblematic, tonic, vastly profitable joyride and Broadway smash.

A couple of years ago O'Horgan went to work on another La Mama Troupe tour, augmenting the company with people from various "Hair" productions, working toward the actor/ musician/dancer synthesis he has been seeking for years. In mid-rehearsal he split with Ellen Stewart, renaming the company the New Troupe. There were two programs. "Gurton's Apocalyptic Needle" was Tom's own two-act combination of the pre-Elizabethan farce "Gammer Gurton's Needle," with medieval tropes (his word) about the anti-Christ. Two layers of action went on throughout, sacred and profane, in two vivid styles, with the actors playing Tom's music on authentic medieval instruments. I saw the piece in Montreal and in Rotterdam, and it was brilliant, pure theatre, esoteric and jumping, a refinement of the free structure of "Hair" without the topicality and pop mannerisms.

The other program was two plays by Sam Shepard. "Melodrama Play," Shepard's most powerful one-act, is another two-style work, flipping in midstream from bright farce into deadly surrealism. In Tom's version the first part is cartoonlike and not very convincing, but by the end the production comes together with stunning force. In the several times I saw it, I was always shaken by the last moments. "The Holy Ghostly" is a beautiful personal poem of a play, reminiscent of the early Shepard, a finer product of the research into desert hallucination lore that went into "Operation Sidewinder." In it Tom used the large-scale apparition puppets that now reappear on Broadway in "Lenny."

The New Troupe toured American colleges and European capitals for several months, but the work was never shown in New York, the troupe disbanded, and Tom went to Hollywood to make a movie about Lenny Bruce. I thought he was gone, discouraged (as I was too at the time), lost to the movies; a discouraged theatre could hardly afford the loss. But the movie didn't happen. Tom came back and put "Lenny" on

Broadway instead, and since then he has been working hard and fast again, two major productions already this season. He seems in fact to be reviving Broadway, reasserting a faith in the native culture of this city, a thought made explicit in the finale of "Inner City."

Getting to my seat for a Saturday night performance of "Jesus Christ Superstar" was harrowing. The crowd around me, at $15 a seat, were ravenous for their money's worth of distraction, and the show certainly delivers. Tom takes Broadway technology to its limits, and the effect is spectacular, overpowering. The performers, singing to us through an unpleasant, erratic sound system, endlessly handling microphones, stay remote and inaccessible. The production can't really be faulted for vulgarity, which is its basic mode—reminiscent of Béjart, Las Vegas casinos, the Folies Bergères. The show's aggressiveness seems to be obligatory under the circumstances, and though I at times felt bullied and didn't exactly like it, I was impressed by the power and assurance of the machine.

In "Lenny" the crassness and hard sell have to do with the subject and his situation, not just the economics of Broadway. Cliff Gorman's performance is all that it's said to be—I was reminded of Ryszard Cieslak, Grotowski's leading actor, though the conventions are all different. Some of Tom's effects are ridiculous—he is alternately meticulous and slapdash. But the work gets stature from its compassion, outrage, and depth of feeling for its subject, and from Bruce's own stature. I felt out of place in that audience: the show isn't for the liberals who wanted to save Lenny Bruce from himself, but for the same people who bought his act.

Playwrights even more than other artists respond to situations. It's hard to move one's work on to the next level when nothing much is demanded or expected, when there is no potential payoff, and amateurs' tools to work with. Our theatre is littered with playwrights, particularly, who have not gone beyond their first successes because there seems to be no place to go. O'Horgan has gone to Broadway, for now, but the playwrights have been left behind: "Inner City" is not a play but a "street cantata" based on a book of poems by Eve Merriam. (I thoroughly enjoyed it at a preview.) Tom has in no sense sold out—does that phrase still mean something? His work is as idiosyncratic in "Superstar" as it was in "The Maids." In "Inner City" he has considerably softened the sell. He exploits the conventions freely, without reverence or even respect, and remains clearly his own man, no part of the snobbish Broadway scene though at the moment its dominant figure.

We still need an alternative theatre for those of us who feel outside the affluent society and theatre-lovers who can't get in free like me. But this is a practical need, not a moral imperative, and it's good to see and tell Tom's success story. What will happen next?   12/23/71

Off-Broadway
1967–68

The Deer Park

A play by Norman Mailer, directed by Leo Garen, at the Theatre de Lys.

"The Deer Park" is Norman Mailer's play version of his own novel, which you will recall is about a group of decadent, tormented Hollywood types. Novel and play are set in Desert D'Or (Palm Springs), which is Mailer's image for "some not quite definable estate or existence of Hell." We are, we are told, "watching the damned chase after love."

The principal characters are Charles Francis Eitel, a black-listed movie director; Elena Esposito, former dancer, former call girl, his mistress; Marion Faye, pimp, sometime queer, sex-obsessed, satanic representative of despair and evil; Dorothea O'Faye, Marion's mother, vicious gossip columnist, former mistress of Eitel turned chief enemy; Lulu Meyers, movie star, Eitel's former wife; Teppis, movie magnate in the old style; Carlyle Munshin, movie producer, rapacious admirer of Eitel; and Sergius O'Shaugnessy, Air Force flyer and temporarily Lulu's lover. They're a sexy and picturesque group, and Mailer makes a fascinating tangle of their lives.

The technique of the play is no less flashy than its personnel. The action is framed within the drunken memories of Sergius, as narrator and commentator, thus distanced into the past. Each of the two eighty-minute acts is divided into more than forty episodes—some no more than epigrammatic moments, others full-fledged scenes—an electric tote board gives a visible countdown. The action is consecutive but elaborately fragmented; in appropriately cinematic fashion we skip freely among the characters and their stories, here catching an ironic juxtaposition, there glimpsing a revealing bit of background, periodically coming upon a key confrontation. The complicated story requires vast quantities of exposition; broken up like this, it's not so forbidding. Mailer sacrifices the involvement that comes from extended dramatic action but achieves a remarkable compression and speed. Narrator, tote board, fragmentation keep a distance between play and spectator, forbidding us the sentimental comfort of identifying with the characters. We are meant to recognize their reality, but not be taken in by them. Mailer wants us to see his hell coldly. He wants us to feel pity and terror, not sympathy.

He also wants to entertain, and considering these multiple aims, the manic fanciness of Leo Garen's production seems just right. A big showy set by Will Steven Armstrong is backed by a glittering spangled curtain and lit in gaudy colors. The light changes are incessant and spectacular. Snatches of music and sound effects are scattered all along the way. The acting is in a colorful variety of styles, including old-movie characterizing, high Method, and amateur bumbling. Ann Roth has outfitted the cast in costumes equaling Hollywood in color and glamor. All these elements are intricately coordinated, with fine technical precision. My main beef about most plays is that too little happens too slowly and there is too little to look at. Compliments to Garen and Mailer for the busiest production in memory.

The surface, in short, is dazzling. But all this description gives little of the play's flavor, for "The Deer Park" is primarily a Mailer manifestation. The outside of the play is mostly cheap thrills: gossipy intimate peeks at Hollywood high life, snappy theatrics, lavish decor; but Mailer's mark is on it everywhere. The language is the play's distinction. I admire Mailer's idiosyncratic lingo because it so vividly expresses a singular personality. I can't give you a detached judgment of "The Deer Park" because I have never been able to judge Mailer. Mailer the writer is an expression of Mailer the man. I don't know if it's a good play, but it's good, pure Mailer.

I'm all for Mailer. The energy and force of his writing turns me on, stimulates me, excites me. I feel him working the language, using it like clay or paint, making it do what he wants; and he very often gets there, concentrating and charging the words, roughing them up, shaking them loose, until they crackle and flash and dance in your head. At the same time he has some mannerisms that threaten to turn me off: a butch tone, a tough-guy stance that feels self-conscious, overstated, corny; a where-it's-at air that can sound patronizing and preachy; a just-one-of-the-boys pretense of simplicity—"I'll put it to you straight" followed by the fanciest language and twistiest thought you can imagine.

Mailer is a wild man and he's fearless but it still won't do to take him at his word. He comes on so strong, he's so impressive that it's tempting simply to submit, and I'm scared of him in more ways than one. Here goes anyway. "The Deer Park" is pretentious. It doesn't have the depth Mailer claims for it. He doesn't find much more meaning in these rather trashy genre events and characters than you'd expect. The play appeals to the curiosity, not to the imagination. It works as a story, as a vision of hell it is vivid and believable, but it has as little resonance or relevance as most psychiatric case

histories: as an image of contemporary society, it is trivial.
Where Mailer is brilliant is in getting at the meat of individual human feelings, particularly about sex. You can believe these characters actually do it, sex is a real part of their lives, not just a conversational toy or a counter in interpersonal games. Sex in "The Deer Park" has a reality that may be unique on the stage. I don't mean titillating or pornographic, I mean real. Then, unfortunately, Mailer pushes it to mean something significant, and the reality fades away. Yes, you think, that's exactly it (I'm not alone, etc.), then the next minute you don't know what he's talking about. Or maybe it's just me. The fact that I haven't bridged the gulf between feelings and rational meanings doesn't mean that it's unbridgeable; it may even be imaginary. Feelings have a built-in existential meaning that is wordless in essence, and the device for expressing it is not verbalization but objective correlative. What comes through in Mailer's search for meaning is the romantic idea that if you feel something intensely enough it matters objectively. Mailer is a writer of a slightly older generation than mine, and at times the play sounds old-fashioned to me. Several characters have moments of unironic prudishness that are joltingly unhip; it is nostalgia that their romantic fancies and intensities appeal to. There is a rough join between these sentiments and the play's assertive modernity that repeatedly disconcerted me into disbelief.

"The Deer Park" is like Arthur Miller's "After the Fall" in subject matter, dramaturgy, and pretentiousness. I like Mailer's play very much better than I do Miller's. It's a difference of temperament. Miller is solemnly pretentious, always defending his dignity. Mailer is exuberantly pretentious, he gets carried away, he likes going too far, he purposively blows his cool. I am charmed and impressed.

Rip Torn is exquisitely evil as Marion Faye; Will Lee is definitive as Teppis; Rosemary Tory is beautiful, seductive, and completely believable as Elena; and Margaret O'Neill makes a gem of the tiny role of Dorothea. Hugh Marlowe is fine as Eitel, the main character, although somehow Eitel never became as real as what people said about him. I think it's the writing.   2/9/67

The Boys in the Band

A play by Mart Crowley, directed by Robert Moore, presented by Richard Barr and Charles Woodward Jr., at Theatre Four.

The same critics who shot down "The Hawk" have made "The Boys in the Band" into the biggest off-Broadway hit since "Scuba Duba." Although Matt Crowley's play is completely lacking in formal interest, it is exceptionally entertaining, in large part, and it makes an earnest, compassionate effort to speak honestly about homosexual experience.

The pretext is a gay birthday do given by Michael, a spoiled and bratty jet-setter, miserable in his elegance, for Harold, a witty, pock-marked, Jewish, paranoid pot-head, both of them lonely and bitchy in the extreme. The guests are Donald, who reads and goes to the analyst; Emory, a sweet, campy queen; Larry, who is defiantly promiscuous even though he loves Hank, a pipe-smoking schoolteacher who has left his wife to come live with him; Bernard, a tweedy Negro; and Cowboy, a beautiful hustler brought by Emory as a birthday present for Harold. Into this specialized situation comes Alan, Michael's college roommate, who is straight but, at this moment, the unhappiest of them all.

The first two-thirds of the play is largely devoted to characterization and exposition, at which Crowley is expert, resourceful, and brilliantly funny. He waits too long, though—well into the second act—before getting down to business, and the transition is rough. Michael at this juncture imposes on the party a game requiring each guest to telephone the person he has loved most in his life and confess that love. This offers possibilities for cathartic, therapeutic release, but Michael is viciously sadistic about it: everyone is forced to confront himself in the mocking mirror of Michael's self-hatred, and frankly it's hard to believe they would tolerate such treatment. There is much truth in the play's sentiment; Crowley is more toughly compassionate toward his characters than they are to themselves. The play's faults are its pretension to being about homosexuals in general, rather than a particular gay social scene; its implication that these human miseries are symptoms of homosexuality; and its tendency to explain and preach. Still, it is a worthwhile and unusually successful attempt to portray a reality that is too often denied recognition.

The production under Robert Moore's direction is super-professional, with a striking set by Peter Harvey and expert performances by the entire cast. Kenneth Nelson as Michael displays an impressive range, though the script forces him to some irreconcilable extremes. Leonard Frey is incisively witty as Harold, Cliff Gorman gives Emory a remarkable dignity, and the remaining performances—by Frederick Combs, Peter White, Laurence Luckinbill, Keith Prentice, Reuben Greene, and Robert La Tourneaux—are precisely conceived and eloquently rendered. 4/25/68

Red Cross
Muzeeka

"Red Cross," by Sam Shepard, directed by Jacques Levy, and "Muzeeka," by John Guare, directed by Melvin Bernhardt, at the Provincetown Playhouse.

Sam Shepard's play "Red Cross" seems clearer, stronger, better in its revival at the Provincetown Playhouse than it did two years ago at Judson. Then I thought it charming but slight; now I was not only delighted but shaken by it.

A young couple are staying in a cabin in the forest. The girl feels her identity slipping away, fears she is losing her mind. She is called away and leaves the young man alone. He tries to amuse himself with exercise and meditation. The maid comes in to make the beds. He tells her he has crabs, shows her one, asks for help. When she offers to take him to a doctor, he evades her. Instead he draws her into his fantasy life, eventually giving her an exhausting mock swimming lesson. She takes him more seriously than he takes himself; and when she takes the fantasy away from him, making it more real than he ever could, and then departs, he is bereft, desperate. The girl returns furious that she's got his bugs now too, and his psychic wound erupts in actual blood flowing from his head. End of play.

Jacques Levy directed both productions of "Red Cross," and the differences of detail are elusive and subtle. Florence Tarlow repeats her brilliant performance as the Maid with equally stunning effect. Moment to moment, the revival seems less focused, particularly in the girl's skiing speech at the beginning of the play. Yet the total impact is greater, and the theme of the play—the confrontation between two levels of reality, the Maid's and the young couple's, the matter-of-fact and the game-playing—emerges with devastating force. What might be taken for faults in the performances of Marcia Jean Kurtz and Sam Waterston are actually an incisive projection of the characters' alienation from each other and from their own feelings. Besides all this, Levy has a vivid audio-visual concept; immediately upon entering the theatre the audience confronts his vision, the all-white set by Peter Harvey.

John Guare's "Muzeeka" is less successful. An everyman named Jack Argue sells out for the good life, runs away into the army, and commits suicide in Vietnam. Guare has a way with words, but this play, at least in this production, is equivocal in both style and content. "Muzeeka" was originally done at the Eugene O'Neill Foundation in Waterford, Connecticut, last summer, and reports are that it was hilarious. At the Provincetown it isn't very funny, except in occasional inspired moments. It seems rather to be striving for sociological significance, driven by a WASP sense of irrelevance. It is not only irrelevant, alas, but indecisive, uncommitted, and shifty. Or maybe it's the production—I'm not sure the play gets a fair shake. Melvin Bernhardt, the director, seemingly lacks any vision of how to do this play and had to make do with moment-to-moment invention.

5/2/68

Memorable Outliers
1967–73

San Francisco Mime Troupe

"L'Amant Militaire," by Carlo Goldoni, adapted by Joan Holden, directed by R. G. Davis, presented by Students for a Democratic Society and Angry Arts at McMillin Theatre, Columbia University.

I've heard about the San Francisco Mime Troupe for years but saw them for the first time last Friday night, when they performed "L"Amant Militaire" at Columbia University. I was astonished by their excellence. They are committed to "making the theatre, in content and in style, a living radical force." The style of the present production is commedia dell'arte, the content leftist revolutionary protest. It is brilliantly entertaining theatre with a purpose: to stimulate, if not create, revolutionary enthusiasm. Its success was unmistakable. At the end of the first act the players had the whole audience, in Columbia's main theatre, chanting in unison: "Hell, no, we won't go!" At the end of the evening the director, R. G. Davis, left us with the Troupe's motto: "This is our society. If we don't like it, it's our job to change it; if we can't change it, it's our job to destroy it."

The immediate play is a classic eighteenth-century Italian farce. The program carries this note on the Troupe's adaptation policy: "We do not usually set ourselves the task of translating an author's intentions; rather, we exploit his work to suit our own: using what we can and discarding the rest, writing in new scenes and characters, to say nothing of new emphases." What they use this time is the basic situation, characters, and plot—Spain fighting on Italian soil, the Italian mayor conniving with the Spanish general over profits, the mayor's daughter secretly wooed by a Spanish lieutenant, and so on—as well as the exuberant commedia dell-arte style, within which they can ad lib freely. Natural parallels are drawn with the Vietnam War, the draft, capitalism, and other contemporary American actions and preoccupations. The play isn't so much an allegory as a caricature of American society from a draft-age point of view. It isn't diagnostic, dialectical, or even polemical; rather it is a satiric manifesto, a series of gleeful jabs at a society it rejects in toto, a defiant provocation, a celebration of the revolutionary spirit. I was fascinated at the ready response of this college audience; a dozen years ago we wouldn't have dared.

In theatrical terms, the evening is a great success: the Troupe equally emphasizes style, as noted above. "L'Amant Militaire" is a wholly convincing demonstration of commedia dell-arte style—costumes, staging, deportment, all expertly accomplished, assured, zestful. (The program notes: "Our interest in this sixteenth-century form is not antiquarian: we use it because it is popular, free, engaging, and adaptable.") The show is hilariously funny, a vivid, exhilarating evening of theatre, a rare pleasure. The production is a challenge to other theatres to become once again robust, artful, pertinent, and fearless.

My admiration is directed toward the whole enterprise. Without sacrificing distinct personalities, the performers achieve a remarkable unity of conviction and projection within the discipline of the style. Their work should be a reproach to most experimental or political theatre groups working in New York and, I hope, an inspiration.

11/9/67

And They Put Handcuffs on the Flowers

A play written and directed by Fernando Arrabal, at the Mercer Arts Center.

Prolific Spaniard Fernando Arrabal's extraordinary "And They Put Handcuffs on the Flowers," which played for some months earlier this season at the Extension, has now been revived at the Mercer Arts Center. The work is a blazing, shocking outcry against prisons and tyranny, specifically the particular tyranny and imprisonments that followed the Civil War in Spain and are still in force. "I've been to Spain," a woman near me said after the play, "and now I'm sorry." The connections are left to us to make: the play is not polemical, not politics, it is an act of witness, a situation statement, a response to the author-director's own life experience.

From the image of three men in a constricted cell and a central story leading to the grisly execution of a man who in his youth twenty years ago worked for decent lives for his people, the play expands outward and inward into the dreams, desires, and wrecked lives of the prisoners. Much of its potent energy reflects sexual repression, invoking the life force that cannot be stopped, as the roots of flowers can and will break concrete. The play recounts prison horror stories in a violently expressive style. In one grotesquely hilarious, horrifying sequence, a prisoner is blinded, castrated, and fed his own testicles. He goes into a ghastly ecstasy that further enrages the authorities. Then an obscene, lascivious Christ appears to him and miraculously heals him. "You must have been very miserable in there to have had such weird thoughts," someone says.

Arrabal uses many approaches to tell the play's stories, from simple recitation of facts to satire to ritual. There is tenderness in the play too, in the intense proximity of the men, in mutual recognition of the madness they are driven to, in their dreams of freedom and love. Mostly, though, the play is, as Arrabal says, a shout.

It is passionately effective theatre. Arrabal as director uses sound, light, and space freely for expressive impact. The action moves all over the theatre, from the midst of the audience to the far distance. Duane Mazey's lighting, mostly in harsh, clashing colors, comes at the action from exaggerated angles. The elements are deployed with bold directness and put together with vitality and sensitivity.

Arrabal takes the actors to the limits of their ability, and the performances are strong and committed. Ron Faber displays a spectacular range in the most varied role, a daring, extravagant, thrilling performance. George Shannon and Peter Mahoney are excellent as the other two prisoners, and Baruk Levi is remarkable as Christ. Ellen Schindler plays the condemned man's wife, pleading for his life to a succession of sweet-talking Pilates. There is a wonderfully comic and strangely tender scene in which a muzzled Faber communicates with Patricia Gaul by manipulating her breasts. Muriel Miguel is a rambunctious whore, Andrea Lazar a young girl who simply recites facts, ugly shameful facts. It is a deeply beautiful play that speaks with the voice of necessity. 4/27/72

In Search of the Cobra Jewels

A play by Harvey Fierstein, directed by Donald L. Brooks, at Bastiano's Studio, 14 Cooper Square.

During the first-act finale of "In Search of the Cobra Jewels," at the opening last Wednesday, H. M. Koutoukas, who plays the central role, cut himself delicately and deliberately with a razor blade, just deeply enough so blood oozed out on his arms and face. Harvey Fierstein's play is transparently about Koutoukas himself, in the personage of Noel Swann, poet and playwright in flirtation with Death. It is, further, a direct rip-off of Koutoukas's distinctive style as a dramatist—aphoristic, euphuistic, picturesque, tormentedly romantic, sentimentally nostalgic. The opening-night blood-letting introduced too much reality onto the stage for my taste. I was sickened and horrified. Koutoukas's gesture, though reviving an ancient sacrificial mode of theatre, seemed to go beyond art and call art worthless, and it had the effect of nearly destroying the play.

The audience didn't seem to be paying much attention anyway. At intermission hardly anyone seemed to have noticed what had just transpired before our eyes. The opening scenes are set at the West Village trucks where gays gather for impersonal sex. The main action has to do with a camp cobra cult inspired by the Maria Montez movie "Cobra Woman." Because of this homosexual ambience, the play is taken by the gay audience to be entirely frivolous, its life-and-death agonies nothing more than occasion for theatrics. Actually, at some level it hardly admits, the performance is in dead earnest.

Fierstein's play, though clever and sometimes perceptive, is not convincing when it gets serious. For all the talk about despair, what is actually shown is self-dramatizing depression and self-destructive exhibitionism. Real despair in art takes into account the ironic energy of spirit that propels it into expression. Fierstein writes lines like "Nobody wants you when you're old and gay." Wait and see. Nobody wants you when you're old and straight either. Nobody ever wants you for long. "I want to die," people keep saying, but to call that

despair is pretentious. It's just morbid.
Once again Donald L. Brooks has done a production that so unnerves me that I can hardly talk about it coherently. Once again he has concocted an indecipherable mixture of brilliance, ineptitude, and pathological acting-out. Agosto Machado gives the most striking performance, hilarious, stunningly original, with an outrageous but impeccable eccentricity of timing. He is paired in most of his scenes with misleadingly named Flash Storm, who can't act at all. Harvey Tavel plays Death with cutting wit and relentless conviction. Mario Montez is full of fun as the Cobra Priestess. Ronald Tavel lends his presence in a gleamingly cold, cruel monologue and song. The chorus, first as truck suckers and fuckers, later as wiped-out remnants of the run-down snake church, participate in some energetic and imaginatively staged production numbers. The singing is generally poor.

Brooks certainly has a flair for raw theatricality. His work persistently confronts subjects, styles, and personal equations which to others appear in bad taste and simply too dangerous. First I was entertained, then I was frightened, then I didn't know where I was and my mind was left burning with contradictions. What kind of theatre is that?

10/12/72

The Magic Hype

A play written and directed by Jimmy Centola (Jimmy Camicia), presented by the Hot Peaches at the Peach Pitts.

The Hot Peaches' current show is about the superstar phenomenon of the past decade, Andy Warhol and Jackie Curtis, speed and illusion, self-delusion and self-acceptance, drag and reality. This is the eighth Hot Peaches production but the first I've seen. I found it funny, touching, and warmly enjoyable.

The Hot Peaches are part of a sidestream theatre I have followed for years but never been able to name. It has come to flower in such varied forms as the Play-house of the Ridiculous, the Ridiculous Theatrical Company, "Vain Victory" and Jackie Curtis himself, H. M. Koutoukas's and Anthony Ingrassia's plays, Taylor Mead, Holly Woodlawn, Candy Darling, the Cockettes, the Angels of Light. Warhol tapped it for a time. Its influence has been wider than its immediate audience; its rock division includes Alice Cooper and David Bowie. Its message is freedom from values outside the self, its method provocation through defiance and mockery of repressive convention. Its character is sexually scrambled, polymorphously perverse, generally gay. It uses drag in all its aspects, from playful dressing up, both to explore and to please, to full-time acting out of a fantasy self. At its best, its decorativeness is not only a diverting front but a theatrical sharing of self: the masks of "normalcy" are replaced not by bare faces but by new, home-made mask faces that express the spirit.

"The Magic Hype" shows three beings sent from heaven (the Egg Factory) to occupy the pits of freak-out street-people earth-existence. The play takes these beings through much of the scene I've been talking about. They meet a drag queen who announces, "I'm not a man. I'm not a woman. I'm a drag queen," whose philosophy is, "Take your fantasy and make it real." They go to a rehearsal of the Happy Hippies (read Angels of Light), who dress up and prance around to old movie songs, and are turned away: "No room at the inn," the Hippies sing, and this subtheme of holiness rejected runs discreetly through the whole play. Randy Whorewall discovers them when he needs tacky trash for a baked beans commercial. By the time he dumps them, one has completely gone off into playing the blonde goddess, another makes a lonely drinking spectacle of himself, and the third is on speed. After they get together for a play called "Hollow Happiness," two are recalled to the Egg Factory; the third is last seen shooting up in the tongue.

The production's awkwardnesses don't contradict its artfulness. The Peaches' loft theatre, the Peach Pitts on West Twenty-Fourth Street, is tiny but comfortable, their technology crude but unpretentious and effective. The Hot Peaches are part of what they are talking about but too aware of themselves to be lost in it. The show is a brave examination of something they love and rises through frivolity to a strong, compassionate truthfulness. Ian McKay is brilliant in the Jackie Curtis role, funny and sometimes shockingly real. Camicia (calling himself Forever Amber) is honest, charming, and beautifully direct, especially in the final song, "There Ain't No Easy Way Down." The play seems very much a company effort, and almost the whole cast show a fine sensitivity and concern in support as well as in their big moments. Luke Viglucci is helpful at the piano and wrote most of the songs, which are fine. 11/1/73

New Forms
1967–73

Environmental Theatre

"Victims of Duty," a play by Eugene Ionesco, directed by Richard Schechner, at the Players Theatre of Le Petit Théâtre du Vieux Carré, New Orleans.

Richard Schechner theorizes about "environmental theatre" in the current issue of *Tulane Drama Review*, which he edits. He demonstrated his concept in a production of Ionesco's "Victims of Duty" that I had the pleasure of seeing last weekend in New Orleans.

The evening was announced as "an athletic event," and from start to finish the audience was deliberately mystified about what they were involved in. Schechner went to extraordinary lengths to break down the distinctions between audience and actors, life and art. Even the start and finish were altered in form. The audience was confronted in the lobby with an exhibit of photos and documents about the production, participants, and various victim-of-duty themes, accompanied by movie and slide projections and taped sound collage, and left to wander on their own into the "theatre," a large, squarish room without chairs or formal seating arrangements. Carpeted platforms and staircases had been set up in a complicated pattern, vaguely sloping down toward the center. Various piece of prop furniture were scattered about. One stood, sat, squatted, or reclined where one chose.

In the middle of the dimly lit room was a brighter area

New Forms 1967–73

where half a dozen people (the actors) were finishing dinner—salad, dessert, coffee—and conversing among themselves. When I came in the room was full of people, most of them talking. Schechner took me over and introduced me to the cast. I drank a cup of warm coffee with them before finding a place to sit.

When they began speaking loudly enough to be heard, the audience shut up and listened to them facetiously discuss the difference between alienation and detachment. Gradually everybody left except Choubert and Madeleine, the characters of the first scene, and they segued into actually doing the play. I can't imagine what people who don't know "Victims of Duty" thought was going on.

It was performed all over the room, in acting areas, on the prop furniture, sometimes wandering about. Spectators had to get out of the way. Movies and slides were projected onto three walls, their content related to the play in ways both specific and expressionist. Tape collage sounds were similarly scattered about the space and similarly used, and some of the speeches were amplified. When, as often happened, the actors were not visible or clearly audible, attention could shift to the other media.

The action of Ionesco's play involves a quest that takes Choubert "up" and "down," the former some kind of psychoanalysis, the latter an expansion of consciousness or "trip." Beyond the basic metaphors, this production dramatized the distances involved by sending Choubert searching through the audience. Near the end, the Detective torments Choubert by stuffing bread into his mouth, chanting, "Chew, swallow." At the conclusion (after the victimizer has been killed, himself a victim of duty) this was extended into forcibly feeding bread to the audience. As a good number of us were quietly chewing, the actors quietly disappeared. The titles were replayed, the tape sounds rose in a crescendo of frenzy, projections were going on all three walls, and the audience was on its own again. The sound and projections continued until all were gone: you couldn't see all of it. In the lobby had been hung a curtain through which the spectators had to pass one by one to get out. On it was painted a quotation from another victim of duty, Eichmann.

Usually attempts to alter the actor-audience relationship are limited to breaking down the fourth wall, actors invading the audience or bringing spectators up onto the stage. Here the whole room became the stage, and the audience was on it—and "in" the play—along with the actors. This resulted in a provocative and engaging experience, if only because so much was going on, play included. I'm not sure what it all means; Schechner has theories involving the increasing theatricality of everyday life, new sensory modes and patterns of attention, new technology, and so on. To his great credit is the fact that the production attracted and engaged audiences of people, most of them young, who ordinarily have little interest in theatre.

As a concept, environmental theatre is consciously anti-literary: Schechner believes we are in a transition "between a theatre where things come from words and a theatre in which words are part of the event." By "words" he presumably means the play, though in fact a play, though written in words, is more than words, it is the formal blueprint of a structured event and experience. You can't be anti-literary without first believing that drama is literature. A good dramatist isn't thinking mainly of literary values, whatever those are, he is thinking of the theatrical event. Words are just "part of the event" to the playwright as well. This is my new "auteur theory" of theatre.

I don't think this was a good production of "Victims of

Duty." It might be described as a very good happening on the same themes as Ionesco's play, using Ionesco's words and structure of action; or as an environment in which "Victims of Duty" was a dominant element. The play was there somewhere and quite adequately acted, but it was subservient to and generally obscured by the formal enterprise of the production. Several episodes in the play were brilliantly staged; what came across finally was not the play but the production.

I wish this didn't sound like a put-down; it's really just a difference of inclination. Contrary to Schechner, I think the text of the play is "the first thing, the original impulse and final arbiter." If he doesn't think so too, then why hang onto the words at all, why call it "'Victims of Duty' by Eugene Ionesco"? Still I think what he accomplished was terrific. If he did little service to Ionesco, he served dramatists of the future by extending the limits of conception. And that is a rarer and more urgent service to the theatre. 5/11/67

Scott Burton

Scott Burton's "Behavior Tableaux" enjoyed a single performance last week at the Whitney Museum. The work consisted of eighty-eight tableaux vivantes for five tall men and several pieces of plain furniture, the tableaux separated by blackouts. The audience was seated at a distance from the performers, who wore plain shirts, trousers, and shoes and had their features toned down with makeup. There was no dialogue, no sound, and the piece moved at a measured, slow pace, lasting somewhat longer than an hour. At one side of the stage was a door, near it a bench, in the center a table with four identical chairs (later joined by a fifth), against the far wall a bare flat cot. The tableaux were far from uniform in character. Some were motionless, some included movement, some were long, some short, some embodied abstract relationships, others were explicit though formalized pictures from real life. A middle section of the work dealt with four men in relation to a leader. Later the content became more emotionally accessible in a section about one man rejected and abandoned by the others, left in painful isolation. By the end the group had reassembled, though in a depersonalized interchangeable mode.

I have seen a number of Burton's theatre works over the past three years. He did five pieces at Hunter College that included specific explorations of theatrical ingredients, movements, and perceptions isolated from narrative content. Several of his Street Works are described and pictured in the current issue of *TDR*. He performed as part of a show at the Architectural League by sleeping in the lobby and later acting out his dream (walking naked through Manhattan streets). I saw a beautiful work he did at the Wadsworth Athenæum in Hartford, consisting of motionless tableaux performed by three young women. These were abstract and systematic, but those at the Whitney were psychological and quasi-narrative; the piece was not dry or cold but dynamic in design and stirringly alive. In Iowa he presented an environment of household furniture arranged like rooms outdoors in a wood amid the natural growth, and a theatre work of living statues on a revolving stage. Last year he offered eighteen widely varied pieces at Finch College including a novella in slides, furniture pieces, a movie, the rape of the Sabine women in sound, and the static, dramatic "Manikins and Thunder."

Burton's work goes beyond so-called conceptual art in its lyricism, delicacy and care of design, and intensity of feeling. Last week's piece at the Whitney had a very narrow range of expressive means, a flat emotional surface, yet the succession of controlled, often ambiguous images resonated mysteriously and warmly with a distinct personal sensibility. One feels both the integrity of the work and through it a clear contact with the life of the artist. The Whitney piece was relatively massive and relentless, its emotional content bleak; other pieces have been more openly playful and full of light. Burton's work is elusive but hardly as difficult as it sounds, always intelligent, attractive, seductive, and fascinating.

4/27/72

Richard Foreman

"Evidence," the latest work of Richard Foreman's Ontological-Hysteric Theatre, is playing at Theater for the New City on Bank Street. This has been a rich couple of weeks for art theatre, what with the series of events at the Whitney, Foreman, a new manifestation by Robert Wilson's Byrd Hoffman School of Byrds, Meredith Monk posing, singing, moving a little, and I don't know what else. These artists come to theatre with some other art's sensibility and social life, making performances that don't resonate to the traditional theatre vibe, that to those expecting drama or entertainment often seem (and may be) perverse and uncommunicative.

I saw Foreman's first piece four years ago at the Cinematheque, then missed the intervening work, including "Lines of Vision" and "Hotel China." "Evidence," according to a repeated tape-recorded announcement, "consists of material that could not be made into a play." Specifically, it is two hours of stage animations from the notebooks in which Foreman's earlier works were written and sketched.

The theatre set-up looks grim—bare walls, bare light

bulbs, found furniture in a spare, rigid arrangement, taut white cords crossing through the air, a blackboard on the upstage wall, most surfaces painted in dull browns, the whole effect anti-decorative, leading one to expect maybe an abstract court-martial. Foreman's ads convey this same grimness and suggestion of horror, and I approached the work with low hopes. "Evidence" surprised me with its amiability, funky gemütlichkeit, deadpan wit, and personal directness. It is indirect too, as a given of the style, and the night I was there roughly half the audience trickled away during the performance, having failed to tune in. I found it consistently interesting, charming, and enjoyable.

It is almost a play. Max is at home alone, trying in a very spaced-out fashion to write a play. This is the play he is writing. Ben comes over, thrown in through the window. They refer to Rhoda. The speeches are broken up, dialogue all but obliterated. Slow. Incongruities. Metronomes, a blinking light, a drum, a buzzer, quacks to set off time. A beautiful woman downstage petrified, pointing. Later a picture falls off the wall and engulfs Ben. Objects are shown to the audience. Music. Acts and objects come from real life but are transformed: this is an art not of juxtaposition, like collage, but of transformation. Long looks at the audience. More cords (straight lines). Lamps. Tilting tables. Cigars. Cardboard boats. Meticulous craft, no illusion.

Here are a couple of quotes from Foreman's notebook (the script):

"1) Basically—audience waits for something to happen.

"2) Find a way to make each moment a denial of what is (let something go in your head).

He calls the show a "tightly packed sea of void-lets."

These are the art thoughts behind the work, and aside from their content they have a cold, negative character that is misleading. Ontologically Foreman's work is another story: full of feeling-content and constantly surprising. Never settling down for long into any fictional reality, it runs the danger of turning into art about art, but turns out instead to be a documentary of the artist's existence in time. Foreman has developed a personal idiom of persuasive integrity, a distinctive and effective craft. Whether you can dig it probably comes down to whether you respond to Foreman's person as here made manifest. There he is.

The actors are excellently self-possessed and convincing in this intensely disciplined style: Jessica Harper, Dempster Leech, Kate Manheim, George McGrath, and Robert Schlee.

5/4/72

The People Show

I am in the thick of directing Ronald Tavel's extraordinary new play, "Bigfoot," which opens at Theatre Genesis this week. Although it's hard to give much head space to critical thoughts at the moment, I want to say something about the People Show, four people from England whose performances at La Mama the past two weeks were original and wonderfully exhilarating. The People Show began in 1966, and the work has been developed in all kinds of performance situations. Both of the shows given at La Mama were structured on a series of visual images, extended by the presence of the actors, actions and words (not quite as improvisatory as they sounded), music both live and prerecorded, and a forceful use of real-life objects and materials.

People Show 44 is a dream of flying and death, approached from different angles in a series of explorations that accumulate power and beauty. Mark Long presented himself to the audience with wild self-assertiveness, making a fool of himself attempting to fly. Michael Figgis played the horn and told a long, painful story about the short, high-flying, painful career and life of Frankie Lyman. Laura Gilbert appeared in a long white dress with grisly blood-stains down the front. José Nava emerged from a huge pile of leaves. More: an evocation of the Charlie Parker memorial concert; two white doves, one caged, one free; a window shattered, a brick wall broken down; Nava lying face down in the leaves while Gilbert strokes his buttocks; Long meanwhile having chopped up and cooked a chicken, which is finally presented for eating to the audience.

People Show 39 centers on a long monologue by Long, illustrated by chalk drawings all over the floor, walls, set, and piano, about London, his wife who died in 1935, their trips to the white cliffs of Dover to make love. Other elements are a small, neat room in which Nava, as a rabbit breeder, reads and treats himself with a sun lamp; an incredibly ramshackle upstage house that collapses when Long enters from it; an elevated grassy lawn on which Gilbert makes herself a cup of tea, plays croquet, and swings on a swing, sometimes screaming. Late in the piece Nava brings in a wheelbarrow of sand, which he dumps off the "cliffs" onto the naked "body" of Long's improbable wife; more sand, which he sets up in little mounds with flowers, among which Long lies sunbathing; gravel, which he dumps on London. An enormous packing case is opened to reveal a tiny world of white mice, which Gilbert transfers onto a lumpy white stuffed "body" hanging in the middle of the space, where they eerily crawl about while Nava dumps more sand on the head of Long, who is breathing through a plastic hose held by a member of the audience.

Beautiful. 11/2/72

Peter Schumann

The puppets of the Bread and Puppet Theatre are magnificent, from the towering giants to the tiny finger puppets, Peter Schumann's staging is marvelously inventive and performed with a fine matter-of-factness, the work's integrity is beyond reproach, and the originality of style unquestionable. Yet the company's new major work, "That Simple Light May Rise Out of Uncomplicated Darkness," which is playing for a few more days at St. Clement's before the group goes home to Vermont, is frustrating in the same way much of the past work has been, the fault magnified by its size. It's not just that the performance is slow, though most of it is. Rather it's a willful insistence in the way the images are presented, a heavy didacticism that forces the audience to look at each image longer than they want to, as if to absorb some moral message.

What the message is, beyond the obvious, remains unclear: the present spectacle indicates very poetically that there are dark forces on the loose, and the meek may just possibly inherit the earth. Many of the images are absolutely extraordinary; some are banal. Schumann weights them equally with time until even the finest of them become boring and unaffecting. What is vivid is the first appearances; the repetitions do not increase but dissipate their resonance and power.

The few light, swift moments are successful: a tea party for a group of clouds, a mountain of furniture with a miniature man watching tv. Costumes and props as well as the puppets are miraculously simple, witty, and evocative. But too much of the progress is leaden, blunt, lifeless. There is something dead about the shapeless black and gray clothes that cover almost all the actors (puppet-handlers). The pointedly ugly noise the company makes as music, banging on tin cans and the like, gives way too seldom to beauty. The production opens into color, life, and gaiety only at the very end, when a complex transformation of images turns the stage into a kind of surreal fairground, and a jolly circus band comes strolling out from behind the audience, passes through, and is gone.

12/21/72

Meredith Monk

"Education of the Girlchild," an opera by Meredith Monk, presented by the House at Common Ground, 70 Grand Street.

Meredith Monk's "Education of the Girlchild" demands an active interest from its audience and rewards it with an unaggressive but richly evocative series of images. Monk's is a highly personal, lyrical theatre style. Its character is serene, centered, with a sly sense of humor, a fairy-tale boldness of imagination, and an active emotional life. Derangements of everyday movements, dissociated time, deadpan theatrics, and nonexplicit characters and events comprise a non-story that seems to lead through a real person's life on the inside. It does not lead somewhere, as narrative pretends to do, but compounds its unity from diversity. Monk's work isn't trying to do something to the audience; it is simply showing itself, from various angles, with a brave directness, and so showing us our world. We are there, watching, doing it with them.

It is a cunningly artful show. Many pictures stick: a half-dozen women in white sitting round a table, none alike, all strangely beautiful; a mad gray-faced royal queen raving, gabbling, and shrieking while other women pad back and forth in veils, cooing and chirping; the figure of Death, a spiky blue-painted woman accompanied by a bouncy blue goblin; and the woman in the red hat, a goofy, suspicious, down-to-earth intrusion into the hush of art. The slow, sure movement of the work is sustained and shaped by Monk's cyclical music; the singing extends the range of known sounds. There are almost no words; this "opera" is in another language. Monk's presence is contained, unassertive, sympathetic. She is sweetly forceful and mystically remote in her complete yielding to her own world.   11/15/73

Robert Wilson

"The Life and Times of Joseph Stalin," an opera by Robert Wilson, presented by the Byrd Hoffman School of Byrds at the Brooklyn Academy of Music.

After twelve hours of Robert Wilson's "The Life and Times of Joseph Stalin" it's hard to find fast words anywhere near adequate to what you have seen, heard, thought, and felt. The idiosyncratic seven-act "opera" is so rich and spectacular, its progress through time so stately and antic, the magic of Wilson's art so suave and self-contained, the huge cast's devotion so eloquent, that merely to list the ingredients of any one sequence would exhaust this little column of space. Any of dozens of its movements might be singled out, any number of theoretical generalities proposed—but you won't get what it is except by going to see it. I recommend that you do, in its two more performances this weekend at the Brooklyn Academy of Music. It is a unique and beautiful theatrical art.

The work is something of a retrospective of what Wilson and his Byrd Hoffman School of Byrds have done to date. The first four acts, lasting from 7 p.m. until around 2 a.m., have been seen here before as parts of "The Life and Times of Sigmund Freud" (1969) and "Deafman Glance" (1970). Close followers of the work can compares these with the earlier versions. The basic mode is enormous, elaborate, slowly moving tableaux vivants, huge set pieces in which all kinds of often incongruous elements interact. The acts and their various prologues and inner scenes are like giant living paintings with sound, with vast backdrops in painted perspective and fantastic, elaborate costumes. Wilson revives the scenic conventions of old-fashioned theatre as well as inventing conventions of his own, always making their concreteness consciously felt.

But here I go generalizing, and this is an art of the relentlessly particular.

The scenes from earlier pieces are all quite changed. The beach, which begins it, has acquired an extension out over the orchestra pit that remains through the work, with patient watchers' heads sticking up through holes in the sand. The beach scene has grown even richer, its famous dance of the mammies to the "Blue Danube" rendered almost ephemeral by night lighting. There is a little more open comedy than before, and the group's specialized vocal work has been highly developed. Alan Lloyd and Igor Demjen make music of all kinds work integrally in the stage life; in this sense it is an opera. The sound level is quiet. Speech is generally low-key and multilayered, often unintelligible.

Meanwhile the eccentric, apparently arbitrary "art" elements have been kept, serving to hold it all together, to reinforce the sense of something more, to enrich the texture. A runner in red runs across the stage every few minutes almost the whole night. Even more abstractly, a bunch of chrome hoops strung on a cable high above the audience are periodically adjusted slightly with a long pole. There

New Forms 1967–73

is always so much going on that even at the long night's deliberate pace the eye never catches up with it all. Some of it is continually changing, some of it always stays the same. You get interested in watching something on the left side of the stage—a giant turtle, maybe—and when you look back over on the right, everything is different. A new backdrop will slowly fly in and the whole reality be changed.

The Victorian drawing room scene has lost some of its momentum and menace, but I had the feeling Saturday was an off night on that particular set.

I went out to dinner during the third act, but I remember how incredibly beautiful the cave scene was in "Sigmund Freud," and later regretted having missed even a minute.

When I came back, Medea had apparently just murdered her children, and their bodies were being carried out by Joseph Stalin. The forest scene, Act IV, apparently the whole of "Deafman Glance," is extraordinarily beautiful, strange, and long, lasting a good three hours and tripping everybody right out.

Wilson's work doesn't have the loose focus of all-night theatres in Asia, which leave room for naps and picnics; the Brooklyn Opera House seats keep you watching the stage and sitting up. I expected to be uncomfortable, but I wasn't. It seemed quite natural to sit in a theatre all night. (But I hope this doesn't start a trend: the next day was lost.) Amazingly, my attention was held throughout. Once my normal bedtime had passed, I gave in and liked it more and more.

There are three acts new to New York. (They have been shown separately in Paris, Persepolis, and Copenhagen.) The temple scene, in a beautiful setting inside a pyramid, is devoted largely to dance, exhilarating loose-limbed bounding and turning choreographed by Andrew de Groat, while Wilson-as-Stalin inside a glass booth talks, laughs, comments, and carries on, later replaced by another Stalin who lectures on dialectical materialism. (Other things are happening too.) De Groat's virtuoso whirling dance is a high point. Wilson's on-stage presence whenever he appears is both powerful and likable; his focus is implacable, and his bold whimsy breaks through the solemnity that sometimes threatens the performance, setting an example of grace.

Act VI, described as a Victorian bedroom but looking more like a hospital ward, is comparatively coherent and emotionally direct, though stylized. An old man in a hall of mirrors seems to be dreaming—or perhaps the images plainly express his state of being. He goes through a repetitious struggle of counting while the white-clad sleepers move about him, in and out of their beds, carrying candles in white lanterns. At moments it is abstract patterns, at moments completely silly, at moments powerful as nightmare, real as people's lives.

I found myself drawing conclusions, thinking the work was getting simpler and overcoming its tendency to morbidness. But the last and latest act is imagistically and formally as intricate as anything Wilson has done, and by the end grew somewhat grating, possibly on purpose. The backdrop represents a landscape of craters and angled peaks. One sequence, the dance of the birds, is incredibly ridiculous. There are a couple of dozen of them, and they really look nothing like birds. You clearly see that they are bent-over people in preposterous ostrich costumes doing ridiculous choreography; but the image keeps working, the mind keeps lapsing, you keep finding yourself watching a bunch of big weird freaked-out birds on Mars or someplace even stranger. It's really funny the tricks it does on your head.

Where was I all last night? Among the happy few. You may not like or approve of this kind of rich, precious theatre, but there it is if you want it.

What is performed and witnessed doesn't translate into anything else. I knew, even when I was paying close attention, that I wasn't actually "following." I didn't know what to follow; I didn't know if there was anything to follow. I didn't even try to make sense of it. It's in another language, one that has meaning on another level than this one I'm playing with at the moment. It's a slow, heady language, its content accumulated through years of work, elusive as any esoteric communication. In a sense it is a projection of Wilson's mind. But it deliberately goes beyond that, calling itself a school, initiating devotees, reaching back to a deeper level of theatre. Wilson is making mysteries.   12/20/73

Personalities
1972–74

Allen Ginsberg

Allen Ginsberg's magnificent poem "Kaddish" has been made into a moving theatre piece by Robert Kalfin at the Chelsea Theatre Center in Brooklyn. It is strangely rare for emotion to be expressed or induced by the theatre these days. Most of what I see, no matter its degrees of skill, is cool if not cold. Passion turns into bombast if it's there at all, hate is pathological, and love is sex or sentimentality. It is difficult to feel involved in plays that deny their characters' emotionality. I too seldom find myself drawn out of my own feelings and preoccupations into an engagement with the people on the stage.

"Kaddish" cuts right through all that. The force is in its subject, which is Ginsberg's remembered experience of his mother, Naomi, who was mad. The meaning, dimensions, and effect of that madness are the matter of the play. Its heart is Naomi's suffering and Allen's compassionate inability to relieve it, his implicit need to get on with his own life.

At the beginning of the play, while her husband Louis is away teaching school in Newark, Naomi, convinced that Louis is poisoning her and that she needs a blood transfusion, persuades Allen, still a young boy, to take her to a rest home—where she acts so crazy nobody can get any rest. She has already spent time in Greystone State Hospital, and had shock treatments, and lost her figure. She goes back to Greystone, fighting Louis in terror and desperation. She comes home and gets crazy again. She tries to poison herself with iodine. She runs naked and hysterical out into the halls. It's impossible. Time passes. She moves to the Bronx to live with her sister Eleanor. Louis divorces her. But Eleanor has a heart condition; Naomi's paranoid intensity is killing her. Allen, now a student at Columbia University, commits his mother to the hospital, there's no place else for her to go. More shock, more horror, ever more. Agonizing visits from her sons, Allen and his older brother Eugene. At last Naomi dies in Pilgrim State. At the end she has a vision: "The key is in the window"—she passes it on to Allen, who passes it on to us.

What is this madness? Naomi comes to America, marries, learns to play the piano, joins the Party, raises two sons, and is taken over by paranoid fear. Gradually the madness becomes her personality—she shares her delusions as other people make conversation. Incarceration and shock therapy are punishment for giving in to terror. You can't even say it destroys her: crazy or not, she is a person, hers is a life.

The poem is Allen's heroic coming-to-terms with this incomprehensibly awful experience that dominated his youth. The play transmits enough of it to be effective and memorable. The first act in particular is stunning. Kalfin's production employs videotape projections in triptych form on a large upstage screen, the best dramatic use of video I've yet seen, and a great advance over slides and movies. (Video is by Arthur Ginsberg and Video Free America of San Francisco.) The story is told by a variety of means: brief sections of the poem spoken by Michael Hardstark as Allen in his twenties; vignettes and scenes acted out live on the bare stage with simple settings and expressive lighting; and projected sequences shot on location. Live and recorded sound are subtly interwoven, and fragments of music are eloquently used. The projections evoke the places and period of Naomi's life and give the play a documentary feel, a sense of contact with its factual origin, that adds to its power and makes possible, most of the time, a coherence and flow of action through disjointed space and time. Sometimes, as in Naomi's flip-out in a Lakewood bus depot, the projections are distorted into nightmarish visions, taking us inside her mind.

As Naomi, Marilyn Chris gives a great performance of astounding range and detailed virtuosity and depth of feeling. The last vision of Naomi at Pilgrim State, grey, shriveled, crippled, will haunt me for a long time. Bennyt Averyt's lighting of that scene is superb. There is good honest work by other actors too: notably Jerrold Ziman as Eugene, Michael Hardstark sounding like Allen and looking just like photos of him at college age, Glenn Weitzman as Allen younger, Michael Vale as Louis, Jani Brenn as a nurse. The emphasis, as it should be, is on Naomi and on Allen recalling her from a hard-won, necessary distance with abiding love.

There are flaws and limitations to the production. The theatre was rebuilt for "The Screens," and the audience sees "Kaddish" from awkward angles and distances; the actors are not always coherently related to the projections; the stage space is formless. The projections occasionally—as in the closeup replays of the climax, when Allen in exasperation strikes his mother—distract from and undercut the stage action: that moment as acted was shattering and should have been let stand. The cinematic montage technique breaks down when the vignettes are too thin and spaced apart. Maybe we see too little of the sane, accessible Naomi—in the play she is always mad. The play can't contain the complexity and resonance of the poem or even attempt its ecstatic heights and elegiac grandeur. For that you must read the poem or/and listen to the poet's recorded reading of it.

"Kaddish" is the first thing I've wanted to recommend in a long time, the first play in months to reach through my urban insensitivity and critical ennui and help me remember that we are responsive human people in this world, we suffer, we feel joy, we care for one another or lose ourselves.

2/17/72

Charles Stanley

"Highways and Byways," dance theatre by Charles Stanley, music by John Smead, at the Construction Company Dance Studio.

Charles Stanley's "Highways and Byways" is a concise, persuasive work of dance theatre done in a large, light space sparely decorated with cats and Stanley's collages. Stanley moves and speaks and John Smead plays harmonica. After a brief verse prologue—"Proceed to plough the fear-filled field"—Stanley moves, organizing the space according to the placement of ceiling lights, through a serious of places and personae. He is hitchhiking and singing blues, he is a kid hiding from the sheriff, he is the sheriff's sexy wife, he is an old woman complaining, he is the artist wondering, "Can I make anger in an art work or only innuendo?" It's not that simple, there are richer possibilities than the words delimit; yet this work's modest form contains that earnestness and an amplitude of experience as well as Stanley's strong presence. Smead draws astonishing sounds and varieties of music from the harmonica, an integral, impeccably complementary part of the piece.

10/12/72

Gertrude Stein

"The Mother of Us All," the opera by Gertrude Stein (text) and Virgil Thomson (music), directed by Elizabeth Keen and Roland Gagnon, at the Guggenheim Museum.

Those who have suspected (probably in secret) that Gertrude Stein was not a real writer but a chic, personally potent verbal trickstress can have their minds clarified by her opera "The Mother of Us All." Most of her plays are so antic in form and manner as to be hardly plays at all: they have to be produced abstractly, the words projected in images related by sensibility, not sense, images that subtly suggest emotions, attitudes, even action, but ever tease at the edge of whimsical nonsense. "The Mother of Us All" is built on a cute, cunningly structured scenario by Maurice Grosser, within which (so I imagine the process) Stein made her wonderfully concise, clever, illuminating words. The libretto has her special charm and sophisticated taste in abundance, and the witty, playful, insistent Stein style is in full flower. (By contrast, Leon Katz's adaptation of "The Making of Americans" at Judson, abetted by Al Carmines's music, made her sound corny, heavy-witted, like a bad writer.) "The Mother of Us All" is a vivid portrait of the late-nineteenth-century feminist Susan B. Anthony and the climate of her times, simultaneously making its own forthright, passionate statements about women and men and men's society.

"What are men?" Stein/Anthony asks, and answers, "Yes they have kind hearts"—they help us up when we fall, when our house catches fire they come to put it out—"but they are afraid." The hen is afraid of the hawk, but "she is only afraid for her children; men are afraid for themselves." She says, "Men want to be half slave and half free; women want to be all slave—or all free." And recognizes, "Men are afraid but if I were to tell them so their kindness would turn into hate." It couldn't be more direct.

The story is mostly about Anthony's fight for suffrage for women and blacks, struggling on even knowing that the men in power will not vote her laws. There are charming sub-plots. Indiana Elliot marries Jo the Loiterer at the end of Act I, but she will not take his name; though Jo supports the feminist cause, "No loiterer has a vote." Later she does take his name—becoming Indiana Loiterer—and gives him hers. Daniel Webster is in love with Angel More though she is dead; she appears throughout, part angel, part ghost, part ingénue, a vision from another world. John Adams is wooing Constance Fletcher but can't kneel to her because he is an Adams. Later he does, she goes blind, and he sings, "Here you are, blind as a bat, beautiful as a bird." A high point of Act II is the announcement, "I have just converted Lillian Russell to the cause of women's suffrage."

The performance at the Gugenheim Museum attains a polite perfection that finely matches Virgil Thomson's witty, pretty, exquisitely wrought music, but it doesn't create much theatrical energy. Much of the fault is with the theatre itself, which was built as a lecture auditorium with no allowance for theatrical magic. The production is relentlessly conventional, smugly efficient but unimaginative. For all the effort that went into the staging, it comes off as a concert version of the opera. I feel nothing but admiration for the musicianship and comportment of the small orchestra and the cast. The major and minor roles alike are presented with craft, intelligence, and finesse. 12/7/1972

Joseph Chaikin

In 1963 Joseph Chaikin and fifteen or twenty actors, along with a handful of playwrights, directors, and critics, began meeting every week in a borrowed loft at Third Avenue and Thirty-Fourth Street to explore acting and the nature of theatre. Joe was a close friend of mine. I admired his acting in Brecht's "Man Is Man" at the Living Theatre, where he led a few acting classes before the new group formed.

Today, ten years later, I have been reading around in Joe's book, *The Presence of the Actor*, and reading Michael Feingold's recent interview with him in the *Times*. I read that the Open Theatre is disbanding, that after a decade of transformations it will exist no more.

The loft group became the Open Theatre. Joe tried not to be its leader, but it was inevitable. His kind of leadership was indirect, a matter not of asserted authority but of the sheer force and perseverance of his presence. For some years he tried to keep the group a laboratory, to hold back the obligation of performance, of presenting "finished" works. He was wholly committed to research, to process, wholly at odds with product. At the same time he was always, I think, hungry for recognition.

I was frustrated by the way he worked. Though we argued a little about theory, what it came down to was temperament, personal tempo, work methods. Everybody who tries to work together confronts these issues. Joe would offer his workshop what he came to call "pebbles," fragmentary impulses, glimpses of possible ways to work, and the actors were remarkable in being able to do something with them. A few of them would get out on the floor and build something, and as soon as Joe saw a little bit of result, he was ready to move on to something else. To me the work was maddeningly inconclusive; I wanted to keep after a problem until it was fully explored, but Joe loved questions more than answers. Strangely, I thought he was working too fast, superficially. Looking back on it now the tempo of work seems luxuriously unpressured. Joe insisted on moving at his own speed. In those early days there were several directors, and the group showed work-in-progress versions of numerous short plays, demonstrated exercises that have since become basic theatre vocabulary, did two commercial productions (Jean-Claude van Itallie's "America Hurrah" and Megan Terry's "Viet Rock"), and, independent of Joe's work, produced a series of plays at La Mama. The more recent ensemble works that have established the Open Theatre's reputation and influence and Joe's eminence as a director, are "The Serpent," written by van Itallie, "Terminal," written by Susan Yankowitz, "The Mutation Show," and "Nightwalk." The group also presented Beckett's "Endgame," directed by Roberta Sklar, with Joe giving a remarkable performance as Hamm.

I first got to know Joe Chaikin a year before he started the Open Theatre, in the spring of 1962, when he starred in a movie I was directing and shooting from a script by Peter Hartman. On the second day Joe didn't appear, and it turned out he was in jail, having been arrested with Judith Malina and Julian Beck in one of the first civil-defense protests in City Hall Park. He began wearing the broken-gun symbol of pacifism and nonviolent resistance. I was sympathetic but not engaged, still thinking that if I got over my "neurosis" everything would be normal again. Joe became deeply involved in anti-war actions. This consciousness informed all his work with the Open Theatre as well as the group's evolving structure. Our little movie turned out to be another "pebble." Doing it we found things, each for himself, other than what we were looking for.

In Joe's book and in the later Open Theatre works the fragments are finely polished and rich in implications, but always fragments. "Nightwalk" is marvelous for the assurance of the staging and the authority of the style, the brilliant, often cold intensity of the performances, the sharpness of satirical observation, the exquisite detail of the acting work, superbly balancing abstraction and presence, comedy and lyricism, seriousness and play. The company works with the efficiency and near arrogance of a surgical team.

Joe and I once wrote the opening scene of a play together too. Gradually our paths diverged. I was hurt by his animus against critics; I was struggling to find the morality and sincerity in my own way. Joe always seemed more moral, more sincere. He was angry with me for criticizing his work in a book I wrote. I often felt critical of the Open Theatre's work, though recognizing its quality. I felt involved in it, almost possessive about it. I felt that the work always aimed beyond its achievement, that it was self-important. In practice that has been its virtue, the concern for deepening experience, the burning sincerity, the commitment to the necessary truth, even if it is impractical, disturbing, or ridiculous. To work with Joe was to be in his power, and I was not strong enough to see the other side of that coin, that we are all in each other's power or alone, and so I resisted.

At the same time I realize he gave expression to many perceptions and views I have come to take for granted. We agree, for example, that the commercial arena is no place to do the kind of work that interests us. We agree that theatre, because we are investing it with our lives, must face the whole world and strive toward that life beyond anything we can yet imagine, that life we already know.

The later Open Theatre tended not to do plays but

group works, with Joe rather than a playwright acting as the formative intelligence, often with a writer as part of the process. The method has been to work on a theme—in "Terminal," death—with everybody bringing in their own experiences and intuitions. The group process and the historical moment produced the generally dark character of the expression; maybe joy and delight are too private in our America to be found in this social way of working. The shape of the performances has been the shape of Joe's mind, not "dramatic," not building to conclusions like nineteenth-century symphonies, but constantly attentive, constantly questioning, constantly renewed.   10/18/73

Jackie Curtis

"Glamour, Glory, and Gold," a play by Jackie Curtis, directed by Ron Link, at the Fortune Theatre.

Jackie Curtis is back, starring in a revival of his play "Glamour, Glory, and Gold." Jackie first came before my eyes as a chorus boy in Tom Eyen's crypto-Egyptian musical "Miss Nefertiti Regrets," back in the mid-sixties when La Mama was on Second Avenue and *The Voice* was on Sheridan Square, and I've always had a soft spot for him. I went to see "Glamour, Glory, and Gold" with some trepidation, having found it grating in its first realization some years back at Bastiano's Cellar on Waverly Place. The late Candy Darling starred in it then. Now Jackie plays the lead role himself, and comes through with a performance that demonstrates his specialness. His talent is ineffable and contradictory—he is somehow truthful and touching even when the material is trashy and patently false. Graceful in his clumsiness, beautiful in his plainness, in control of his knockabout freedom, he plays a woman without pretending to be a woman.

His play too is built on contradictions. Its story of Nola Noonan, hash-slinger to stripper to star to pitiful has-been, is a time-worn cliché and a projection of the very fantasies Jackie, Candy, and other sex-switching pop show people have made their lives on for the past few years; it is a second-hand rose of a fantasy in the first place, half mocking and contrived from careers that were themselves contrived by the star system and the economics of sexual frustration. The play is half mocking about itself even while it is itself: the publicity for it says Jackie Curtis *is* Nola Noonan. So you don't know how to take him, her, or it. It is these ambiguities, and his spirit, that give the work its character and interest.

It sometimes gets strident, relying too steadily on the comedy of insult, but more often it is charming, whimsical, knowing, and hard-boiledly tender. Ron Link's production is snappy and energetic, playing into the fond Hollywood routines with style and relish but not getting lost in them, nicely underlining the surreal, expressionist imagery that is Curtis's special language as a dramatist, maneuvering the small, skillful cast through the Eyenesque collage of a narrative with swift assurance. Andrew Amic Angelo, remarkable as a whip-wielding movie director, unleashes an amazing tirade of denunciation after Nola fails in her comeback. Estelle R. Dallas is flawless as Nola's tough, loyal girlfriend. Jeremy Abbott, Madeleine Le Roux, and Paul Vanase, who complete the cast, are all good. 4/4/74

The Ridiculous II
1972–73

The Trojan Women

Donald L. Brooks's all-male, gay-oriented production of "The Trojan Women" opened last Thursday at the Theatre of the Lost Continent on Jane Street. The Euripedes play is one of the awful masterpieces of world literature, set amid the ashes of fallen Troy, where the surviving women are awaiting transshipment as concubines and slaves to the conquering Greeks, who are themselves to be victims of the gods' revenge on the long voyage home. Misery is the play's only emotion, pity and terror the only possible responses. It is the great anti-war play, a blunt, unequivocal demonstration that war destroys losers and victors alike. It is also an anti-imperalist play: the ten-year siege of Troy was a first Greek attempt to colonize Asia Minor. And it is a play that sympathizes with the enemy.

Brooks attacks this material with camp, razzmatazz, and ridiculousness—and much of the time it works very well. Where the production goes wrong is where it takes itself seriously. Being serious and taking oneself seriously are not the same things, of course. Jackie Curtis is quite serious as the interpolated Hera, Goddess of War, in a silver lamé minidress and combat boots, posturing and making moues in front of projections of war atrocities from ancient times to the present. Mario Montez is serious as Cassandra, although the audience laughs at him. He plays her like Ophelia, casting demented gaiety to the rubble, and he rises above the audience's frivolous mockery with a strangely noble sincerity. Ondine is a serious Poseidon, his cobweb-painted face stuck through a giant seashell. Surrounded by writhing tentacle arms, he delivers the prologue with impressive force and solemnity and a delicate, saving twinkle in his eyes. The irony all three of them project is there in Euripedes. As Sartre has pointed out, "In 'The Trojan Women' the gods are powerful and ridiculous as the same time." The same can be said of the heroes—of Menelaus, at least, who fought about Helen for no higher reason than romantic vexation. Gods and men have been naughty, and Brooks does not violate the play in being naughty with it—or provoking the audience's naughtiness with a charmingly nude Talthybius (Don Wyckoff). (But an exotic dance of three veils, climaxing—is that the right word?—with an asshole display, is outright burlesque.)

Naughty may be the right word for the behavior of gods and men, but their triviality doesn't trivialize the misery they have caused—and this is the problem of the production. Brooks wants it both ways. It is in the "serious" performances, particularly that of Bill Maloney as Hecuba, that the production goes wrong. Maloney hits one note of bottomless grief at the start of the show and wails along on that same note throughout. It is a long and wordy role, and while it is initially affecting, it becomes gratingly tedious. This rendition of the great text, which often looks like an unwitting parody of grand classical acting—the real thing is much cooler, more calculated in its effects—makes us grow sick of Hecuba, who turns into a self-pitying hag, hardly the character Euripedes wrote. Harvey Fierstein as Andromache, after a striking Callasesque beginning, similarly overpowers the role with emotional fervor, so that one comes to feel bullied by the acting. Grover Noel, his smiling brown face refulgently haloed in black frizz, is ambling and unintelligible as Helen. Ondine's Menelaus might be more subtle, but his exasperated withdrawal behind a newspaper seemed the only thing to do. The Chorus, led by Harvey Tavel, tend to play their lines with passionate feeling which, because of their jarring accents and lack of acting ability, sounds silly and amateurish. It is when the incongruities are cultivated and controlled that they make sense. Art is first of all deliberate; when these actors come on like traditional tragedians they simply look inept

Brooks does not hesitate to connect Troy to Vietnam, or to suggest a similar future in ashes for us. The sheer vulgarity and decadence of the proceedings amounts to some kind of point. He contrives powerful theatrical effects, including the strobe-lit chorus movements at the beginning of the play, and uses recorded music well. The production is most successful when it makes direct use of its discontinuities. This Menelaus is a modern general, and the *Times* he reads is today's. 3/16/72

Eunuchs of the Forbidden City

A play written and directed by Charles Ludlam, presented by the Ridiculous Theatrical Company at the Theater for the New City.

Charles Ludlam's new work is a historical epic chronicling the long, ruthless, bizarre career of Orchid Yehonala, the Manchu concubine who became Tsu Hsi, the last Empress of China. I'm at a loss how to convey the idiosyncracy, charm, and distinction of Ludlam's style. The play is conventional in form, harking back to such fine classical models as Racine and W.S. Gilbert—restrained, dignified, almost stately. At the same time it is, by its own claim, ridiculous. The text is pieced together out of clichés, scraps of movie dialogue, and fragments of literature both trashy and beautiful. It relishingly mocks and frolics in chinoiserie. The dialogue is freely garnished with anachronistic, frivolous, straightforwardly funny jokes, and the presentation of the story breaks down from time to time into startlingly salacious romping.

Along with strategic nudity and sex-switching, there are theatrical devices ranging from the most sophisticated to the most childlike. This delicate combination of artful, knowing discipline with playful ebullience gives the work its special flavor. The play is long and spacious in form and performed with relaxed assurance and suave clarity. Its content is gratuitous, with no concessions to contemporary relevance. Instead, though clearly ridiculous, the work achieves a kind of classical nobility and serenity.

Ludlam and the core members of his Ridiculous Theatrical Company have been working together for some years now, and the central performances are superb: Black-Eyed Susan as the concubine Empress; Lohr Wilson and Ludlam as principal eunuchs; Lola Pashalinski as the co-Empress; John D. Brockmeyer as the Son of Heaven; Bill Vehr as the Pearl Concubine. Some of the others, newcomers to the company, in smaller parts, are not very good, but their limitations don't matter much. Theatre is an art of limitations, suggesting worlds, not actually going there. It is startling at the end of "Eunuchs of the Forbidden City" when the cast take their bows: there had seemed to be many more than this dozen.

There are exquisite, wonderfully liberating moments in this play. I remember particularly a breathtakingly extraneous and delicious disquisition on jade, the shocking love scene between the Empress and the Chief Eunuch (Ludlam), who fucks her with the Great Seal; the Chief Eunuch's theatrically dazzling comeuppance. Lohr Wilson created the handsome oriental setting and gorgeously elaborate, witty costumes.

Be warned that the sight-lines are terrible; get there early and sit down front or you may be unable to see much of the action. 4/13/72

Sissy

A musical with book and lyrics by Seth Allen, music by Michael Meadows and Seth Allen, directed by John Vaccaro, presented by the Play-house of the Ridiculous at La Mama.

"Sissy" is a brilliant success. This latest manifestation of the Play-house of the Ridiculous under John Vaccaro's direction is an ebullient, madcap musical. What it's all about I can't tell you—nothing, everything, everyday life, nothing. It's enough that the script's vapidities are an excellent basis for these players' art, allowing Vaccaro the room for his sometimes brutally irreverent, distractingly decorative, and elegantly vulgar stagings. Even after seeing "Sissy" twice I can hardly remember any action or thought. Most of what's said is offhand, perfunctory, cool to the point of emptiness, reflecting shared values but committing none of its own, a pastiche of public private jokes and post-camp borrowings. I am struck instead by the stage images and the wonderfully original and energetic performances. Vaccaro has assembled a first-class cast of those most developed in his unique style, and the staging is his most likable work in a long time, overflowing with comic invention, sardonic humor, and enthusiastic presence, largely free of the crudenesses and forced desperation that have made some of his recent work incoherent and grating. "Sissy" is entertainment.

The setting, designed by Vaccaro and Russell Krum, is dominated by a large diagonal ramp at the back, up which Wee Robin Pennings, looking indirectly but strikingly like

Marlene Dietrich in drag, rides a giant turtle through the length of the play, profiled protosurrealistically against a backdrop of the Paramount mountain. Below the ramp is the low door of a giant safe, through which the rest of the cast appear and retreat. Up left is a Coke machine, above it a sequined Heaven; up right an area in which a quartet of unruly types called Rifkins incessantly act out commentary, as rude as it is witty, on the center stage goings-on. Not to be neglected as more than scenery is Elsene Sorrentino, fetchingly posed between wisecracks as Mona Lisa herself in a picture-lit gold frame.

There are casual plot continuities to provide a semblance of momentum—a distressed mother looking for her baby, Superman seeking change of a dollar—but what really keeps it together is sheer style. The makeup alone is a lesson, a Play-house of the Ridiculous trademark that has inspired other theatres from the Cockettes to Béjart and is ever more frequently appearing at parties. Glitter predominates. Ruby Lynn Reyner's red-glittered lips are only the start. Otto Erotica's half polka-dotted pink face is a brilliant creation; John Albano goes from outrageously ugly lopsidedness as Kansas City Bummer to ravishing silver, white, and tinsel when he reappears as the Coke Angel; Michael Arian transforms himself past recognition in a dazzling multiplicity of roles. The whole cast is into it, the details are fully elaborated, and this exuberant intricacy is but a symptom of a style that is a constant feast for the eye. The costumes by Bernard Roth and Janet Wolfman are identically extravagant, the images pushed beyond clarity to a loving fullness and madness of invention that encourage the eye to roam everywhere with amazement. John P. Dodd's lights achieve stupendous saturations of pink and contribute an extraordinary rhythmic energy with their fine-tuned, baroque chromatic fantasies. Add to the visual density the slides and films by Bill Gamble and dual video monitors. Ruby Lynn Reyner is terrific both in her songs—"Bad Sex" and "The Power of Art"—and in between, not so much playing a role as a non-stop series of routines. She is brittle and bouncy, bravely buoyant through all indignities, unsentimental and demented yet a most generous and personal performer. Michael Meadows is a poignant Superman, isolated in his sincerity amid this population of thrill-crazed, cynical decadents, yet matching them in madness. Michael Arian stops the show with his grandly proportioned rendition of "Big Spade Sailor," incorporating a la Elvis a long spoken bridge that reveals itself incredibly to be Blanche's Moon Lake Casino speech from "Streetcar." He is equally effective as an Eskimo singing "Cold Power," during which the rest of the cast come up the aisles to pass out creamsicles and Kools. Gordon Bressac sings "Do You Know the Feeling" beautifully, creating a genuine lift. The band, called Paranoia, is subtle and solid, the chorus sings in tune, and Richard Weinstock's arrangements give "Sissy" the most together sound of any Vaccaro show to date.

It is impossible not to wish there were more substance, more sense; Seth Allen's book expresses mostly an aloof, post-personal, overstimulated worldliness, though a sweetness of temper just below the surface saves the show from being hard. It is formally linked to "Hair" and to former Vaccaro productions, musical drama and revue merged into a free-form succession of numbers linked by moment-to-moment high associations, sustained by style alone. The weak moments, as a result, are shockingly empty, and neither the progress to the finale nor the finale itself seems sufficiently inevitable. Yet end it must. I had a great time and intend to go back for more.   11/16/72

Corn

A musical written and directed by Charles Ludlam, music and lyrics by Virgil Young, presented by the Ridiculous Theatrical Company at the Thirteenth Street Theatre.

Charles Ludlam and his Ridiculous Theatrical Company are back. Their new show, "Corn," is lovable and health-giving. From the baleful Island of Lost Love of his now-classic "Bluebeard" to the preposterous court of Tsu Hsih, last emperor of China, in last season's "Eunuchs of the Forbidden City" (what a title!), Ludlam transports us now to Hicksville, prototypical hill-country home of the feuding Hatfields and McCoys. Lola Lola, a big-time country music singer, has come down from New York City to put on a free concert, explaining to her dubious manager, Dude Greaseman, "Unless a country singer stays close to her roots, she's just another pop-art product." To accommodate the Woodstock crowds that are expected, she needs the neighboring cornfields of both the warring clans. Maw McCoy and Paw Hatfield won't hear of it, but two of the younguns are in love—"a regular backwoods Romeo and Juliet." Rachel, who is dumb, communicates with Ruben through the language of the flowers, which Lola fortunately understands and translates. Aunt Priscilla, benevolent faith healer and former midwife, ultimately straightens the whole thing out, ending the feud, effecting a wedding, curing Rachel's muteness (alas), and setting the stage for Lola's concert.

Ludlam has constructed the play with even more than his customary wit, decorative richness, and expertise, lightly turning every dramaturgic trick to the end of sheer delight. The good humor and transparent ease of "Corn" are irresistible and, it seems to me, an admirable direction for this talented company to have taken. The contrast with the two other leading practicioners of the "ridiculous," John Vaccaro and Ronald Tavel, is telling: both are occupied as much with pain as fun, Vaccaro's latest work hard-edged, cynical, sprinkled with bitter put-downs of humane values, Tavel's probing with the sharpest intellectual tools toward a disorientingly difficult vision of the unresolvable. Ludlam says, "I think it's time we all got back to corn again." "Corn" is on the side of common sense, good eating, consummated love, and wholesome entertainment. When the cast unites for a straightforward square dance, it is the purest exemplary action.

The play is made to these actors' measure, and the performances are flawless. Towering, gangling John D. Brockmeyer is a sight and a half as Maw McCoy, brilliantly matched with a clean-shaven Ludlam as Paw Hatfield. Ludlam is the most amiable of presences, and the scene in which, aided by several others, he flies writhingly through the air is comparable to the unforgettable seduction scene in "Bluebeard." Lola Pashalinski, generously proportioned and warmly sincere, is splendid as Lola Lola, and in the final song—"I've been a loner all my life, and I won't cheat myself now by starting a love affair with you"—reveals a great radiant beauty. Bill Vehr makes a nice contrast as her citified agent Dude and doubles resplendently as the nurse. Black-Eyed Susan is earnestly twitchy as the speechless Rachel (and hideously shrill once she is cured). Robert Beers is an adorably sincere Ruben/Romeo. Richard Currie and George Osterman are funny as the other two hick kids, Moe and Melanie, and Ma Uory in full skirts and bonnet is all faith and fun as Aunt Priscilla. The excellent sets and costumes are by Edgardo Franceschi. The play is sprinkled with good straight country songs by Virgil Young, performed with easy assurance by the Lucky Stars, a trio featuring Roger Acorn as lead singer. Among the show's best qualities is its hassle-free, unrushed, yet never flagging pace, most difficult to achieve. Ludlam is a master. 11/30/72

The Magic Show of Dr. Ma-gico

A play by Kenneth Bernard, directed by John Vaccaro, presented by the Play-house of the Ridiculous at La Mama.

Kenneth Bernard's new play, "The Magic Show of Dr. Ma-gico," is a shocking vision of evil, a metaphoric projection of the world peopled by gross caricatures of kings, queens, courtiers, princesses, gleefully displayed for their disillusioning lesson by the king-puppeteer-magician-god, Dr. Ma-gico. Yet it's no grosser than reality, we are meant to see, for the play and production have a malicious elegance and cold-blooded viciousness that must be taken as passionately moral in order to be tolerable.

This is the third of Bernard's plays to be produced by John Vaccaro's Play-house of the Ridiculous (the others were "The Moke-Eater" and "Night Club"), and it shows the company in a serious humor, its special visual opulence, glittering and color-saturated, its parodistic sexuality, its brazenly mannered performing style, all applied with control and coherence. There is a conviction to it that really gets your attention. It's like a slap in the face from a beauty.

The play is structured in a series of episodes, simultaneously the tricks and turns of a magic show, diversions at a decadent court, and parables of Dr. Ma-gico's teaching. The playwright makes a point of never stating his point straight, instead teasing, goading, and challenging the audience to discover it. The play is certainly coherent—it tries and fails to get off the subject of royalty; it is nasty to the core—but its sense is in the action, not the argument. Dr. Ma-gico, here embodied in a tall, cruelly beautiful, fiercely sensual woman, is something of a dark guru, a counter-illusionist. What makes the spectacle disquieting is its air of being presented for our enlightenment.

When a lover tells his beloved he would die for her, she tests his love by transforming herself into a suppurating hag and biting off his cock. A prince seeking an enchanted princess meets a preposterously clumsy ballerina and an odd king who croaks like a frog, and kills the wrong one. Esmeralda, wooed by Quasimodo, dies from horror. In one episode the cast confront the audience in eerie, gorgeous stillness. In another they dance. The outrageous, awful vision is never compromised, its beauty the servant of its corruption, its humor satanic.

The cast, mostly pseudonymous, are fully into the style, self-effacingly collaborative in the chorus, though relentlessly idiosyncratic, and most of them have stand-out roles in individual episodes. Vaccaro's company has never looked better. Sierra Bandit dominates as Dr. Ma-gico, the stunning central image. There are striking performances by Golda Rush as Esmeralda, Elsene Sorrentino as the Old Lady and the Queen, and Belle Pavlov as the hilarious, pitiful dancing Fairy Princess.

All elements of the production must be singled out for admiration. Richard Weinstock's high-class, expert music for cello, clarinet, saxophone, piano, and tympani contributes immeasurably to the evening's seductiveness. Bernard Roth's costumes, mainly in black and white, mythologize the images, registering and parodying the archetypes the author so knowingly plays upon, and lending the production a classically elegant solidity of style. The makeup, done by the company, is extraordinary. Carolyn Lord's choreography fills the play with buoyancy, setting the stage swirling with the formal patterns of courtly dance, the action emerging from the movement as if the whole pageant might be idle fancies during a gavotte. Charles Terrel's setting with its black and white checkerboard floor and reflective metal walls is hard, cold, decorative, and elegant within La Mama's encroaching bare brick. David Adams's lights make a volume of living radiance, the rich and lurid colors laid like nerve warps on the achromatic imagery. 3/22/73

Notable Playwrights
1972–73

Murray Mednick

"The Hunter," a play by Murray Mednick, directed by Kent Paul, presented by the New York Shakespeare Festival at the Public Theatre.

"The Hunter" by Murray Mednick is a beautiful and complex play. "It's all real," says the Hunter, "it's all the same real." But this real is multilayered, dense-textured, with echoing, hauntingly mysterious spaces in it and hallucinatory overlaps. The language, spare, hip, deceptively casual, circles and returns with ritual insistence. The four characters are set against the night in emblematic relief.

The center reality of the play is two men, Lee and Harry, who are spending a night out in the woods, sleeping on army cots in what may be a cemetery—there is a single headstone on the stage—and may also be a battlefield of the Civil War. They are wearing castaway uniforms, but they are at the outset peaceful men. Lee is obsessed with a woman who has let him down; Harry, who would rather sleep than hear the horny details, tells him, "Obsession is low-level awareness."

A gunshot is heard, and into the scene stumbles the Hunter, lost, carrying a twelve-gauge automatic shotgun and the hawk he has just killed. The Hunter is middle-aged and deranged. Lee and Harry are appalled at his killing the hawk with his supergun, but he keeps the gun on them.

There is a creepy, growing menace in his genial but flippy behavior. He keeps flipping back to the Civil War, reciting ghastly battle facts with obsessive relish. Finally Lee and Harry, frightened and furious, play into his military fantasies, get his gun away, overpower him, and nail him to a handy tree.

Act Two brings a woman into the scene. Marianne, a vision in fringed buckskin and boots, enters toting a watermelon and shoots it open with her revolver. The headstone has moved; it now reads, "I keep thinking it's Thursday." The crucified Hunter is in fine fettle, babbling history and heading into a final delirium. The strange fact that he doesn't bleed makes them doubt his reality. In the foreground Lee is getting it on with Marianne, who gives him her gun. They go off stage to ball, leaving Harry to entertain the voyeur Hunter with a high-flying monologue about Orgasm, Dreams, and Death, which come to the Hunter all at once.

In Act Three the Hunter is dead, the tree is gone, and Harry and Lee have each other covered with the two guns in a paroxysm of paranoia. The corpse is starting to smell, but neither of the men will let down his guard so no one can bury it. Marianne is on Lee's side of the stalemate, finally openly urging him to shoot Harry, but he can't quite do it. At the point of maximum pressure she splits. Lee and Harry are in effect alone again as at the beginning of the play; but now they have guns pointed at each other, and even without a reason for hostility, it's not so easy to drop their guard. The only way out of one obsession is into another. They dump the body of the Hunter, and finally the visionary level of the play takes over completely. They share a vision of a ghost black army all in white, speaking of it in unison, while behind them emerges a vision of white cemetery crosses, and white crosses of light come swarming upon them out of the darkness as the black army forever advances.

The play works by the superimposition of images and

themes; the ambiguities are spaces in which the images resonate. It is about men together and the special power in an intimacy of equals: they unite against an enemy, they are set against one another by a woman. It becomes the Civil War, brother against brother, driven by obsession and desire. The connections make themselves, they don't have to be spelled out. The play goes beyond meanings into passionate, knowing theatre poetics. The crosses are not symbols. It doesn't make "sense" to crucify the Hunter, but when it happens it is inevitable, as if crosses exist to become an image at this moment in this play.

The production at the Public Theatre only goes part of the way. All the pieces are in place, but Kent Paul's direction is limp. The relationship between Lee and Harry has no excitement in it. Theoni V. Aldredge's costumes are fine, but the set by Ralph Funicello and lighting by Spencer Mosse are too conventional-minded. The play needs, and lacks in this production, a hyper-sensitive awareness of the crucial present moment in and between the characters and the possibility of magic. Douglass Watson is excellent as the Hunter, filling out a difficult, basically static role with convincingly crazy energies. Kathleen Cramer has the definitive looks and swagger for Marianne but is a bit off-hand with the lines. Robert Glaudini is likable and long-suffering as Harry, with a certain detachment from the role, but Michael Hadge as Lee struck me as too boyish and tentative, and the two men's changing relations seemed acted, artificial, instead of burning up out of the depths within Mednick's powerful play.

6/1/72

Robert Patrick

"The Golden Circle," a play by Robert Patrick, directed by the author, presented by the Spring Street Company at 119 Spring Street.

Playwright Robert Patrick's comedy "The Golden Circle," written in the mid-sixties, is partly based on his experiences with the Caffè Cino and its dizzyingly varied community. The lavish production by the Spring Street Company, under the author's direction, is vindication and apotheosis of Patrick's work, in which he is true to himself even at cost of being unfashionable.

The play uses twelve characters, modeled on the signs of the Zodiac, to express a particular view of human nature—that the dynamic of interrelating character types makes inevitable and self-perpetuating the conflicts and shifting harmonies of society. "If there is a lesson to the play," in the author's words, "it is that all the people doing what they have to do could have been a great deal nicer to each other." This affectionate and generous spirit redeems Patrick's world.

The play opens with a prologue in heaven in which the twelve, dressed alike in pretty shifts, sing and dance together in a turning circle. As their personalities differentiate and begin to clash, the patterns of movement shift—and Patrick's staging takes off into sheer brilliance. The prologue reaches and sustains an amazing momentum of hilarity through pure kinetic invention. The figures fall to a proto-earth, where, as if in Eden, they act out the genesis of civilization. Most of the action is about power plays and the question of who will be leader., although one of them says, "I don't know why we should follow the leader. We're not going anywhere!"

The play is performed in an extravagantly imaginative,

decorative, daffy setting by Charles Terrel, lovely, witty costumes by Bobby Kubera and Jack Gilbert, and splashy, seductive lighting by David Andrews. The cast play with youthful enthusiasm and a fine responsiveness to each other. Almost everyone has a vivid character and a cleanly cut approach to it. Kenny Norris is terrifically funny as Ego (Aries), small, confused, but fiercely self-assertive. Denny Leone as Snake (Scorpio) is deliciously vicious. Terry Talley is charmingly put-upon as Justine (Libra), Matthew Diamond is summarily outrageous as Mediak (Aquarius) when, in a climax of frustration, he takes to self-flagellation. Nor are the others to be slighted. The production is a delight.

10/5/72

Rosalyn Drexler

"The Bed Was Full," a play by Rosalyn Drexler, directed by Barbara Forst, at the Moving Company, 46 Great Jones Street.

For some reason Rosalyn Drexler's wonderful plays are not often performed, so it's a rare pleasure to see her farce "The Bed Was Full." The action makes a dizzy kind of domestic sense, though the ingredients seem haphazard: an intermittently obsessed painter, the goddess Kali, a count who wants his gloves steamed, a marital spy and Jesus freak, and an urbane though disheveled married couple. What makes the play such a pleasure is its warm good nature and fullness of feeling and its exuberant freedom with language. In this homey loft production under Barbara Forst's clean, relaxed, zestful direction, the cast romps through the play to everyone's delight. Willy Nickels as the Count and Pauline Walsh as Vera are particularly comical. Jerry Chesnut has some memorably funny, odd moments as Joel, and Josh

Carle is a likably bumbling Lewis. Kali and the painter are played without much conviction, which robs the play of some resonance and connection. But what's there is so much fun that I shouldn't quibble. 10/12/72

Arthur Sainer

"The Thing Itself," a play by Arthur Sainer, directed by Crystal Field, at Theater for the New City (Jane Street).

Arthur Sainer's new play "The Thing Itself" is a combination melodrama and trip inside the head, a comedy full of sorrows, a reality populated with whimsical archetypes. By contrast with last year's "The Celebration: Jooz/Guns/Movies/The Abyss," an epic of the whole history of the Jews, this work is personal, a series of home-movie images of ordinary events extended into pop-paranoiac fantasy, controlled by a tender, comical, original sense of self. The production is an impressive step forward for Theater for the New City, its emerging company, and director Crystal Field.

The play is in one long act divided into innumerable fragments, some of them swift glimpses of isolated actions and images, others fully developed scenes. The play centers on one Louis Nerval, a writer—he sometimes types, throwing away many pages he has written—and his friends and neighbors. The action moves about the theatre as it moves about the city. The principal neighbor is "ailing." We meet him on the street at the beginning of the play as Louis goes about his harried, preoccupied errands. Before long Louis comes to the man's hospital room and, "to do you a kindness," shoots him in his bed. The principal friend is Harold Queer, a food-obsessed pimp to Althea, a splendidly human and self-indulgent whore. There are also Louis's girls, the pretty, collegiately sensitive, self-involved Bettina and an alarmingly aggressive pre-pubescent, neither of the least use to Louis in getting his work done or head together.

The play's forward progress is elusive but unmistakable. Saying, "I'm moving toward coping with the thing itself," Louis seems to be descending into the spiritual hell of isolation. Though he is exquisitely sensitive to those around him, he can get nothing from them. It is a trajectory reminiscent of Ionesco's "Victims of Duty," though less laborious, of Chaplin, of the French Symbolists; Louis never loses his sense of absurdity, the playwright never loses his sense of humor, and the characters go on with their lives. The neighbor's wife repetitively laments the loss of her husband and the world's indifference, then transforms from drab to beauty when enough time has passed. Althea receives her clients one by one and takes them on surprising trips. She and Harold meet at Horn and Hardart for a buoyantly charming production number: there are lively songs and incidental music scattered throughout the play. Harold is being pursued for unspecified reasons by two farcically sinister detectives. When they catch him and torture him sufficiently, he fingers Louis. The detectives tip their hats politely as they pass Louis in the street; he doesn't know what to think. The neighbor at length recovers from his ailment, and everybody comes to the party to celebrate his return. Some of what Louis has experienced is evidently nightmare or delirium, which seems to clear the air. After the party Louis catches Harold raiding his refrigerator and, such the suspiciousness that has accumulated in the atmosphere, Harold impulsively shoots him. The event is tragic, or another intrusion of nightmare, or perhaps he has done him a kindness, we do not know.

When Louis theorizes about art he comes out for the "theatre of mistakes." He treads the edge of sanity—though claiming "insanity's not my strong point"—not out of pathology or in quest of art but because everything really is that way: look around. The form of Sainer's play is the same as its content. It is not an easy play. It doesn't impose or accept the conventions of sense that insulate us from disorientation. But it isn't in any sense forbidding: when Louis "takes a walk inside his head," he takes us along. The play is at every turn inventively diverting and warmly generous of spirit.

George Bartenieff is remarkable as Louis. Occasionally he rants through passages of heavier language rather than making sense of them, but in every other way his performance is superb: disciplined, idiosyncratic, varied, adventurous, subtle, extravagant. In the "walk inside his head" sequence he goes amazingly far out, yet never for a moment loses control. Jordan Charney is full of fun as Harold, and Jacque Lynn Colton is a treat as Althea: both bring exceptional zest to their performances and show a fine understanding of Sainer's wit. Kristen Steen as Bettina, Mark Duffy as the neighbor, and Renata Mooney as his wife are outstandingly good; so are Arthur Rosen, Jerry Jaffe, and David Tice as Althea's three clients. Rick Shannin's lighting takes us from place to place with crisp, forceful precision. The witty costumes are by Jon Teta and Evelyn Schneider. Jim Kurtz, Cosmos Savage, Arthur Rosen, and David Tice provided the multifarious songs. Crystal Field's direction is unusually clean and efficient, whisking the images before us and disappearing them as if by magic, losing nothing of warmth, homeyness, and heart. 12/14/72

Jeff Weiss

"...*And That's How the Rent Gets Paid, Part Two,*" a play by Jeff Weiss, at La Mama.

Jeff Weiss, virtually alone, makes a remarkable range of theatre. Two other actors appear briefly, strangely, like crazy characters on the street. A few objects are set up—a clothesline with odd things hung on it, a ladder, a chair, a table with a candle, a candy rabbit, a seashell. It's less a set than a collection of amulets, or the furniture of the playwright-actor's mind. Tight preoccupied spotlights melt from one color to another, grudgingly picking him out of oblivion, making the eyes work to see as the mind and sympathies are drawn to follow though shocked, appalled, frightened—and then in the next instant all is bright, outwardly sensible, the pity and terror all but gone, and we are watching broad, hilarious satire or, for all we know, a play.

"...And That's How the Rent Gets Paid, Part Two" is another visit with Jeff Weiss at home in his imagination and at loose in the world. It's a horror show, and simultaneously a display of astonishing virtuosity. The show is basically a collection of skits. He picks up the shell and holds it to his ear; it becomes a telephone and he's in the middle of a conversation. He goes to audition at the Pubic Theatre (sic) and becomes half a dozen characters—the fiercely brisk stage manager; a growling, swaggering male hunk with such balls he can't cross his legs; a dotty aging actress who sings a whole mad medley of show songs; a jive black actor who disintegrates before our eyes into pitiful strung-out pleading: "I need a job real bad"; and "Jeff," meek, sincere, innocent, meaning only to do his best, not an image but a person. Also a character on the stage, don't forget. A little glimpse of

Greenwich Avenue: a middle-class Village gay gets talking to a well-built stranger, a sweetly shy, innocently enthusiastic, healthily physical Finnish gymnast visiting New York; back at the man's apartment the Finn slowly transforms into a calculating psychopath, rapacious, ultimately murderous. The fact that Weiss does it by himself deliteralizes the unacceptably factual, makes it play out in our heads like a nightmare—it's not really happening, but it feels more real than if it were. There are quite a few more pieces, large and small, and at intermission Weiss, in yet another charming, fast-talking character, sells peanuts to the audience. That's how the rent gets paid, and the peanuts are good.

Weiss is a phenomenally skillful actor, presenting each of the many characters he creates with breath-stopping verisimilitude. Gross caricature dissolves into stark reality. He is always playing at the brink, at the outer limits of what is possible, permissible, bearable, scaring us repeatedly by how close he comes to the stark facts our art usually conspires to ignore. He plays treacherous games with our dulled sympathies: he enters down a fortuitous staircase, trips, falls, and you're sure he's hurt himself. No, he's acting. If it were real, who would get up and help him? There is a didactic edge to his trickery. You are brilliantly entertained, then suddenly someone is being terrorized, crushed, killed, and you don't know who's doing it, who's the victim, who's the passive passer-by. Again and again, often at extremes of intensity and psychic risk, the latest mask is suddenly not a mask but a person's face. You think he's crazy, he's gone too far out, and then in a flash he has juxtaposed that reality with two or three others equally demented but different, linked by impeccable technical control.

It's like a circus act or a gypsy con, and thus a very basic form of play. It is intensely personal, the imaginative and emotional levels as strong as the physical. Weiss is a great idiosyncratic performer, in a class with Marcel Marceau or Lenny Bruce. His persona is demonic and frightening. Sometimes he certainly goes too far and is really offensive; his hypersensitivity and preoccupation with horror are sometimes hard to swallow. One part of the second act, in which Graham Timbs convincingly takes part, reminded me of Leonard Melfi's "The Shirt," and seemed gratuitously violent. Often too, though, it is a pleasing art. The program concludes with Gertrude Stein's "As a Wife Has a Cow," which Weiss reads magnificently.

Past Tense: Jeff Weiss's "... And That's How the Rent Gets Paid, Part Two" played last weekend at La Mama at the bitter hour of 1 a.m. and word comes to me now that the run has not been extended. I guess he made the rent. Watch for him next time around. 4/26/73

Theater for the New City
1972–73

Petit Cabaret Solennel
The Discovery of America

Short theatre pieces by John Herbert McDowell, Arthur Williams, Ann Harris, Diane di Prima, and George Dennison, with music by Al Carmines; and "The Discovery of America," a play by Diane di Prima, directed by John Herbert McDowell, at Theater for the New City (Jane Street).

The early to middle 1960s seemed then and seem now to be a classical moment in the downtown theatre/dance community, and a selection of delicacies from that moment is now on view at the Theater for the New City. The evening was put together by John Herbert McDowell, a composer, choreographer, and director who has been responsible for an incredible quantity of theatre work through the years, an essential and formative figure in the Off-Off-Broadway scene from the start, and through his dance scores a key connection to the dancers responsible for much of the formal innovation. McDowell is an expert composer with a rich sense of fun and devotion to the integrity of the moment. All this, and the impulses that gave theatre new energy a decade ago, has been submerged of late in the necessary rush to consolidate lives and careers (by securing State Arts Council grants), and it is an occasion of joy to see some of it resurfacing intact.

The first half of McDowell's evening, "Petit Cabaret

Solennel," consists of half a dozen pieces. Several are slight—a charming processional, a song, a finale, and Arthur Williams's clever playlet "The Convert," crisply acted by Renata Mooney, David Tice, and Crystal Field.

Field and her husband George Bartenieff, who run the Theater for the New City, bring back sweet and other memories with "Patter for a Soft Shoe Dance," a gem of the 1964 Judson Poets Theatre season. George Dennison's words mocking Ginsberg, Mailer, and the fads of the time— then obscure, soon to take over—manifest the age with rare precision and wit; Al Carmines's piano score is tuneful and delicately sardonic; Remy Charlip's staging is delicious in its understatement and clarity; Field and Bartenieff perform with élan and eight years more qualification for the earned perspective the author intended.

Most remarkable of the pieces in this cabaret is "Did He Go to Scarsdale?," one of a dozen or so monologues Diane di Prima wrote about her friends to be performed by themselves. (A group of these pieces, collectively titled "Monuments," constituted the last production at the Caffè Cino before it was closed by the License Department in the spring of 1967.) McDowell performs the piece without pants, as it shows him, the text a series of states of mind, personal quirks, everyday obsessions, patterns of relationship, accidental incident, strategies of survival; the writing is brilliantly factual, witty, sharp, free, loving, unsparing; James Waring's staging is by turns abstract, debonair, outrageous, and inescapably direct; McDowell's performance is an extraordinary act of bravery, a complete giving of himself. I was moved to tears.

The second half of the evening is "The Discovery of America," a three-act verse play written by di Prima in 1960, with new lyrics added last summer. McDowell has given it a splendid production with a huge cast of bats, cows,

Puritans, priests, princess, dragon, assorted historical and literary figures, and a swamp. The writing (sensibly inspired by Stein) is free to the point of nonsense, yet sustains itself by tone and texture, bringing to mind an entire early-learned American history, charming yet strangely tragical. The staging—in which McDowell was aided by choreographers Elina Mooney and Cliff Keuter—flows along with it faithfully in a nearly uninterrupted parade of invention, full of delight in the stage and presence of people on it, meeting and completing each image as it goes by. The pace flags vaguely after the mid-point, once all the characters have been introduced, but the ending is exquisite. The aesthetic involved values the amateur, and the performers are satisfied to do what they can: they have the immediacy, charm, and presence of an ideal community theatre. The costumes by Charles Terrel and Carl More are a remarkable and delightful achievement in themselves. Rick Shannin did the varied, effective lighting.

10/5/72

Gossamer Wings

Free theatre by the Angels of Light, at Theater for the New City (Jane Street).

    The new Angels of Light extravaganza is committed to beauty, freedom, and happiness through self-expression. The passive audience doesn't get to have as much fun as the hyperactive people on stage—or is it that we don't know how to enjoy ourselves? I was overwhelmed by glitter and sequins and tinsel during the first part, not having seen such Oriental splendors this side of Chinese opera (the Angels are a lot faster). Somewhere in the middle, after a dozen solos, production numbers, and costume changes by the numberless cast, one of the climaxes turned into a distribution of wine and fruit (bananas and apples) to the audience, who momentarily came to, realized where they were, and smiled back at the performers. After that came a series of exquisite solo dances, each extravagant and brief. Then we sparkled out again on a musical circumnavigation: "By the Waterfall," "Caravan to India," "Bombay Baby," a glimpse of China, a snatch of "Carmen," "Golden Earrings," and a plunge into the cardboard flames of Hell. I get a little dazed with the insouciant succession of happy exotic choruses, and I was glad to see in this Angels production some beginnings of regard for pacing, some opportunity to register the individual presences. The Angels place supreme value on each performer's developing and displaying his or her own fancies, the commonalities of style being joyfulness and outrageous decoration.

Highlights include: Crystal Field singing "Everything's Coming Up Roses," joyful, dauntless. As she segues into "We're in the Money Now," the chorus of Angels seems to be vomiting into the footlights! Rocky Road rules in both his evening's incarnations, caveman and Ice Queen, high on his connection with the audience, simultaneously fabulous and friendly. John Herbert McDowell is Zeus in the title song from "Hello, Zeusy," high-kicking sublimely down the staircase and singing a right-on "Wow!" Hibiscus in silver sequins climaxes a deadpan Harris Family patriotic medley with a straight, feelingful "Remember My Forgotten Man" over the glittering body of his lost soldier love. And more, more, actually too much more. 10/26/72

Ten Best Martyrs of the Year

A play by Seymour Simckes, directed by Crystal Field, at Theater for the New City.

Dick Brukenfeld fell victim last week to *The Voice*'s current plague of production problems. The missing part of his review of "Ten Best Martyrs of the Year" said it was one of the worst plays he had ever seen. I, on the other hand, thoroughly enjoyed it. The fact that a particular critic doesn't like or doesn't get a play can either mean it's no good or that it isn't his cup of tea. Some people don't like tea. It's terrible that we *Voice* critics are the only way many theatres can reach their potential audience. The whole critic setup breaks down in a situation of so much diversity, when different theatres serve different gods and caesars, seek different publics, speak different languages. I'm being very polite about this. I actually feel the *Voice* theatre section has a responsibility to the theatre scene it helped create. We're not its judges, we're part of it, we should be its defenders. We shouldn't shoot things down just because we don't like them.

"Ten Best Martyrs of the Year" is a play by Seymour Simckes about ten rabbis impaled on a dilemma by the Emperor Hadrian, who tells them he will kill all their people unless they martyr themselves: "Either you ten or your whole nation except you ten." It's an old story; the situation has a timeless profundity about it, and when Rabbi Akiva, the Man, goes to heaven to confront a God who has gone into a mysterious coma, the resonances are mythic.

Simckes's play is extraordinarily strange, its historical and philosophical solemnity enlivened by all kinds of stylistic intrusions, linguistic frivolity, and almost hysterical inventiveness. Or so it seems in Crystal Field's lavishly detailed production. Her use of trapdoors for entrances and exits gives the play unique movement, and the other parts of the production have the same fresh practicality. There are some awkward performances in the large cast, but the actors' devotion to what they are doing makes up for that. Theater for the New City eschews slickness, and their dauntless, rough and ready way has flashes of real immediacy and life. Arthur Rosen, self-effacing in the masked role of Akiva, makes us feel the extreme courage of a modest man's challenge to stupid fate. George Bartenieff offers a series of rich cartoon pictures of a very crazy Hadrian. There are elements of genius in his work, moments so vivid and original that you long for fewer lapses into distraction. Lee Kissman is deliciously funny as Suetonius, the Emperor's secretary. Roger Trefousse is charmingly real as a Stoic, and Mark Duffy and Hugh Jackson are funny and sinister as Gabriel and Michael.

11/8/73

Last Columns
1974

State of the Theatre

Last night I dreamed that the Caffè Cino had fallen down. What a relief! In reality the tenement building at 31 Cornelia Street stands intact, the narrow storefront that was the magic space of theatre used these years as a storeroom for French antiques. In my dream the side of the building had collapsed; the shops next door were gone, replaced with others. Josie, the landlady who used to bang on the ceiling when the late show got too forceful, had a new balcony on her narrowed second-floor domain and sat there surrounded by mattresses and white petunias. I walked down Cornelia Street polishing windows.

I have been working day and night on my own play, "Prussian Suite," which opens this week at Theatre Genesis. I haven't seen anything. I haven't wanted to see anything.

An Italian journalist recently asked me to write something short about the present state of our American theatre. This is what I gave him:

Theatre reflects the national confusion. It's as if we don't want anything expressed: exposure of truth only adds to our embarrassment. There is no room in our lives for passion, or no belief in it, and fun only comes in expensive packages. Nixon loves Debbie Reynolds, Rockefeller and Reagan back Carol Channing, Liza Minnelli packs the Winter Garden as Barbra Streisand did with "Funny Girl," without benefit of a vehicle.

A number of idiosyncratic theatre artists—Robert

Wilson, Meredith Monk, Richard Foreman, a few more—opt for brilliantly objectified personal visions. They are variously anti-theatrical, studiedly playing against most essentials of the tradition, such as the generous esprit of performance, the vitality and variety of natural rhythms, the comforting clarity of narrative, the free possibility of entertainment. They hold the audience in a trance and present their shows as art objects. Similarly, they are anti-drama, excluding personal interchange from their stages or abstracting and aestheticizing it to death.

The "new" styles have been dubbed Visual Theatre, as if theatre were not always visual. Theatre is multisensory, social, collaborative. These beautiful experiments in isolating its modalities appeal to us as connoisseurs. Theatre becomes private, self-valuing, esoteric, like communication among scientists.

These few are sustaining the spirit of experiment, but the theatre meantime has gone to sleep. The fine ensemble work of the past decade has penetrated the university and intellectual theatre while vanishing from the public stages. The disbanding of the Open Theatre this winter seems to mark the closing of that era in New York, as the departure of the Living Theatre in 1963 ended the possibility of a committed poetic theatre Off-Broadway, as the end of the Caffè Cino in 1968, after Joe Cino's death the year before, broke the wave of enterprising new playwrights. A busy, compulsively productive scene sprang up in the wake of all that, but it is continuing now mostly on administrative momentum and vague careerism.

The people who might be exhilarating performers are languishing because nobody knows what's worth doing. Sam Shepard and possibly a few other playwrights keep getting better, going deeper, speaking more fully. Theater for the New City, the Ridiculous Theatrical Company, and a few other troupes keep paying some authentic homage to the Muse. The life force is here, of course, but its present form is discontinuous, unsupported, amorphous, its morale unmentionable. So theatre continues to express its community. 1/31/74

My Big Week

Some Music by John Herbert McDowell, at Judson Memorial Church; "Freaky Pussy," a musical by Harvey Fierstein, music by Ronnie Fierstein, directed by Harvey Tavel, presented by the New York Theatre Ensemble at the Arena Theatre; Ekatherina Sobechanskaya Dances with the Trockadero Gloxinia Ballet, at La Mama.

John Herbert McDowell put on a retrospective concert of some of his music at Judson Church last week and created an occasion of great joy and positive energy. McDowell has been a prolific and ubiquitous composer for downtown theatre and dance for the past ten or fifteen years, as well as a choreographer-director, sometime dancer and actor, and ever-helpful, encouraging presence and friend to art. The Judson concert was a rare opportunity to listen to his music. It sounded great.

I used the word "great" advisedly. The big new piece, "God Has Gone Up With a Shout," had that kind of beauty, force, and conviction. Dedicated to four friends of the composer who have died, it is a setting for chorus and chamber orchestra of texts from Robert Louis Stevenson, the Book of Revelation, and Arthur Williams. Great intensity of feeling is conveyed in expertly resourceful music, as American as Ives, alive with McDowell's warmth, whimsical humor, and exuberance. To have written so affirmative a work in response to death is an act of immense courage and generosity.

The other major work on the program was "Modulamen," a mini-concerto for harpsichord and string quartet that dates from 1962. Played with concentration and brilliance by Stoddard Lincoln (for whom it was written) and the strings, the piece carried the listener on a remarkable mood trip, deep into the dark and out again. I wish it were available on record; I'd like to hear it again.

The concert was structured with an easy-going but sure-handed theatricality, with a number of "Processing Pieces" chanted by a large and engagingly varied chorus walking through the space ("processing" as in procession); solo songs; tape pieces; opera excerpts; and musical resources ranging from pipe organ and harp to toy piano. The concert ended with "Lyra Davidica," a rousing hymn-setting for audience participation that had everyone singing "Alleluia!" The lucky audience was left screaming with joy and admiration.

***

"Freaky Pussy" has been denounced in Phebe's more than any play I can remember. Harvey Fierstein, the author and star, certainly asks for it. His opening night audience included most of the people who invented the genre he is crudely exploiting, if it exists. His vulgar tastelessness seems to be a clumsy copy of some clumsy thing I can't quite identify. His ambition is shockingly naked. He declares himself to be a "star" but in a second-hand style that only rarely worked for its creators.

I wrote a straightforward put-down of "Freaky Pussy" for last week's *Voice*, but it got left out of the paper. In the meantime I've had a couple of phone calls and a long, mind-boggling letter from Fierstein, as well as an extra week's worth of the publicity campaign or whatever it is. I'm getting caught up in it: somehow all this "scene" energy makes the play's painfulness really disturbing.

Here is what I wrote last week:

The play is set in the men's toilet of the Broadway-Lafayette subway station. Blanche Yankowitz (played by Fierstein) works there as a prostitute; the other caricaturish, crazed people are her clients and competitors. Into this hellish underworld come Stanley and Stella, Blanche's twin sister, who set the place up as a restaurant. (There is no satire of Tennessee Williams, merely the borrowing.) The action is mainly a series of hysterical altercations between Blanche and everybody else. Various songs and musical numbers are performed, and a series of murders or suicides are committed in the toilet booths.

Fierstein is a disciple of the playwright Ronald Tavel, and most of the writing consists of word-play and puns, successfully concealing meaning, Tavelian in manner but without Tavel's wit, depth, and skill. The imagery owes most to the dramatist H. M. Koutoukas, especially his sewer fantasia "With Creatures Make My Way," but without Koutoukas's heart and love of beauty. The play is performed (especially by the author) as if it were screamingly funny, though most of its jokes are camp clichés, its content composed equally of self-indulgent ugliness and shallow despair. We all may sometimes need to roll in the gutter, but not for our careers. Fierstein's problem as an artist is not to succeed in this style but to get free from its dead hand.

Sitting close to the actors, the audience at "Freaky Pussy" are forced to smile back at them out of general good will. The vision Fierstein and his collaborators show us is nasty and pitiful, though, not amusing or titillating. Taken seriously, they seem to be agents of the dark forces, perhaps unwitting but still to be resisted. To go along with their entertainment is to conspire in a cynicism and despair that seem affected, repulsive, and unnecessary. At the end of the play, which is mercifully brief, Fierstein drops the grand-dame manner to sing simply of what seem to be his own feelings. The moment would be touching if one hadn't already been backed into the corner of rejection. Even if you accept the truth of this nightmare vision, it's hard to enjoy having it inflicted on you.

At this moment in the writing of this review (last week) Harvey Fierstein calls me on the telephone to ask if I know who's covering his play for *The Voice*. We are both listening to "Porgy and Bess." The conversation is friendly, though I tell him I am writing negatively. "I think it's strange," he says, "that people get so upset about a little sexual suicide."

Clio Young, toothless and enormous in his dress, adds the transcendent realness of a true performer. Luis Macia is an arrestingly peculiar Stanley. Ruth Brandeis and Maxine Albert have some effective moments as Stella and Anna Magnetic. But it's really impossible to come to terms with such self-contradictory material. Fierstein, snappily growling out asides and one-liners, striding about striking poses, and raging through tirades, presents more of a personality than a performance. The actors seem almost unthinkingly thrown together, and Harvey Tavel's direction is sketchy at best. Donald L. Brooks made the play a handsomely elaborate set that fills without shaping the wide-angle space of the Arena Theatre, giving a panoramic view of what ought to be intimate and claustral. This kind of mismatch between style and content, this abuse of reality, is somehow at the heart of the play's exceptional disagreeableness.

***

The downtown gala of the week was the appearance by Ekatherina Sobechanskaya and the Trockadero Gloxinia

Ballet at La Mama for three midnights. Larry Ree and his troupe of male ballerinas are better than ever, and the program was full, varied, and tasty. The form is travesty, but in the event it has remarkable charm and beauty, thanks to the disciplined sincerity and graceful faux-naïve humor of the dancers. The classical group ballets—a "Russian Snowflakes" and a "Raymonda" third act—are outlandishly comic and strangely enchanting at the same time, an exhilarating combination of effects.

Among the highlights were a fiery "Firebird" excerpt by Anthony Alfonso, danced with chunky insouciance by Tamara Karpova; an elaborate "modern" group dance in the Graham manner by Olga Plushinskaya, "The Tragic Heart of Gloom and Despair"; and a brilliant pas de deux between Sobechanskaya, majestic in a towering wig, and a tiny danseur noble. What makes the performance so enjoyable is the feeling of love, the sense that the dancers are casting aside doubt and making their fondest dreams come true. Their humor is not mockery or self-deprecation but awareness. This is not just camp, it is homage.   2/28/74

Dialogue with Arthur Sainer
On Richard Foreman

"Pain(t)" and "Vertical Mobility," two new works written and directed by Richard Foreman, presented by the Ontological-Hysteric Theatre at 141 Wooster Street.

Smith: Richard Foreman's theatre work has a powerful negative magnetism. He has a major critical reputation; but I can't find anybody willing to go see his new work with me. I can hardly get myself to go. He is doing two new pieces, and the press release insists: BOTH PIECES MUST BE

SEEN. I went to "Pain(t)" like a good boy, but when time came for "Vertical Mobility," I couldn't face it. "Pain(t)" was painful without evident purpose. Foreman's new buzzer is much louder than the old one, and the music amplification is crude and brutal. I didn't mind being bored. I expected that. "Particle Theory" was boring, but I liked it. "Pain(t)," though, is not only boring, it is aggressively unpleasant. I felt assaulted, not in the name of anything such an assault might be relevant to, but in the name of art.

Sainer: I understand, I think, what you're feeling. My own experience with Foreman's work is that while watching it I want to be both there and not there, I find the work tremendously exciting and tremendously...maybe not boring but enervating. But I also don't mind the "boredom," it's relaxing, it allows me to be there almost in whatever way I please. It's also this very freedom, this ability for the spectator to be so separate from the material, that seems to me a virtue and a liability. I maintain my freedom but I feel disconnected. Also I worry for the sense of community, and I'd like to explore that a little later.

The aggression you felt in "Pain(t)" I also felt but as a new phenomenon in Foreman's work. Other people have had to point out to me examples of aggression before I become aware of them: the buzzer, the stage lights that glare into the audience, the sexist nature of "Pain(t)." But I can accept the aggression as simply the way Foreman wants it, I can accept the truth of that aggression.

Smith: But why put yourself in its path? I feel myself being co-opted into a critical conspiracy. There's something weird about it when I take theatre seriously as a critic but wouldn't recommend it to anyone as a friend. The new Foreman has me confused. I'm tickled by his sensibility, I recognize the twinkle, I like the audacious idiosyncrasy of what he does, I admire the care and consistency, I can appreciate the home-theatrics aspects, the loft, the air that this is just something Richard and his art-world friends got up to amuse themselves. I think it's funny. But this time I felt a sourness, I saw a cold, maybe contemptuous look in the actors' eyes. I suspect it is a product of the foundation funding, the establishment of this work amid the high decor of the West, which makes people capitalize on their styles rather than keeping them alive. There is a contradiction between the original eccentric charm of Foreman's work and the grimness of the present experience: the uptight seating, the aural assault, and the subject matter of "Pain(t)," which is the anguish and craziness of being an artist.

It takes itself so seriously! When the Living Theatre does "Seven Meditations on Political Sado-Masochism," I expect it to take a certain discipline to put myself in tune with the work, but that's because it's an attempt to think about things that are horrifying, implicating, deadly serious. The solemnity of the event is appropriate to the subject. Foreman, though, is concocting an intellectual divertissement. He is intelligent and sophisticated and subtle, and he shows that the pain artists go through is in large part self-important and ridiculous. But the pain he inflicts on the spectator is real.

Sainer: It's interesting that you see the new Foreman work as grim and solemn.

Smith: Not the work itself but the experience of seeing it.

Sainer: I see it as positively lighthearted. "Vertical Mobility" and "Pain(t)" are positively romps in the park compared to an early work like "Total Recall," which offered little movement, where the movement and sound shared the sense of a Robert Wilson night in Catatonia (a place I just made up). Perhaps the ugly character you're sensing in the new work related to the speeded-up dynamics, to the fact that characters are beginning to move and speak at life-time speed. At that speed, aggressive vibrations may seem more blatant than at slower paces. The "charm" aspect in Foreman doesn't contradict our sense of grimness—your sense of grimness, but mine too. I tend to see the work as a field of sober energy with joyous bubbles rising. The bubbles are almost aberrations, but they are forces released by the general sobriety of his vision and not contradictory elements. I recognize that audiences find some moments very amusing and they laugh, but laughter hardly ever seems to me an appropriate response to Foreman's work, it just seems to be beside the point. The craziness never seems to me crazy in the context of what he's doing, because as a matter of fact it's all crazy. It's as serious as the Living Theatre, but it's a private seriousness, the concerns are aesthetic, philosophical—phenomenological, I believe—and not cosmically serious as the Living Theatre's are. Maybe that kind of seriousness has its inappropriate aspect when one considers the crisis of the world—forthcoming mass starvation, ecological disasters, the growing corporate stranglehold on the world's people, and the like. Maybe that's why I feel uncomfortable and restless and bothered by a community of people watching the Foreman work like so many rabbits in a trance. At its worst the room takes on a self-congratulatory air. But there's something else, an integrity which I find morally beautiful, and a sense of constant discovery which always excites me. In "Vertical Mobility" there are visual verticals, crosses, spire-like constructions, aural vertical images that have to do with events like flying, and these verticals suggest that the world we inhabit is open to being re-seen, reconstructed. It's a way of reconstituting phenomena, and it's lovely. But I could do without being assaulted by the buzzer. I have a friend who slept through "Particle Theory" except when she would be wakened intermittently by the buzzer. Maybe the buzzer is akin to the forte chord in Haydn's "Surprise" Symphony. Maybe it's there to get you back into consciousness, I don't know. Anyway, she keeps asking me how Foreman and his buzzer are.

Smith: Yes, or it's like being hit with the stick in Zen meditation—you don't mind that it hurts, in fact you welcome it. But that's not the point, as your talk of verticals reminds me. The buzzer, like the metronomes and other repeated sounds, is a structure delineator. It's one of the ways Foreman reminds us that what we are seeing is a contrived art event rather than a spontaneous real event. But I already know that. I know time is passing without Richard hitting me over the head with his buzzer. The alienation devices were invented to puncture a soppy sentimental identification response, but now it's all turned around, and our emotions—irritation and resentment—are stimulated not by the reality content but by the art mechanics. Foreman's strategy is bizarre, making a career on works that drive people away. The voyeuristic seductions of "Pain(t)"—the beautiful naked women in the French-postcard poses—are part of this pull-push process, balanced by the increased hostility. It feels, though, more like acting-out. I don't think his vision is so sober, I think it's playful and frivolous and comic. For me the most convincing thing in "Pain(t)" was the low-down vaudeville sequence in which they tried to shove the word PAINTER up Rhoda's ass. I can enjoy expressions of sheer fuck-you hostility, healthy and politically apt or not, just for vitality and exuberance. But the style, in its present hardened form, doesn't so often release the spirit as crush it. Whether or not you liked it, it was worth seeing at least one Foreman piece just for the idiosyncrasies, but now I'm stranded. What are we congratulating ourselves on? Being in the know and ahead of the crowd? Being tough enough to take it?   4/11/74

Ave atque vale

Spring is here already, end of another phase of death and rest, beginning of another cycle. Why are our city lives patterned contrary to nature's time: we are frantic in winter, confused and uncertain in spring, we go somewhere else and take the summer off if we can, and in the fall, when the sun's energy is fading, when the whole world around us is lying back and laying low, we rev ourselves up and start all over again. I am going to Denver, to get in one last lick of work before the season ends.

Some changes haven't happened. I keep reading my state of mind as theatrical critique: my life has become a theatre journal. A strange pattern has caught me this year. I have got stuck downtown, out on a particular limb of the tree of theatre. I moved to Brooklyn last year hoping to get some perspective on Manhattan, to see more of its theatres, concerts, museums, ballets, even movies and more of its life than my own East Village neighborhood. It hasn't worked.

I made it to Carnegie Hall one time in a carload of friends. The Mahler was starting as we panted up the last flight of stairs into the top of the top balcony: that was the rush. We took one of the musicians downtown afterwards for asparagus and wine and music talk. We had the top down, and ran out of gas on the FDR Drive and left the car and walked.

I saw Maria Callas at last, in concert at C. W. Post College on Long Island, long past her prime, still a great theatre artist.

A friend and I went to the Metropolitan Museum once, late in the day. We had a sandwich in the Junior Museum and listened to two old men talk. We saw a terrific bunch of little watercolors and an overpoweringly rich exhibition of women's evening dresses from my mother's girlhood. The guards did a bullying number on us on the way out.

I saw three movies, "Day for Night," "The New Land," and "The Three Musketeers." I loved the first two; the third seemed to be an imitation of itself, its sly self-mockery amusing but disengaging, irresponsible. Oh, and I also saw a high-political Godard film, "A Thing or Two I Know About Her," which was unbearably pretentious. Such attitudinizing!

My extratheatrical friends who go to plays for the pleasure tell me they are getting discouraged with the theatre. I don't know what to recommend. I have the impression that lots of good work is going on that I haven't seen.

I haven't seen anything at the Public Theatre. I haven't seen any of Joe Papp's productions at Lincoln Center. I haven't seen anything on Broadway except "The Visit," which I didn't like. I haven't seen much at the Circle Rep, WPA, Theatre at St. Clement's, or even Theater for the New City. I haven't seen anything at the Manhattan Theatre Club, the Cubiculo, Clark Center, or the Roundabout. I have never seen anything at CSC. I didn't see anything at the Chelsea Theatre Center this year. I didn't see any of the English productions. I didn't even see "Moon for the Misbegotten," which I know I would have loved.

What is the meaning of this? Am I turning into Jonas Mekas? One evening last fall I caught myself running along Eleventh Street toward *The Voice*: I had ten minutes to deliver my column and get to a theatre clear across town, and there were no taxis. Running. Wait, I thought, this is crazy, and I slowed down. I didn't go to that play, had dinner instead. It doesn't make sense to go to the theatre crazy, hungry, head full of the day's rush. I don't know what bearing a critic's responses can have on anybody else's. You have to postulate a well-organized life, and who has time for that?

I kept a selective but fairly constant eye on the season at La Mama. It seems to take two or three nights a week keeping abreast of what old friends and colleagues are doing and taking in the major events, essentials like the Living Theatre, the Bread and Puppet Theatre, Robert Wilson—the list would go on to include Peter Brook, Richard Foreman, Meredith Monk, Jeff Weiss, Tom O'Horgan, Andrei Serban, the People Show. (This is a season when the playwrights have not been much in evidence and the Open Theatre has stopped performing.) This leaves little time to be open to anything new, and sets a high threshold of attention. The thing is, there has been a great broadening of theatre activity, making the categories (Off-Off and such) all but useless, making any kind of particularizing overview consuming if not impossible. The various *Voice* critics seem to have their arenas: Julius Novick for Broadway, Dick Brukenfeld for Off-Broadway, Michael Feingold for classics and literature, Arthur Sainer for the political and the avant garde—and me for what? I won't try to say. I'm just playing with words.

It gets serious, though, when so many lives are caught up in it, when subsidy becomes a form of welfare, when humane values become confused with aesthetics, when art has to sell itself to bureaucracy and the audience is neglected. I myself like to make theatre the way I like to play music, for the moment. Tell me a story and let me put my thoughts away.

4/25/74

Index

Joyce Aaron, 52
Jeremy Abbott, 289
Roger Acorn, 299
Charles Adams, 56
David Adams, 301
After the Fall, 149-154, 249
Agon, 49
John Albano, 294
Edward Albee, 15-20, 21, 24-28, 82-88, 203
Maxine Albert, 323
Theoni V. Aldredge, 303
Anthony Alfonso, 324
Becklan Algan, 14
Alice in Wonderland, 47
All Day for a Dollar, 199-200
Billie Allen, 88
Donald M. Allen, 73
Seth Allen, 293-295
L'Amant Militaire, 254-255
America Hurrah, 285
The American Dream, 19-20
American Place Theatre, 188-190
...And That's How the Rent Gets Paid, Part Two, 309-311
And They Put Handcuffs on the Flowers, 256-257
...And Things That Go Bump in the Night, 184-186
Jim Anderson, 101
David Andrews, 305
Andrew Amic Angelo, 288
Angels of Light, 260, 314-315
Susan Anspach, 171
Maria Antinakes, 225=226
Mary Anthony, 44
James Antonio, 167
Karl von Appen, 112
Michael Arian, 294-295
Will Steven Armstrong, 247

Fernando Arrabal, 85-86, 256-257
Larry Arrick, 188-190
Antonin Artaud, 216-28
As a Wife Has a Cow, 311
Bennyt Averyt, 280
Hermione Baddeley, 92
Word Baker, 5-6, 79-81
John Bakos, 239
George Balanchine, 49
The Bald Soprano, 34, 73-75, 121-122
William Ball, 158-161
Balm in Gilead, 186-188
Sierra Bandit, 297
The Baptism, 141-143
Eugenio Barba, 234
Claude Barbazon, 193
Jared Barclay, 20
Brunetta Barnett, 12
Richard Barr, 18, 19, 21, 28, 82-88, 250
Julian Barry, 242
Tony Barsha, 179-182
Don Barshay, 193
George Bartenieff, 51, 52-53, 57, 101, 308, 313, 317
Nicolas Bataille, 32-34, 73, 121-122
The Beard, 145-148
A Beautiful Day, 53-58
The Beauty Part, 89-90
John C. Becher, 30, 71, 83, 84, 86
Julian Beck, 101-110, 285
Samuel Beckett, 14-15, 21-24, 28-30, 82-83, 285
The Bed Was Full, 304-306
Robert Beers, 297
Cynthia Belgrave, 12, 88
Carmilo Bene, 119
Jerry Benjamin, 141-143
Robert Benson, 171
Tanya Berezin, 209

Index

Berliner Ensemble, 111-113
Kenneth Bernard, 298-300
Melvin Bernhardt, 253
Eric Berry, 28
Bertha, 82
Bigfoot, 269
George Birimisa, 190-193
Lauren Bivens, 142
Black-Eyed Susan, 292, 297
The Blacks, 11-13
Paul Boesing, 64
Bluebeard, 296
Gary Bolling, 134
Micheline Bona, 121
Sudie Bond, 20, 51, 82-83, 84
Haal Borske, 208-209
Julie Bovasso, 2, 66-70
David Bowie, 260
Jane Bowles, 129-132
Mary Boylan, 202
Peter Boyle, 140
The Boys in the Band, 250-251
Joe Brainard, 143
Ruth Brandeis, 323
Carola Braunbock, 112
Bread and Puppet Theatre, 271-272, 332
Bertolt Brecht, 36, 111-113, 216-218
Jani Brenn, 280
Gordon Bressace, 295
The Brig, 98-101, 219
Richard Bright, 148
Burt Brinckerhoff, 14
John D. Brockmeyer, 293, 297
Peter Brook, 122-128, 216-218, 328
Alfred Brooks, 44
Donald L. Brooks, 196, 205, 257-259, 289-291, 323
Kenneth H. Brown, 98-101
Roscoe Lee Brown, 12
The Brown Crown, 208-209
Lenny Bruce, 241-244, 311
Dick Brukenfeld, 316, 332

Norman Bush, 134
Richard Burton, 162-165
Scott Burton, 265-267
Shelley Burton, 139
John Bury, 220
Caffè Cino, 4, 38-48, 203-215, 233, 304-305, 313, 318, 319
Maria Callas, 329
Jimmy Camicia, 259-261
Denis Cannan, 126
Dominick Capobianco, 183
Josh Carle, 305-306
Carlos Among the Candles, 144-145
Al Carmines, 49-60, 140, 282, 313
Carnegie Hall, 329
Lewis Carroll, 38, 47
Brandy Carson, 39
Nicola Cernovich, 82
Godfrey M. Cambridge, 12
Barbara Ann Camp, 228
Veronica Castang, 142
The Celebration: Jooz/Guns/Movies/ The Abyss, 306
John Chace, 61
Joseph Chaikin, 78, 123, 185-186, 284-287
Wynn Chamberlain, 229
Changes, 242
Carol Channing, 318
Mari-Claire Charba, 229
Remy Charlip, 53-56, 59, 82, 313
Jordan Charney, 308
Chelsea Theatre Center, 278-281
Jerry Chesnut, 305
Chicago, 178-179
Marilyn Chris, 280
Nancy Christofferson, 59-60
Chic Ciccarelli, 101
Ryszard Cieslak, 114-118, 123, 244
Joe Cino, 42-48, 199-200, 205-207, 210-215, 316
Circle in the Square, 8-11
Hampton Clanton, 134

James Nisbet Clark, 73-75
Philip Clark, 208
The Clown, 207-208
Harold Clurman, 95-97
The Cockettes, 260, 292
Ronald Colby, 47
The Collection, 71-73
Rufus Collins, 101, 141
Michele Collison, 183
Jacque Lynn Colton, 205, 209, 308
Frederick Combs, 251
Conquest of the Universe, 229-232
The Constant Prince, 113-118
The Convert, 310
Ralph Cook, 176-179, 182-183
Alice Cooper, 260
Corn, 296-298
Risa Corsin Chamber Theatre Group, 45
Mariclare Costello, 154
Frank Cotner, 141
Cowboys, 176-178
Michael Craig, 220
Peter Craig, 239
Kathleen Cramer, 303
Jane Cronin, 74
Hume Cronyn, 164-165
Mart Crowley, 250-251
Cubiculo, 330
Gretel Cummings, 51, 52-53, 56
Jerry Cunliffe, 239
George Curley, 6
Richard Currie, 297
Robert D. Currie, 24
Steve Curry, 241
Jackie Curtis, 259-260, 287-289
Marcel Cuvelier, 122
Kathleen Dabney, 66
Daddy Violet, 190-192
Robert Dagny, 39
Robert Dahdah, 199
Estelle R. Dallas, 288
Leora Dana, 132

Candy Darling, 260, 287
Donald Davis, 85-86
R. G. Davis, 254-255
Deafman Glance, 276
Deathwatch, 85-86
Denis Deegan, 39-40
The Deer Park, 246-250
Igor Demjen, 274
George Dennison, 139-140, 313
Desire Under the Elms, 8-11
Ken Dewey, 35
Colleen Dewhurst, 9-10
Matthew Diamond, 304
Did He Go to Scarsdale?, 313
Melinda Dillon, 18
Diane di Prima, 139, 312-314
The Discovery of America, 312-314
Billie Dixon, 148
John P. Dodd, 56, 60, 145, 183, 229, 239, 294
Bianca D'Origlia, 120-121
Diane Dorr Dorynek, 225-226
David Doyle, 89
Rosalyn Drexler, 50-51, 305-306
Robert Drivas, 186
Alice Drummond, 20, 85
Mark Duffy, 143, 308, 319
William Duffy, 66
Delia Duke, 183
The Dumbwaiter, 71-73
Mildrid Dunnock, 93
Mae Durnhelm, 209
Dutchman, 133
Ronald Dyson, 241
Sally Eaton, 241
Joyce Ebert, 161
Education of the Girlchild, 272-273
The Eighth Ditch, 140-141
Richard Dow, 196
Dana Elcar, 71
Alex Elias, 94
Michael Elias, 101
Gene Elman, 183

Index   *335*

Embers, 47
Empire State, 211-212
Endgame, 21, 82-83, 285
Erich Engel, 112
Alvin Epstein, 171
Morris Erby, 12
Victor Eschbach, 182-183
Linda Eskenas, 38
Eunuchs of the Forbidden City, 291-293, 296
Euripedes, 289-291
Evidence, 267-269
Tom Eyen, 65-66
Ron Faber, 257
Edwin Fancher, 1
The Fantasticks, 5-6
Michael Feingold, 284, 332
Gene Feist, 85-86
Crystal Field, 57, 306-308, 313, 315, 316-317
Harvey Fierstein, 257-259, 290, 320-323
Ronnie Fierstein, 320
Michael Figgis, 270-271
Warren Finnerty, 101
Firehouse Theatre, 62
Neil Flanagan, 39, 40, 186-188, 209-210
Richard Foreman, 267-269, 319, 324-328, 331
Jo Ann Forman, 228
Maria Irene Fornés, 56
Fred Forrest, 208
Barbara Forst, 305-306
Henderon Forsythe, 73
Gloria Foster, 171
Paul Foster, 47, 201, 235-239, 242
Edgardo Franceschi, 297
Francis Francine, 231
Gene Frankel, 11-13
Frankenstein, 103-107, 182
Ed Franzen, 44
Freaky Pussy, 329-323

Al Freeman Jr., 137
Leonard Frey, 88, 251
Robert Frink, 57
From the Second City, 242
Ralph Funicello, 303
Funny Girl, 318
Funnyhouse of a Negro, 87-88
Futz, 233-235, 242
Roland Gagnon, 282-283
Gallows Humor. 84-85
Bill Gamble, 295
Vincent Gardenia, 83, 85
Rita Gardner, 6
Leo Garen, 133-138, 246-250
Jim Gates, 101
Larry Gates, 161
Patricia Gaul, 257
The General Returns from One Place to Another, 141-142
Jean Genet, 11-13, 85-86
Rudi Gernreich, 222
Alice Ghostley, 89
John Gielgud, 27-28, 164
Jack Gilbert, 302
Laura Gilbert, 270-271
John Gilman, 205
Hermione Gingold, 94-95
Alan Ginsberg, 278-281, 313
Glamour, Glory, and Gold, 287-288
Robert Glaudini, 303
Glocasta, 120-121
Christine Gloger, 113
God Has Gone Up with a Shout, 320-321
The Golden Circle, 304-305
Carlo Goldoni, 254
Peter Goldfarb, 129-132
Rene Gonzales, 66
Stephanie Gordon, 178
Gorilla Queen, 226-229
Cliff Gorman, 242-245, 251
Gossamer Wings, 314-315
Saul Gottlieb, 103

Heller Grace, 224
Beverly Grant, 143, 202, 231
Reuben Greene, 250
Jane Greenwood, 161
George Grizzard, 18
Maurice Grosser, 282
Jerzy Grotowski, 113-118, 123, 234
John Guare, 252-253
David Guerdon, 32
Barbara Guest, 47
Lee Guilliatt, 56, 59
Gurton's Apocalyptic Needle, 243
Tyrone Guthrie Theatre, 183-185
Michael Hadge, 303
Walter Hadler, 182
Uta Hagen, 18
Larry Hagman, 89
Hair, 240-241, 295
Quinn Halford, 228
Norman Hall, 67
Peter Hall, 219-220
Hamlet, 162-165, 172-175
John Hancock, 168-172
Helen Hanft, 66
Happy Days, 21, 28-30
Michael Hardstark, 280
Jessica Harper, 269
Ann Harris, 312-313
Barbara Harris, 94
George Harris II, 228
Walter Harris, 209, 241
Peter Hartman, 144, 285
Peter Harvey, 251, 253
The Haunted Host, 42
The Hawk, 179-182
Gary Haynes, 134
David Hays, 10, 137
David Kerry Heefner, 228
John Heffernan, 28
Henry Street Playhouse, 44
Fred Herko, 30-31, 50
Baarton Heyman, 172
Hibiscus (George Harris III), 315

Eddie Hicks, 181
Gerald Hiken, 7
James Hilbrandt, 228
Arthur Hill, 18
Kenneth Hill, 139
Regina Hirsch, 224
Harold Hobson, 79
Byrd Hoffman School of Birds, 267, 273-277
Dustin Hoffman, 190
Ferdi Hoffman, 186
Jane Hoffman, 20, 84, 86
William M. Hoffman, 42
Hal Holbrook, 156-157, 161
Joan Holden, 254
Anthony Holland, 78
Pat Holland, 199
Ellen Holly, 88
Ian Holm, 220
Christopher Holt, 59
The Holy Ghostly, 243
Home Movies, 50-51
The Homecoming, 219-220
David Hooks, 20
John Horn, 14
Hot Peaches, 259-261
How Come You Don't Dig Chicks?, 190-192
Henry Howard, 101
Jim Howard, 47
Michael Howard, 78-79
The Hunter, 301-303
William Hutt, 28
Icarus's Mother, 203-204
In Search of the Cobra Jewels, 257-259
In the Summer House, 129-132
William Inge, 47
Anthony Ingrassia, 260
Inner City, 241, 245
Eugene Ionesco, 73-79, 262-265
Steven Ben Israel, 101
Istanbul, 193-196

Index

Paul Jabara, 241
Carl Jablonski, 34
Glenda Jackson, 126
Hugh Jackson, 317
Jerry Jaffe, 309
James Jennings, 139, 205
Salome Jens, 152, 156, 161
Jesus Christ Superstar, 241-245
O-Lan Johnson, 182
Scarlett Johnson, 182
Christopher Jones, 52
James Earl Jones, 11-12, 166
Mark Jones, 126
Tom Jones, 5-6
LeRoi Jones, 133-138, 140-143
The Journey of the Fifth Horse, 188-190
Jerry Joyner, 229
Judson Dance Theatre, 34-37
Judson Poets' Theatre, 49-60, 226-229, 313, 320-321
Donald Julian, 61
Kaddish, 278-281
Michael Kahn, 76-79, 87-88
Wolf Kaiser, 112
Robert Kalfin, 279
Peter Kalisch, 112
Tamara Karpova, 324
Leon Katz, 282
Susan Kaufman, 52-53
Elia Kazan, 149-154
George Kearns, 61
Elizabeth Keen, 282-283
Eddie Kenmore, 40
Adrienne Kennedy, 87-88
Lin Kennedy, 38
Jack Kerouac, 1
Walter Kerr, 95-97
Cliff Keuter, 314
Siegfried Killian, 113
Willa Kim, 88
Sally Kirkland, 239
Lee Kissman, 178, 181, 314

Kitchenette, 224-226
Edward I. Koch, 212-213
Kenneth Koch, 82
Arthur L. Kopit, 93-95
Lawrence Kornfeld, 49-58, 139-140, 184-186, 226-229
Jan Kott, 174
H. M. Koutoukas, 47, 197-202, 222, 224, 227, 257-259, 322
John Kramer, 65-66
Jonathan Kramer, 241
Ruth Krauss, 53-58
Russell Krum, 293
Bobby Kubera, 305
Leonard Kuras, 101
Jim Kurtz, 308
Marcia Jean Kurtz, 57, 253
Donald Kvares, 47
Tom LaBar, 211-212
The Magic Show of Dr. Ma-gico, 295-297
Bert Lahr, 89
La Mama, 4, 43, 61-70, 233-235, 269, 284, 293-295, 298-300, 309-311, 320, 323-324, 331
La Mama Troupe, 233-239
Paul Lally, 14
Patsy Lamers, 231
Zohra Lampert, 154, 156-157
William Larsen, 6
Robert La Tourneaux, 251
The Laundry, 32-34
Andrea Lazar, 257
Dan Leach, 192
Deborah Lee, 144-145, 199-200
Dempster Leech, 269
Bobo Legendre, 66
Betty Leighton, 7
Josie Lemma, 44, 318
Lenny, 241-245
Denny Leone, 305
Madeleine Le Roux, 288
The Lesson, 73-75, 121-122

Baruk Levi, 257
Jacques Levy, 153-154
Paul Libin, 168
The Life and Times of Joseph Stalin, 273-277
The Life and Times of Sigmund Freud, 274
The Life of Juanita Castro, 224-226
The Life of Lady Godiva, 222-224
Tom Lillard, 101, 183
Stoddard Lincoln, 321
Ron Link, 287-288
Victor LiPari, 205, 239
Michael Lipton, 24
Liquid Theatre, 242
Dan List, 1
Joan Littlewood, 95-97
Katherine Litz, 140
The Living Theatre, 31, 98-110, 182, 219, 235, 320, 327-328
Alan Lloyd, 274
Tony Lo Bianco, 14
Caroline Lobravico, 40
Michael Locascio, 47
Barbara Loden, 154
Mark Long, 270-271
Look Back in Anger, 1
Larry Loonin, 41
Carolyn Lord, 297
Elisa Loti, 34
Love and Variations, 233
The Lover, 21
Robert Lowell, 188
Jane Lowry, 47
Lawrence Luckinbill, 161, 251
Charles Ludlam, 224, 229-232, 291-293, 296-298
Ludlow Fair, 186-187
Robert F. Lyons, 177
Lyrica Davidica, 321
Galt MacDermot, 240
Leueen MacGrath, 186
Agosto Machado, 259

Herbert Machiz, 92-93
Luis Macia, 323
The Madness of Lady Bright, 39-40
The Magic Hype, 259-261
The Magic Show of Dr. Magi-co, 298-300
Peter Mahoney, 257
The Maids, 2, 101-103, 245
Norman Mailer, 1, 14, 246-250, 313
Judith Malina, 98-110, 285
The Making of Americans, 282
Fran Malis, 34, 74
Bill Maloney, 290
Kate Manheim, 269
Theodore Mann, 8, 168
Claude Mansard, 122
Marat/Sade, 216-218
Marcel Marceau, 311
Marco Millions, 155-158
Julienne Marie, 167
Alan S. Marlowe, 140-141
Hugh Marlowe, 250
Charles Marowitz, 128
Linda Marsh, 34
Norman Thomas Marshall, 228
Nan Martin, 137
Dan Mason, 66
Marshall W. Mason, 38, 42, 186-188, 208
Duane Mazey, 257
Eddie McCarty, 226, 228
Michael McClure, 145-148
John Herbert McDowell, 56, 312-314, 315, 320-321
Gerald E. McGonagill, 74
George McGrath, 270
Ian McKay, 261
Terrence McNally, 184-186
Taylor Mead, 142-143, 231, 260
Michael Meadows, 293-295
Meat Joy, 34-37
Medea, 198-199
Murray Mednick, 179-182, 301-303

Index

Ralph Meeker, 154, 156
Jonas Mekas, 108, 330
Leonard Melfi, 311
Melodrama Play, 243
Murray Melvin, 97
Ignazio Meo, 120
Vivien Merchant, 220
Eve Merriam, 245
Irving Metzman, 210
William V. Metzo, 74
A Midsummer Night's Dream, 168-172
Jo Mielziner, 93
Muriel Miguel, 257
The Milk Train Doesn't Stop Here Anymore, 90-93
Arthur Miller, 149-154, 249
Michael Miller, 239
Liza Minnelli, 318
Modulamen, 321
The Moke-Eater, 298
Moliere, 158-161
Meredith Monk, 267, 272-273, 319, 331
Marilyn Monroe, 151
Barry Montcrease, 67
Mario Montez, 226, 259, 289
Monuments, 313
Moon, 204-205
The Moon Dreamers, 66-70
A Moon for the Misbegotten, 330
Elina Mooney, 314
Renata Mooney, 307, 313
Melba Moore, 241
Robert Moore, 250-251
Inge Morath, 152
Carl More, 314
Robert Morris, 141
Spencer Mosse, 303
The Mother of Us All, 282-283
Maxine Munt, 44
C. Murawski, 148
Murder Cake, 139

Brian Murray, 221
The Mutation Show, 285
Muzeeka, 252-253
My Fair Lady, 49
Marlene Nadle, 12
José Nava, 270-271
Claris Nelson, 38, 47, 208
Kenneth Nelson, 6, 251
The New Tenant, 76-79
The New Troupe, 243
New York Post, 3
New York Shakespeare Festival, 165-168, 172-175, 301-303
Mary Nichols, 66
Willy Nickles, 305
Night Club, 298
Nightwalk, 285-286
Grover Noel, 225
No Exit, 45
Kenny Norris, 305
Lore Noto, 5
Eric Nord, 52-53
John Normington, 220
Julius Novick, 331
Kevin O'Connor, 177-179, 239
Oh Dad, Poor Dad, Momma's Hung You in the Closet and I'm Feeling So Sad, 93-95
Oh, What a Lovely War!, 95-97
Frank O'Hara, 141-142
Tom O'Horgan 233-245, 331
Tim Oksman, 60
The Old Glory, 188
On the Road, 1
Ondine (Robert Olivo), 231, 290
One Way Pendulum, 7
Eugene O'Neill, 8-11, 155-158
Eugene O'Neill Foundation, 253
Margaret O'Neill, 250
Only a Countess May Dance When She's Crazy, 197
Ontological-Hysterical Theatre, 267-269, 324-328

Dorothy Opalach, 224
The Open Theatre, 123-124, 284-287, 319, 331
Operation Sidewinder, 243
Jerry Orbach, 6
John Osborne, 1
George Osterman, 297
Michael O'Sullivan, 160-161
Othello, 165-168
Rochelle Owens, 193-196, 233-235
Pagoon, 47
Pain(t), 324-328
Joseph Papp, 172-175, 240, 330
Dennis Parichy, 42
Estelle Parsons, 132
Particle Theory, 325, 327
Lola Pashalinksi, 292, 297
Aileen Passloff, 31, 55-56, 59
Robert Patrick, 42, 304-305
Patter for a Soft Shoe Dance, 313
James Patterson, 73
Kent Paul, 301-303
Belle Pavlov, 299
Marvin Peisner, 209
Austin Pendleton, 94
Yves Peneau, 122
Wee Robin Pennings, 293
The People Show, 269, 331
The People vs Ranchman, 62-64
S. J. Perelman, 89-90
Petit Cabaret Solennel, 312-313
Avra Petrides, 188
Phebe's, 318
Phoenix Theatre, 73, 93-94
Ben Piazza, 83, 86
Picnic on the Battlefield, 85-86
Harold Pinter, 61, 71-73, 79-81, 219-220, 224
Play, 21-24
Play I Play II Play III, 56-58
Play-house of the Ridiculous, 222-227, 229-232, 260, 293-295, 298-300
Shelley Plimpton, 241

Olga Plushinskaya, 324
Polish Lab Theatre, 113-118, 234
Emanuel Popolizio, 213-214
Porgy and Bess, 323
Beth Porter, 239
Michael Warren Powell, 66, 188, 208, 239
Keith Prentice, 251
Herman Price, 84
Henry Proach, 101
Prussian Suite, 318
Public Theatre, 240, 301-303
José Quintero, 8-11, 155-158
James Rado, 241
Charlotte Rae, 77-78, 90
Gerome Ragni, 241
Yvonne Rainer, 31, 41
Jerome Raphael, 137, 140
James Ray, 73
Marian Reardon, 24
Red Cross, 252-253
Larry Ree, 323-324
George Reinholt, 74
Jeffrey Reiss, 142
Repertory Theatre of Lincoln Center, 149-161
Ruby Lynn Reyner, 294-295
Ronald Ribman, 188-190
Debbie Reynolds, 318
René Ricard, 231
Howard Richardson, 32
Jack Richardson, 84-85
Ridiculous Theatrical Company, 260, 291-293, 296-298, 318
Terence Rigby, 220
Naomi Riseman, 61
Felicitas Ritsch, 113
William Ritman, 18, 24, 27, 73, 88
Rocky Road, 315
Jason Robards Jr., 154, 156
Jerome Robbins, 93
Marilyn Roberts, 239
The Rock Garden, 176-178

Index

Patricia Roe, 73
Paul Roebling, 92-93
Paul Rogers, 220
Roxie Roker, 12
Betty Rollin, 1
Andrew Roman, 59
Vincent Romeo, 84, 86
The Room, 61, 79-81
Bert Rose, 67
George Rose, 165
Michelle Roseman, 140
Arthur Rosen, 308, 317
Rosenkrantz and Guildenstern Are Dead, 220-221
Ann Roth, 132, 148
Bernard Roth, 294, 299
Royal Shakespeare Company, 122-128, 216-218, 220-221
Gregory Rozakis, 188
The Rue Garden, 38
Golda Rush, 299
Anna Russell, 7
Thea Ruth, 74-75
Mitchell Ryan, 167
Alfred Ryder, 129-132
Arthur Sainer, 108, 306-308, 324-328, 331
Saito, 66
The Sandbox, 84
San Francisco Mime Troupe, 254-255
Sarah B. Divine! (Part 1), 65-66
Robert Sargent, 51
Jean-Paul Sartre, 45
Robert Cosmos Savage, 199, 308
Irene Schaeffer, 196
Richard Schechner, 262-265
Evelyn Schneider, 308
Ellen Schindler, 257
Robert Schlee, 269
Harvey Schmidt, 5-6
Carolee Schneemann, 34-37
Alan Schneider, 15-18, 21-24, 24-28, 28-30, 71-73, 82-83

Peter Schumann, 124, 271-272
George C. Scott, 9
Douglas Seale, 7
Separate Tables, 47
Andrei Serban, 331
Tony Serchio, 181
Serendipity, 222
The Serpent, 285
The Service for Joseph Axminster, 139-140
Valda Setterfield, 139
Seven Meditations on Political Sado-Masochism, 108-110, 326
William Shakespeare, 162-175
Rick Shannin, 308, 314
George Shannon, 257
William Shari, 101, 102
Paula Shaw, 228
Martin Sheen, 175
Douglas Sheer, 140
Sam Shepard, 176-179, 203-204, 227, 243, 252-253, 316
George L. Sherman, 85
Tom Shiboca, 224
The Shirt, 311
Larry Siegel, 50
Don Signore, 193-196
Carole Silon, 66
Seymour Simckes, 316-317
N. F. Simpson, 7
Merrill Sindler, 34
Sing Ho for a Bear!, 51-53
Sissy, 293-295
Tom Skelton, 132
Roberta Sklar, 285
The Slave, 133-138
A Slight Ache, 47, 79-81
John Smead, 281
Jack Smith, 222, 224
Oliver Smith, 132
Garnett Smith, 139
Robert Smith, 34
Sue Smith, 56

Richard Smithies, 39
So Who's Afraid of Edward Albee?, 39, 47
Ekatherina Sobechanskaya Dances, 320, 323-324
Arnold Soboloff, 90
Sally Sommer, 181-182
Song of Songs, 58-60
Elsene Sorrentino, 224, 294, 299
Bruce Sparks, 61
Victor Spinetti, 97
James Spruill, 134
Jarrett Spruill, 142
Charles Stanley, 198-199, 208, 209, 281
David Starkweather, 39, 47
Richard Stauffer, 6
Kristen Steen, 308
Gertrude Stein, 49-50, 53-58, 282-283, 311
Frances Sternhagen, 24, 81
Roger Stevens, 93
Wallace Stevens, 144-145
Karole Kaye Stevenson, 66
Robert Louis Stevenson, 320
David J. Stewart, 156
Ellen Stewart, 43, 61-70, 234, 243
Serena Stewart, 1
Tom Stoppard, 220-221
Flash Storm, 259
Lee Strasburg, 151
Sylvia Strauss, 192
Igor Stravinsky, 49
Barbra Streisand, 318
Michael Strong, 156
Louise Stubbs, 12
Sundance (Bucks County), 210
Burton Supree, 56
Caroline Swann, 7, 71
Sandor Szabo, 95
Mary Tahmin, 188
Clay Taliaferro, 67
Terry Talley, 305

Jerry Tallmer, 1-3
Tartuffe, 158-161
Florence Tarlow, 52, 55, 252
Dennis Tate, 188
Harvey Tavel, 224-226, 259, 291, 320-323
Ronald Tavel, 221-229, 259, 269, 297, 322
Barbara Ann Teer, 51
Buddy Teljelo, 67
Ten Best Martyrs of the Year, 316-317
Terminal, 284-286
Charles Terrel, 300, 305, 314
Megan Terry, 62-64, 123, 242, 284
Jon Teta, 308
That Simple Light May Rise Out of Uncomplicated Darkness, 271-272
Theater for the New City, 267, 271-272, 291-293, 306-308, 312-317, 319
Theatre Genesis, 176-183, 269, 318
The Thing Itself, 306-308
This Is the Rill Speaking, 208-209
Luke Theodore, 102
Rob Thirkield, 239
Dylan Thomas, 208
Hugh Thomas, 6
Sada Thompson, 161, 167
Steve Thompson, 101
Virgil Thomson, 282-283
The Threepenny Opera, 111-113
David Tice, 308, 313
Graham Timbs, 311
Tiny Alice, 24-28
James Tiroff, 101
The Toilet, 133-138
Sheindi Tokayer, 52
Michael Tolan, 190
Tom Paine, 235-239
Rip Torn, 10, 145-148, 250
Jonathan Torrey, 39
Rosemary Tory, 250
Total Recall, 326
Roger Trefousse, 317

Index

Elsa Tresko, 66
Trina, 232
Trockadero Glixinia Ballet, 317-321
The Trojan Women, 289-291
Russell Turman, 142-143
Susan Tyrrell, 132
Ultra Violet (Isabelle Dufresne), 231
Lois Unger, 186
Ma Uory, 297
US, 122-128
USCO, 148
John Vaccaro, 141, 222-224, 226, 229-232, 293-295, 297, 298-300
Françoise Vaiel, 122
Vain Victory, 260
Michael Vale, 280
Paul Vanase, 290
Jo Van Fleet, 93
Jean-Claude van Itallie, 47, 285
David Vaughan, 56
Gladys Vaughan, 165-168
Bill Vehr, 293, 297
Jenny Ventriss, 187
Négro Verdié, 34
Vertical Mobility, 324-328
Victims of Duty, 76-79, 262-265, 307
Viet Rock, 124, 285
Luke Viglucci, 261
Joanna Vischer, 139
The Visit, 330
Vistas of the Heart Unveiled, 144
Dashwood von Blocksburg, 224
Waiting for Godot, 14-15, 21, 221
Pauline Walsh, 305
Sydney Schubert Walter, 62-64
Bill Walters, 232
War, 47
Andy Warhol, 225, 226, 231, 259
James Waring, 31, 139, 144-145, 313
Sam Waterston, 94, 253
Donald Watson, 76
Douglass Watson, 303
David Wayne, 156-157

Richard Weinstock, 295, 299
Jeff Weiss, 202, 309-311, 331
Peter Weiss, 216-218
Glenn Weitzman, 280
Ronald Weyand, 74-75
What Happened, 49-50
When Clowns Play Hamlet, 200-202
Alex White, 67
Ruth White, 30
Robert Whitehead, 158
Who's Afraid of Virginia Woolf?, 15-18, 20
Richard Wilbur, 159
Clinton Wilder, 18, 19, 21, 28, 82-88
Thornton Wilder, 208
Gus Williams, 88
Ann Williams, 93
Arthur Williams, 312-313, 320
Tennessee Williams, 47, 90-93, 201, 319
Noel Willman, 90
Willy the Germ, 182-183
Doric Wilson, 47
Lanford Wilson, 39-40, 47, 186-188, 208-209
Lohr Wilson, 292
Robert Wilson, 267, 273-277, 318, 326, 331
Barbara Windsor, 97
Margit Winkler, 224
Joseph Wiseman, 157
With Creatures Make My Way, 322
Peter White, 251
Daniel Wolf, 1
Janet Wolfman, 294
John Wood, 221
Marilyn Wood, 53
Holly Woodlawn, 260
Charles Woodward Jr., 250
Claude Woolman, 161
John Worden, 142
Mary Woronov, 225-226
Irene Worth, 28

Susan Yankowitz, 285
Ching Yeh, 181
You Can Go Home Again, 39
Ruth Yorck, 47, 200
Clio Young, 323
Barbara Young, 182

LaMonte Young, 36
Virgil Young, 296-298
Jamil Zakai, 56
Jerrold Ziman, 280
The Zoo Story, 19-20
Wolfgang J. Zuckermann, 211-212

www.ingramcontent.com/pod-product-compliance
Lightning Source LLC
Chambersburg PA
CBHW062005180426
43198CB00037B/2416